SONNY LISTON

SONNY LISTON

His Life, Strife and the

Phantom Punch

ROB STEEN

JR
BOOKS

First published in Great Britain in paperback 2008 by
JR Books, 10 Greenland Street, London NW1 0ND
www.jrbooks.com

A catalogue record for this book is available from the British Library.

ISBN 978-1-906217-81-5

3 5 7 9 10 8 6 4 2

Printed in Great Britain by CPI Bookmarque, Croydon, CR0 4TD

To my parents, John and Shirley,
and my first niece, Kate Emily

Contents

Acknowledgements

To my profound regret, Sonny's widow Geraldine, suspicious to the last, and forgivably so, declined my requests to participate in the making of this book. Happily, others were more co-operative, notably Davey Pearl, Henry Cooper, Floyd Patterson, Father Alois Stevens, Bill Cayton, Al Braverman, Bernard Poiry, Joey Curtis, Nino Valdes and, above all, Hank Kaplan, who offered visual as well as verbal memories. Ken Jones, William Nack, Colin Hart and David Field supplied invaluable leads, while Peter and Jane McInnes provided coffee, biscuits, endless bookshelves and unresolvable moral debates. And to Anne and Woody, heartfelt thanks for love, patience and encouragement.

I am grateful too for permission to reproduce the following photographs: Associated Press (nos 3, 7), Hulton-Deutsch (15), PA-Reuter Photos (17), Planet News (4, 5, 8, 16) and Topix (6). The remaining photographs and the chapter ends are from the Hank Kaplan collection and from Harry Mullan at *Boxing News*, whose practical help was greatly appreciated.

Most of all, I would like to express my gratitude to Tony Pocock and Neil Tunnicliffe at the Kingswood Press (now Methuen) for showing faith in someone whose only connection with boxing was a grandfather who used to act as ringside doctor at York Hall.

ROB STEEN
London

One

The Sour Science

I was the king of the alley, mama
I could talk some trash
I was the prince of the paupers
Crowned downtown at the beggars' bash
I was the pimp's main prophet
I kept everything cool
Just a backstreet gambler with the luck to lose.

(Bruce Springsteen, *It's Hard To Be A Saint In The City*)

Emphasising the animal in us all, the most telling line in Woody Allen's marvellously cerebral film *Manhattan* is Isaac Davis's suggestion that, in the unlikely event of Nazis invading New Jersey, the locals would be better off returning fire with baseball bats than biting satire. During the same movie, a woman reveals that the only orgasm she has ever experienced was 'the wrong kind'. If Charles 'Sonny' Liston had any luck at all he, too, had the wrong kind. Like Bruce Springsteen's hard-pressed saint, he had the luck to lose. Shackled by chains of disadvantage that imprison most souls for life, he almost broke free. He was granted a second chance. Sadly, he was never really allowed to take it. The late Harold Conrad, who spent endless hours oiling Liston's publicity machine, may have been overly melodramatic when he observed that Sonny 'died the day he was born', but only just. This was a man on whom fortune bestowed a wicked, teasing asp of a smile.

The heavyweight boxing champion of the world enjoys a status no other man can hope to match. He is the king of the alley and the prince of the paupers. He puts the ass into masculinity, the roar into terror. A two-legged billboard promoting the profitability of physical force. The Dean of the Mean. The champ stands alone, unable to delegate, unable to hide behind the strength and commitment of others. Tougher, frequently rougher than the rest, his very existence is wholly reliant on western civilisation's rusty notion of what constitutes a Real Man. In his pomp, Sonny Liston was as real, as fearsome an *hombre* as ever pulled on a pair of gloves.

To say that the acquisition of such symbolic trappings is not without its drawbacks would be something of an understatement. There is the self-delusion: the belief that might can be right rather than trite, that muscle can lift you above the hustle. There is the envy and patronising of others, and the animosity which that brings; there are the principle-shorn pimps and bullshit artists who pick your pocket and peck away at your future, a future already shrouded in a blanket of bruises to body and brain. Few objects of fear are subjected to such ridicule. Few riflemen make such easy targets. It cannot be coincidental that boxing is the only sporting category in the *Guinness Book of Records* that includes a section listing, and by implication canonising, its oldest champions at the time of their death, which must say something (take a bow, Jack Sharkey, wherever you are).

True, the $35.8 million that Mike Tyson and Michael Spinks earned between them for ninety-one seconds' work at the Atlantic City Convention Hall in 1988 would have fed more than 400,000 starving people for a year, inoculated around 10 million children against the six killer diseases, paid for nearly 400,000 cataract operations for blind people in the developing world and raised as much for Ethiopia as Live Aid. But, for every mansion and jacuzzi, there is a Don King lurking in a shadowy corner, hand outstretched, palm upturned with the self-righteousness of a tax collector but with none of the social benefits. At his side, more threatening still, stands that most insatiable and merciless of opponents, the male ego, the monster that drives a man so far through the pain barrier that he fails to acknowledge its presence until the damage is irreversible. As Norman Mailer once put it: 'No physical activity is as vain as boxing. A man gets into the ring to attract admiration. In no sport, therefore, can you be more humiliated.'

It would be nice to think that civilisation has progressed to a stage where the pen really does strike deeper than the sword, but only a ratepayer from Cloud-cuckoo-land would lend the possibility any credence. That said, if sport has a purpose above distracting the proletariat and turning competition into something approaching art, it is to prove that, unlike the nasty, real world, talent, diligence and patience can overcome all; that perfection is a viable proposition. However, as Lord Taylor of Gryfe pointed out when proposing his ill-fated Boxing Bill at Westminster in 1991, the laughingly-dubbed 'noble art' is alone in promoting 'intended violence'. American football, rugby and motor racing may each claim more casualties in any given year but, despite the vengeful gleam frequently discernible in the eyes of prop forwards and tight ends, despite the daggers Ayrton Senna and Alain Prost glare and sometimes thrust at each other, the aim of the combatants is not to beat each other's brains out, nor to shred each other's features, nor to break each other's bones.

In boxing, the *raison d'être* is to hurt your opponent and so sap his resistance. *Nightmare on Elm Street*? Child's play. The most horrific moment in cinematic history is that monochrome shot in *Raging Bull* of blood oozing from the ropes, every drip another ounce of humanity drained from the male soul. Forget all that twaddle about elegant right jabs, Fonteynesque footwork and tactical acumen: hunting aside, pugilism in its essence remains as primeval a pastime as man can ever have conferred respectability upon. After all, in what other cultural activity is the audience's greatest thrill achieved by seeing one man knock another senseless? What other source of disposable income taps so easily into the beast within – and without? Lord Taylor's reasoning seemed sound enough: 'We have long since abolished cock-fighting and dog-fighting. Why are we less sensitive to the greater problems of young men in the ring?'

To call boxing a sport is thus an insult to sport. It may well adhere to the definition of sport as a contest involving bodily exercise. It may even convey a darkly mesmeric beauty when practised by brutal ballerinas such as Muhammad Ali and Sugar Ray Leonard. But the intrinsic ingredients of wit and friendly competition are scarce to the point of invisibility. No one *plays* boxing. Sport reflects reality but also improves on it; in its unforgiving attitude to body and soul, boxing is too realistic. Chance plays little or no part; virtually nothing is accidental. To paraphrase Joyce Carol Oates, within the inner sanctum of the ring the proponents serve as mirrors, each reflecting the Other: the strengths of one are the weaknesses of that Other, and vice versa. Will-power and intellect, granted, are vital components, but the quest for victory over that Other Self calls for a literal bloody-mindedness. The advice of Rocky Graziano's army sergeant in *Somebody Up There Likes Me* rings with chilling clarity: 'Make that hate work for you.'

Purists will dispute such an assertion with all the illogical vehemence of a smoker defending his fix; but the only possible justification for boxing surely lies in the opportunity it affords the less privileged. As the twenty-fourth child of the twenty-five sired by a Depression-era sharecropper, Sonny Liston certainly qualifies with something to spare. 'Boxing gave my brother a sense of purpose,' explained Stuart Watt, whose sibling, Steve, the former Scottish welterweight champion, suffered cumulative brain damage in the ring and eventually lost his life there in 1986. But is that sense of purpose enough? Can we truly justify legitimising violence in order to atone for the murderous indifference which allows us to shrug off poverty as a necessary by-product of the Thatcherite 'natural' order, an order that blithely accepts greed as one of man's little peccadilloes?

The carrot boxing offers is that there are fiscal rewards to match the self-abuse. For its foremost exponents, the workload is not even particularly burdensome. Evander Holyfield fought twice in 1991, and pocketed a cool £15.5 million for his year's labours. Nearly £4 million came from what promised to be a routine defence of his world heavyweight title against a supposed no-hoper whose presence in the top ten of the rankings owed much to official finagling. Yet Bert Cooper, the human sacrifice who ultimately came within an ace of purloining the crown in the third round, was estimated to have taken home less than 4 per cent of his opponent's purse. After the fight, Cooper returned to his hotel with some buddies, ordered a dozen beers at a total cost of $44, gave the waiter a hundred-dollar bill and told him to keep the change. James Lawton's subsequent lament in the *Daily Express* was a heartfelt one: 'They give everything they have in the ring, and out of it. They are mostly a doomed breed. They are used up and tossed away. Often without a tip.' Some, mind, do not exactly help themselves. Having earned in excess of $100 million, Mike Tyson was allegedly down to his last $3 million by the time he was tossed away on a dubious (if possibly deserved) rape rap. The most popular argument against banning boxing for profit (Lord Taylor's intention) thus seems spurious. A return to the disreputable underground existence of yore would not only keep the numbers down, it would also turn heroes into villains.

The public appetite, stoked brazenly by that fountain of vicarious stimulation, television, nevertheless remains hearty, even if the flavour of the dish on offer has changed drastically. Until the 20th century, pain and danger were part of everyday existence, amputations and teeth extractions *sans* anaesthetic merely dropped stitches in life's rich tapestry. To see one's fellow humans suffering in the ring was to relive familiar experiences. Little wonder, then, that Dr Samuel Johnson should have cited prizefighting as a valuable 'art of defence', one that 'makes people accustomed not to be alarmed at seeing their own blood or feeling a little pain from a wound.' Today, though, much of the society that embraces boxing is free from physical pain; hence the rise of therapists and psychologists to help satisfy the need for mental compensation. 'The spectators at present-day boxing matches are mainly people who . . . would not have the first idea what to do if they had to fight for their lives,' the philosopher, Mary Midgley, has contended. 'If they were brain-damaged in the course of their work they'd expect to sue. Of course, our current freedom from pain is an enormous advantage. But its effect for sports like boxing is a most unpleasant shift in the motives available to the spectators

– a shift away from genuine, practical fellow-feeling in a shared skill towards sadistic, voyeuristic fantasy.' And violence, after all, is the new pornography.

Some nations have faced up to this unpalatable truth and acted accordingly, albeit prompted rather more by the inherent perils. Iceland prohibited all forms of boxing more than thirty years ago. For the Swedes, the sight of Ingemar Johansson's left foot twitching uncontrollably after he had been immobilised by Floyd Patterson was clearly traumatic: in 1969, barely a decade after hailing their first world heavyweight champion, they outlawed professional bouts. Norway followed suit in 1982. Yet not even the Parkinsonian symptoms that now assail Muhammad Ali, rendering him utterly unrecognisable from the loquacious thespian who bestrode a generation, have spurred others into taking similar action. Surely Scandinavians cannot have a monopoly on sense and sensitivity?

George Bernard Shaw's weakness for that unlikeliest of sadists, Gene Tunney and, indeed, for boxing in general, did much to dignify the ignoble art among non-disciples, but even he hinted at self-admonishment when discussing his fistic novel, *Cashel Byron's Profession*: 'Out of the savagery of my imagination I wrote the scene; and out of the savagery of your tastes you delight in it.' And it is that savagery that enables us to urge these men onward in their missions of destruction. Paul Gallico rejected all notions of virtue: 'I have covered boxing, promoted boxing, watched it, thought about it, and after long reflection I cannot find a single thing that is good about it either from the point of view of participant or spectator.'

Many will refute the contention that Shaw's addiction was an affliction at all. 'I have always considered that boxing really combines all the finest and highest inclinations of a man – activity, endurance, science, temper, and last, but not least, presence of mind,' wrote Lord Lonsdale in 1915, a period when anything not connected with trenches, Gatling guns and mustard gas must have seemed positively beneficial. A century earlier, in his inaugural volume of *Boxiana*, published in 1812, Pierce Egan defined boxing as a 'manly sport' alongside bull-baiting, cock-fighting, cudgelling and wrestling. 'To those, Sir, who prefer effeminacy to hardihood – assumed refinement to rough Nature – and whom a shower of rain can terrify . . . the following work can create no interest whatsoever,' ran the dedication. 'But to those persons who feel that Englishmen are not automatons . . . *Boxiana* will convey amusement, if not information.' A dozen years later, it was Egan who first referred to the 'Sweet Science of Bruising'. To those refined, effeminate automatons among us, and many more besides, the subject of his amusement has never been more than a sour science.

To be fair, that sourness lies not so much in the nature of boxing as in the machinations outside the squared circle. These are embodied in part by those who keep the bones together by glamorising the 'sweet science' and, worse still, perpetuating the myth of nobility. Not just the media, but polemical writers such as Hemingway and Mailer, men imbued with a commensurate streak of machiavellian machismo. Neither are the authorities free of culpability. The reduction in the length of certain championship bouts from fifteen to twelve rounds was laudable, even if one suspects that the motivation owed more to society's shrinking attention span and the ennui that succeeded the Ali era. Medical strictures, logically enough, are less stringent than they might be: were every fighter to receive the scrupulous attention accorded horses, say, the fall–out would probably nuke the industry.

At the very least, it would appear sensible to allow a doctor to examine the contestants after every round. Sensible, that is, to everyone except those in charge. Resistance toward regular weight checks is equally inexplicable. During the build-up to a fight, a boxer may put his body through dietary hell in order to tip the scales at the requisite poundage, endangering himself in the process. Simon Brown's preparation for his World Boxing Council welterweight title defence against Buddy McGirt in 1991 highlighted the lengths to which some are willing to go, and the extent of the consequences. Having been 2st overweight eight weeks earlier, the Jamaican went without food for the four days immediately prior to the contest, trained in a rubber suit, then shed the last few ounces in a steam room on the morning of the official weigh-in. After surrendering his crown on points, Brown spent the subsequent weekend in hospital, suffering, according to the Nevada Boxing Commission doctor, from total dehydration and exhaustion as a direct result of his determination to meet the 10st 7lb limit. Mad? Possibly. With due deference to George Foreman and Larry Holmes, career lifespans are relatively short, the incentive to make every pay-day count all-consuming.

The obscenely thick skin of our creature, however, is formed by the puppet-master pariahs, the managers and matchmakers, the promoters and bookmakers, the endless layers of Mr Fixits. As a British Medical Association working party acknowledged in 1984, 'The pressure of "big business" is the most formidable obstacle to the banning of boxing.' These men take the lion's share of the prize and the lamb's share of the risk. Courage ranks among the most admirable of virtues, but in what other spheres of everyday existence is so much courage demanded of so few by so many yarn-spinning yellow-bellies? Then there's that most engrossed of bystanders, the gambler. With no more than a couple of steeds in the stalls, boxing is his concept of heaven. The temptation to pre-arrange outcomes, correspondingly, is exceedingly powerful.

And heaven help the naughty marionettes who refuse orders. In January 1991, shortly after he had failed to capture the World Boxing Council international super-middleweight title (it often seems as if there are more world championships on the market nowadays than holes in Blackburn), a scan indicated that Lou Cafaro had sustained brain damage. He promptly announced his retirement. A couple of days later, he was shot in both arms. A come-back is not anticipated. Sometimes, admittedly, the puppet-masters go to the other extreme and come over all warm and protective – although only a hypersuspicious mind would conclude that that fire at the Indianapolis hotel housing three jurors in the Tyson trial constituted anything more than metaphorical evidence.

As puppets go, Sonny Liston was Captain Black to Joe Louis's Captain Scarlet, The Hood to Ali's Scott Tracy. Depicted as a misanthropic fool incapable (which he was) of reading a book, let alone a cheque, he was the ultimate tool. Here was the cosh used by organised crime to steal the world heavyweight title from Floyd Patterson and, more pertinently, from his manager, Cus D'Amato. A plucky, eccentric soul who smelled foul play in the consommé and steadfastly refused to kowtow to the gambollers and gamblers who pulled the strings, D'Amato it was who later rescued the teenaged Tyson from the slough of despond, if all too briefly.

Sonny's was the era in which officialdom began to take its big stick to boxing's vulnerable, not to say inviting, backside. The increasing infiltration by criminal and monopolistic tendencies following the growth of the television gravy train in the late 1940s had prompted the emergence of an enthusiastic reformer in the shape of Estes Kefauver, a fiercely ambitious Tennessee senator with unabashed designs on the presidency. Keen not to be outshone by the House of Representatives' investigations into purported violations of trade in baseball, the Senate set up a sub-committee on antitrust and monopoly, allowing Kefauver, as chairman, to find a focal point for his public crusade against organised crime. This ultimately resulted in a series of essentially futile Senate hearings into professional boxing between 1960 and 1964, at which Sonny and his benefactors were among the chief witnesses.

With so much at stake and so many oars eager to steer the ship clear of murky waters, it is perhaps less than surprising that the next time a Senate committee trawled the depths of ring corruption was fully three decades later, in August 1992. The two-day hearings were prompted by a bout between James Toney and Dave Tiberi in Atlantic City the previous February, Senator William Roth pushing for an investigation following allegations that Toney's split-decision victory stemmed from the bribery of the judges by the Mafia. 'I sadly saw how the majority of fighters – depending upon their respective levels of talent – are viewed by their promoters,' Tiberi volunteered. 'Some are considered prime ribs, others pork chops, and the less talented [as] scrapple, but rarely are they recognised as human beings.' Among the other key witnesses was Bobby Z, an integral component in the FBI sting that uncovered a veritable nest of vipers, who explained that the involvement of the Colombo, Genovese, DeCalvalcante and Cleveland families came about because they all knew that, otherwise, 'Don [King] will steal you blind'. Michael Franzese, formerly a powerful capo in the Colombo family, testified that King, along with the New York civil rights activist and Senate candidate, the Reverend Al Sharpton, had happily struck deals 'with organised crime guys'. In Franzese's estimation, 'professional boxing [is] a prime target for organised crime.'

Other witnesses were more concerned with the official bodies that purported to be running boxing. Evander Holyfield informed his inquisitors that he had been forced to pay the World Boxing Council (with which he claimed King has close ties) nearly $300,000 for his title defence against Larry Holmes, and a further $300,000 to the International Boxing Federation and the World Boxing Association. Bob Arum, Ali's one-time promoter, dismissed the Mob connection, laying the industry's ills at the door of the three 'sanctioning authorities'. 'These guys are all crazy,' he scoffed. 'It's a great racket. You collect sanction fees, you don't account for the money . . . Bobby Lee [the IBF president] is the best of them all.' For his part, King sought the refuge of the Fifth Amendment on no fewer than eight occasions, refusing to respond to allegations that an annual $52,000 fee was paid out of Mike Tyson's earnings to the promoter's daughter, Debbie, for her services as president of the Tyson fan club, together with a similarly hefty consultancy payment to King's sons, Eric and Carl, and $100,000 per fight to their mother, Henriette. Tyson, reportedly, is now bankrupt. The upshot was that Senator Roth and Senator Joe Biden introduced legislation to establish a national corporation for professional boxing and to protect boxers' rights. *Plus ça change*. . .

The connection between boxers and criminals is timeless and unsurprising, the link too natural, the mutual dependence too great. Were physical violence a more respectable means of earning a crust, there would be no need for a ring, still less gloves or a referee, although the stakes, of course, would be vastly inferior. As it is, in this two-horse race, the first past the post is a potential Mill Reef or Secretariat. The temptation to bask in the same glow in the unsaddling enclosure is powerful, the lure of securing a return on one's wager irresistible.

That Sonny Liston became one of boxing's most bankable mounts is in no doubt, even though his fame (or should that be infamy?) was founded on just four fights, two of which he lost under circumstances that have fuelled almost as many conspiracy theories as the assassination of John F. Kennedy. Neither can there be any question that there have been few sourer sporting chapters than his, and surely no more damning indictment of boxing's heartless wheeling and dealing.

Despite the antipathy I now hold, I grew up idolising Gene Tunney, as much for his singular sense of purpose as for his mastery of ringcraft psychology. Here was someone who transcended the archetypal, identikit image of a boxer. Like Ali, Tunney managed to pacify the pacifists. But, whereas Ali did this through matchless charisma and canvas arabesques, Tunney did it largely by getting out while the going was good, achieving his goal then marrying an heiress and returning to the comfortable upper middle-class life he had never really left behind, to all intents and purposes unscarred. Sure, he had it easier than most, but here, in defiance of all my squeamish, moralistic posturing, was nevertheless a boxer worth celebrating.

The other substantial link between Tunney and Ali is that both dethroned champions who had appeared to own an indefinite lease on the entertainment world's hottest property. The tenants in question were, respectively, Jack Dempsey and Sonny Liston, modern-day Minotaurs deemed invincible by judges and victims alike. Dempsey's story has been well documented, but it seemed distinctly odd that no one had written a book about Sonny apart from A. S. 'Doc' Young, whose presciently-entitled portrait, *The Champ Nobody Wanted*, surfaced just after his subject first stole the heavyweight title from Floyd Patterson. It was never published in Britain, has long been out of print and, in any case, featured very little direct input from the man himself. Research soon revealed the cause of the void. No one knows for certain when Sonny entered this mortal coil, let alone when he shuffled off it, still less why, or even how. So many of those closely involved with his career have either passed on or have elected not to tap their memories, that any attempt to join up all the dots is destined for failure.

The title of Young's book remains most apt. Had Clay-Ali not surfaced when he did, Sonny could have set the civil rights cause back twenty years. Although James Baldwin hailed him as 'a sweet guy', other influential black voices proffered a different interpretation when the National Association for the Advancement of Coloured People (NAACP) pleaded with Patterson not to defend his title against Sonny, fearing that a champion, and hence a representative, of his sort would do irreparable damage to their mission. Yet it was his past, more than any lack of support for the cause, that prevented him from becoming the figurehead Ali became. Only rarely are the criminal class allowed to slip the yoke of their misdeeds.

Sonny remained a captive from gun to tape, his relationship with the law as widely reported as Jackie Kennedy's taste in blue serge skirts. Note, though, the change in criteria since he started out: these days, flirtations with the judiciary are almost a prerequisite for a boxer to get noticed and so clamber from the teeming mass of so-so sluggers. Yet, while it remained an essential ingredient in his climb to the uppermost rung of his profession, Sonny's image was of the unwanted neanderthal kind: a fearsome, intimidating presence contorted by illiteracy and hawked around by the unscrupulous salesmen who smoothed his path. Hardly the sort likely to find favour with a black populace requiring a cleaner, more erudite model to project to the racist white world of the early 1960s.

Sonny declined to be 'the tame nigger they all want me to be', an understandable if costly denial of the need for pretence that incurred the wrath of the white establishment and constituted a source of immense embarrassment to a black America seeking to alter the preconceptions of their oppressors without recourse to the confrontational philosophy of Malcolm X and his ilk. If Sonny was acutely aware that a price would have to be paid for this rejection of compromise, the extent of the sum astounded him. 'I didn't expect the President to invite me into the White House and let me sit next to Jackie and wrestle with those nice Kennedy kids,' he once confided to his friend and long-time sparring partner, Ray Schoeninger, 'but I sure didn't expect to be treated like no sewer rat.' 'All he ever wanted was for people to look up to him and call him "champ",' Schoeninger lamented. 'But they never did. If he'd had an education he could've been anything he wanted. Sonny had a real sharp brain.'

It would indeed be unfair, not to say fallacious, to depict Sonny as some punch-drunk pug incapable of rational thought or civilised deed. For one thing, few boxers have sustained so little damage in the ring over the course of a career. For another, he could fight his corner verbally with the same incisive power he brought to bear on the chins and ribs of his prey; even Norman Mailer depicted him as the 'Prince of Hip'. 'I have never met an athlete in baseball, basketball or football who is smarter, more intelligent than Sonny Liston,' proclaimed Jose Torres, the one-time world light-heavyweight champion whose typewriter proved as insightful as his fists were spiteful. 'But Sonny Liston was a man who could not articulate his ideas.'

'He was a pussycat,' declared Joey Curtis, now president of the American Veteran Boxers' Association. Curtis trained alongside Sonny in Philadelphia when the latter first stepped out. 'You should have seen him with the kids. Boy, did he love 'em. But he was easily led. If you said something was blue when it was pink, he'd believe you.' Those in attendance when Mickey Duff brought him to Britain on a promotional jaunt in 1963, by contrast, regarded Sonny as an oversexed tomcat. In fact, one flagrant association with a white prostitute in Las Vegas caused neighbours to wonder whether he was a pimp. For Sonny's predilection for the female form was unashamedly open, almost self-mocking. Once asked how he psyched himself up before battle, he retorted by saying that he would simply imagine that his opponent was the only thing that stood between him and a night with Lena Horne. By general consensus, though, here was simply a henpecked husband given to behaving like a mischievous boy when his steadfast, matriarch-wife, Geraldine, was out of earshot.

An intensely private, self-conscious man who would do anything to avoid eye-to-eye contact outside the ring, Sonny was forever glancing over his shoulder, and understandably so. His initial spell in jail as a teenager left him a target for myopic law-enforcers all over America, so much so that he spent much of his life hopping from town to town in a mostly fruitless attempt to find a place to lay his hat. If he found solace in the arms of wiseguys such as Frankie Carbo and Blinky Palermo, links that merely hardened public disapprobation, it was because he had no other refuge: such was his reputation, as convicted felon and fistic colossus, that only those with extreme influence could obtain opponents for him. Interestingly, Sonny once told Davey Pearl, a constant companion over the last five years of his life, that 'Blinky was nicer to me than any other manager I ever had.' The Cosa Nostra, it could be argued, are little more than over-zealous, largely ruthless businessmen with a heightened sense of filial duty. 'This is gonna be a Cosa Nostra till I die,' John Gotti once promised. 'Be it an hour from now, or be it tonight, or a hundred years from now when I'm in jail. It's gonna be a Cosa Nostra.' Yet there are whole rafts of American society willing to make offers that cannot be refused. As Colonel Fletcher Prouty, the director of special operations during the Kennedy era, once told journalist Clancy Sigal, 'We [Americans] operate a permanent Murder Incorporated ready to wipe out any good President.'

Whatever the perceived wisdoms about wiseguys, the US state athletic commissions were far from sympathetic. Not once in an eighteen-year career did Sonny fight in New York. For much of that time, he was *persona non grata* in a cluster of other states, California included. Obtaining a licence was a perennial struggle, particularly in New York, where he never succeeded. In all, he fought only fifty-four times as a professional; by contrast, Harry Greb was unbeaten in 178 contests between 1916 and 1923 alone. A further measure of this handicap was that it took Sonny nine years to land a shot at the world title; to take one example of life at the privileged end of the spectrum, Pete Rademacher, the (white) Olympic heavyweight champion of 1956, contrived to do so in his very first professional contest.

It is hard to be a saint in the city, but Sonny Liston was the saddest of sinners. Robert Wyatt, a wheelchair-bound musician, once remarked that his greatest regret was getting himself born 'without really thinking the thing through'. Sonny might have shared those sentiments. He didn't die the day he was born; he checked out what was on offer and went the day after. The world spent the next forty years trying to bury him.

Two

Born to Run

On the strong and cunning few
Cynic favors I will strew;
I will stuff their paw with overplus until their spirit dies;
From the patient and the low
I will take the joys they know;
They shall hunger after vanities and still an-hungered go.
Madness shall be on the people, ghastly jealousies arise;
Brother's blood shall cry on brother up the dead and empty
*   skies.*

(William Vaughn Moody)

A flimsy piece of paper fluttered from an immense hand, clutched with a tenderness more becoming a butterfly with a broken wing. On it, Sonny Liston fondly imagined, was the proof he needed, finally, to silence the assembled media in San Francisco's Cow Palace. Rarely can a birth certificate have meant so much. See, it proclaimed. Charles 'Sonny' Liston is 36, not 40, or 42. Is that good enough for all you bums who keep mocking me?

It was July 1968, fully fifteen years after Sonny had first used that liassic left paw to win a professional fight. And no, the bums were not satisfied. According to the document, one generally decreed to be bogus, he had been born on 8 May 1932, as he had been claiming for umpteen years. The age issue, just one of the quiverful of projectiles hurled at this fleshy dartboard, had assumed such paranoiac, obsessional proportions that Sonny, who originally insisted that he was born two years later, had growled at reporters some years earlier, 'Anybody who says I'm not 30 is callin' my momma a liar.' Helen Liston, though, remembered a different arrival date for one of her innumerable offspring, albeit with only a modicum of certainty: 'I think it was the 18th of January 1932. I know he was born in January, in 1932. It was cold in January.' Years later, she dispensed with this memory of a chilly winter's night and confused matters still further by referring to Sonny having been born on 22 July 1927.

That the official certificate has never been found should come as no surprise; barring a member of Sonny's parole board who claimed to have it but failed to supply any evidence, it appears never to have existed. Delivered by midwives, children born to black families in Arkansas during the Depression were frequently left unrecorded, unwanted statistics buried beneath a pile of prejudice. Helen Baskin had given birth eleven times before she married Tobe Liston, a fellow-child of farming stock from Montgomery County, Missouri. Sonny was the last but one of his twenty-five offspring. The couple moved to Arkansas in 1916, subsequently renting land (share-cropping, in other words) from a black farm operator, Pat Heron. The farm lay seventeen miles from Forrest City in Eastern Arkansas, fifty miles west of Memphis and 100 miles or more from Pine Bluff, the town Sonny would claim to hail from when he gave his first interviews. His parents' life together was pure hand-to-mouth. 'The boss man,' Helen recalled, 'got three-fourths of what you raised.' Aside from toiling side-by-side in the cotton-fields, she and Tobe raised peanuts, corn, sorghum, molasses, sweet potatoes, hogs, cows and chickens. 'We had to raise what we ate, and then buy shoes and clothes.' Home was 'a shabby, little, old four-room house, and it was cold.'

In *The Souls of Black Folk*, first published in 1903, W.E. Burghardt DuBois – whose doctoral dissertation at Harvard, *The Suppression of the African Slave Trade*, was acclaimed as 'the first scientific historical work by a Negro' – waxed lyrical over the cotton-fields:

'Have you ever seen a cotton-field white with the harvest –

its golden fleece hovering above the black earth like a
silvery cloud edged with dark green, its bold white signals
waving like a foam of billows from Carolina to Texas across
that Black and human Sea? I have sometimes half-suspected
that here the winged ram Chrysomallus left that Fleece after
which Jason and his Argonauts went vaguely wandering into
the shadowy East three thousand years ago; and certainly
one might frame a pretty and not far-fetched analogy of
witchery and dragon's teeth, and blood and armed men,
between the ancient and the modern quest of the Golden
Fleece in the Black Sea. And now its golden fleece is found;
not only found but, in its birthplace, woven. For the hum of
the cotton-mills is the newest and most significant thing in
the New South today . . . To be sure, there are those who
wag their heads knowingly and tell us that the capital of the
Cotton Kingdom has moved from the Black to the White
Belt – that the Negro of today raises not more than half of
the cotton crop. Such men forget that the cotton crop has
doubled since the era of slavery, and that, even granting
their contention, the Negro is still supreme in a Cotton
Kingdom larger than that on which the Confederacy builded
its hopes. So the Negro forms today one of the chief figures
in a great world-industry.'

By 1932, however, it was doubtful whether Tobe and Helen Liston
regarded themselves as part of a great world-industry. If, for the
sake of argument, we accept Sonny's word, his delivery came amid
an ominous period in history. A day earlier, at the Rothschild
Foundation in Paris, the President of France, Paul Doumer, had
been approached by a White Russian *émigré* with an avowed hatred
of communism. 'This is only the beginning,' cried the interloper,
Gorguloff, as he fired his revolver, mortally wounding Doumer.
The growing power of the Master Race was represented by Max
Schmeling, the then heavyweight champion of the world; two
months later, Adolf Hitler's National Socialists became the domi-
nant voice in the Reichstag. In the United States, unemployment
was surging toward 9 million; by August, it would hit 11.5 million,
paving the way for Roosevelt's landslide election victory in
December. Even the Automobile Association of America had run

out of gas. The good news? In Texas, an 18-year-old typist, Mildred Didrikson, was a couple of months away from being immortalised as 'Babe' at the Los Angeles Olympiad, her reward for becoming the first, and thus far only, athlete to win golds for running, jumping and throwing. In Chicago, Al Capone was still getting used to life behind bars after receiving an eleven-year sentence for tax evasion, while New York was growing accustomed to life without another gangster megastar, Jack 'Legs' Diamond, gunned down in his sleep the previous Christmas. The sighs of relief were even more pronounced the following April, when scientists announced the development of a vaccine against yellow fever.

'Ain't he got big hands for such a teeny-weeny baby?' The midwife's response to Sonny was nothing if not insightful. 'He's going to be a boxer.' Although his maternal grandmother, Martha, was a tall woman, and the paternal grandparents, Alexander and Fanny, could boast some sizeable relatives, neither mother nor father had the sort of build one might expect. Indeed, the 5ft 5in Tobe, according to the 5ft 1in Helen, 'was awful thin'. Sonny, in contrast, was teased unmercifully for his size as soon as he began to attend school, an activity that was soon turned into an infrequent occurrence by Tobe. Yet Helen played down Sonny's professed recollections of incessant beatings: 'He went [to school] a little bit, whenever his daddy let him. But his daddy always had a job for him and the others to do, rain or shine. Their daddy put him out there to work as soon as he was 8 or 9. He said if they [the kids] could go to the dinner table they could go to the fields. He didn't whip them as much as people say he did. But he hollered at them a lot. The biggest thing he did was whoop and holler. He whooped and hollered so much, nobody paid any attention to him.'

Sonny's recollections were more painful when he related them to the *Chicago-American*: 'I can understand the reason for my failings. When I was a kid I had nothing but a lot of brothers and sisters, a helpless mother, and a father who didn't care about a single one of us. We grew up like heathens. We hardly had enough food to keep from starving, no shoes, only a few clothes, and nobody to help us escape from the horrible life we lived.' Urged, no doubt, to heighten the drama for publicity purposes, he later told *Ebony* magazine that he had run away following one fierce whipping, only to be administered with another lashing upon his return. 'My father worked me hard and he whupped me hard. If he missed a day, I'd feel like saying, "How come you didn't whip me today?" School? That wasn't for me. The kids made fun of me because I was so big, and I would start fighting.' Sonny later referred to St Francis County as 'a ghost town' when describing his closest encounter with fear. 'One night, me and my brother walked toward the river. The moon was so bright it looked like day, and when we came to the top of a hill we saw a man walking back and forth – only he didn't have any head. My brother says, "Where's his head at?" – but he didn't wait for an answer. I wasn't really scared. I was just running to keep my brother from being scared.'

Helen left the nest, such as it was, during the Second World War. Crop yields were low when she heard on the radio that there were jobs aplenty in St Louis, where 'they'd pay you while you learned'. She went to work in a shoe factory and rented two upstairs rooms in a house on O'Fallon Street. Four of the children would eventually join her there, including Sonny, who was 13 when he stole enough money for a bus ticket and sped off in pursuit of some maternal warmth, unable to bear his father any longer. 'A town,' wrote Pete Hamill of the *New York Post*, 'of con-men and hustlers, drifters and pimps, the flotsam and jetsam of a war, a town where a big kid could get jammed up,' St Louis scarcely proffered itself as a desirable meeting-place. The way Sonny told it, he figured that all he need do was ask someone, and they would point him to his mother's home, and the someone in question apparently turned out to be a wino. Helen saw the reunion in less idealistic terms: 'He arrived at night. The police put him in a place where I could find him. The police in St Louis will take care of a child.' Monroe Harrison, an early manager, also praised the local cops for picking Sonny up from his sleeping-place in an alley and taking him downtown, where the boys in blue 'gave him a place to sleep, and fed him bologna and crackers. They kept him with them for three days. They liked him – he did little chores – and he liked them. He didn't want to leave.'

Helen found Sonny a job in a poultry house, and later on an ice-wagon. She also encouraged him to attend night-school in an attempt to compensate for his lack of education. Sometimes she tagged along to see if he actually attended, but 'he didn't go like he should have'. This had much to do with the way the shy, hulking, illiterate teenager was scorned by his fellow-pupils. Put in a class with children five years his junior, he endured their taunts for a year before embracing the streets. Sonny explained his lack of scholastic endeavours when interrogated by Senator Estes Kefauver during the professional boxing hearings of 1961: 'Other kids seen me coming out of – I was such a large boy – other kids would see me coming out of such small kids' rooms. So they would make fun of me and start laughing, and I started fighting. Then I started playing hooky and, from hooky, I led to another thing, so I wound up in the wrong school . . . the house of detention. I was about 14. My mother, she got me out, and then, well, I figure – she got me out, and I went right back for the same things. I went back to the same thing and wound up in a bigger house this time.'

The drift toward crime was hastened by Sonny's experiences when he joined a construction gang. 'Those guys treated me like a man. They thought I was one because I could work as hard and as long as they could, and I could do more than hold my own in a fight. It was a tough bunch. Many of them had been in jail, and others were headed there. But they were the only friends I had and they influenced what I did and thought. I never knew there were other kinds of people. I'd heard of Negro doctors and lawyers, and outstanding businessmen, of course, but how was I going to get with them? They were educated, refined people. I wasn't educated and knew I wasn't refined.'

Precisely why Sonny was sent to the house of detention is uncertain. He maintained it was because of truancy, others that it was assault. Monroe Harrison may have been talking about the same incident when he recalled Sonny taking $5 from a boy who had been sent to the grocer's for some shopping. In the event, he was given a lecture and released into Helen's custody. At 16, he took part in a caper planned by a local gang: 'We broke into this restaurant about 2 in the morning and got away. But, after we'd gone ten blocks, we decided to stop and get some barbecue, and then the police came along and barbecued us.' Released on probation, and already weighing a whopping 200lb, he was quick-tempered and far from chary about using his fists. The gang hailed him as 'the No.1 Negro', and he was characterised as 'evil'. His strength, according to Harrison, was such that he could lift the front end of a Ford, just to prove a point.

At the outset of the 1950s, Helen left St Louis for Gary, Indiana, returning briefly to St Francis County en route 'to make two crops with the kids'. Sonny, meanwhile, had been arrested for six muggings, one of which had earned him the princely sum of a nickel. One victim was struck in the mouth, knocked down and robbed of $6. A second reported being beaten by three men who dragged him into an alley where they relieved him of $9. A third said he was pulled into an empty parking lot to be deprived of $45. In Sonny's case, crime did not pay very well.

The descent to armed robbery was inexorable. In the late spring of 1950, a St Louis restaurant was robbed. Two people were found beaten up, for no apparent reason. Sonny, now 18, was caught and sentenced to serve five years in the Missouri State Penitentiary at Jefferson City. Convictions were obtained on two counts of robbery and two of larceny. 'They say he confessed,' said Helen. 'I don't know.' To his credit, Sonny never sought absolution via excuses. 'We were just always looking for trouble. Someone says, "Let's stick up the restaurant," and we did. We never got a chance to count the loot. I don't know how much there was in the haul. There were four of us, and we never split it up or anything. We just did the job like the stupid, crazy, bad kids we were.' A member of the St Louis police force, who chose to remain anonymous, later summed up the hole Sonny had dug for himself. 'Going to the can was the best thing that ever happened to him. If he hadn't gone to the can he would never have met Father Stevens, and if he never met Father Stevens he never would have learned to box, and if he hadn't learned to box he'd be dead of a bullet in the back.'

The sentence began on 1 June 1950. Communists had displaced Nazis as Public Enemy No.1; the Cold War was hotting up. A week earlier, French troops had been attacked by Viet Minh in Dong Khe. The USSR refused to apologise for shooting down a US plane over Soviet-occupied Latvia. On 25 June, North Korean troops invaded South Korea; twenty-four hours later, American air and naval forces were ordered to intercede, an act speedily supported by the UN. Along with two other senators, Joe McCarthy, capitalism's very own avenging angel, had been denounced by President Truman for sabotaging American foreign policy. Still, at least the underdogs were peeping over the parapet: in March, the House of Representatives had voted to admit Alaska as the forty-ninth state, while the US soccer team, almost a contradiction in terms, were preparing to shock Matthews, Finney and their supposedly incomparable Co. in the World Cup. Joe Louis had retired, leaving the heavyweight boxing division as open as it had been since the mid-1930s. According to a study, only 46 per cent of British households had the luxury of a bathroom, and petrol prices had just risen to three shillings a gallon, the highest for thirty years. Even so, the twin spectres of Depression and the Second World War were receding in the memory; indeed, the Blitz seemed light years away when Frank Sinatra strolled into London for his first night on a British stage. Medical breakthroughs, meanwhile, were providing a constant source of cheer: the world's first kidney transplant was performed in Chicago on 17 June. In Brooklyn, a 65-year-old New Yorker was twice pronounced dead during an abdominal operation, only to surface for a third time and live, courtesy of a revolutionary new technique known as the heart massage. Whether Sonny had similar recuperative powers remained open to question.

Three
Redemption

I have very little idea what it was that attracted me to boxing in the first place. No one in my immediate experience ever had the least interest in it. What started as a little fooling around at the Y [YMCA] soon turned into almost an obsession . . . I wound up sparring the first night with a fellow who outmatched me pretty badly in experience. I took a three-round beating, never letting him knock me down, but taking plenty of punishment, mostly jabs that landed on or around my nose, which I was sure must be broken by the end of the second round. After practice, the trainer told me I had a hell of a lot of heart. Don't blow your nose, he said, or your eyes will be black, and be here tomorrow. Driving home I knew that "heart" meant crazy or stupid or both . . .

(Letter to Joyce Carol Oates, reproduced in *On Boxing*)

Jake La Motta became world middleweight champion because he didn't care whether he died in the ring and fought accordingly, with reckless abandon. He felt he deserved punishment for murdering a man in a robbery, a crime, as it transpired, he never committed. Mike Tyson's stated aim, meanwhile, was to catch his opponent on the nose and 'try to punch the bone into his brain'. Not that he stopped there. 'I feel so good when you're in pain. I'm always thinking about taking an ice-pick and sticking it in somebody's ear or stabbing somebody in the eye, just biting them or ripping their lips off,' the bull-necked gryphon informed Jose Torres.

Given that you cannot really dabble in anything so serious, so nasty, so unforgiving as boxing, do you have to be crazy to practise it for a living? A little. Stupid? Perhaps. Hungry? Certainly. Anger helps, too. So do accidents of birth. It cannot be entirely coincidental that, for the past four decades, the black man, the perennial whipping boy of American society, has all but assumed the freehold on the most glittering bauble in show business and, more importantly, the foremost emblem of western masculinity. And prior to that, too, when Jack Johnson and Joe Louis bestrode their respective generations during the first half of the century. As a way out of the mire, boxing constituted an escape hatch before Elmore James ever dusted his broom. Until the mid-1950s, bashing away the blues was infinitely more profitable than singing them.

Before tracing how Sonny began his evolution from errant cub to grizzled 'Bear', it seems appropriate to outline the genesis of the stranglehold he would seek to perpetuate, one that in Norman Mailer's estimation made being 'a black heavyweight champion in the second half of the 20th century . . . not unlike being Jack Johnson, Malcolm X and Frank Costello all in one.' It was Johnson, a former stevedore, who first confirmed the white oppressors' worst fears, namely that black men *were* better endowed – with manly attributes. Johnson gilded the lily as well, habitually celebrating his victories in the arms of one, or more, white women. Yet, in 1809, virtually a century before the 'Black Menace' finally cornered Tommy Burns in Sydney, Tom Molineaux had become the second American – and first black – to fight for the heavyweight championship when he challenged, resolutely if fruitlessly, the British master craftsman, Tom Cribb. Even before that, in the late 18th century, 'The Black Terror', Bill Richmond, had pulverised all but one of his British foes, losing only to Cribb, and that after a grim contretemps lasting an hour and a half.

Not until the 1890s, however, was a noted coloured heavyweight, the West Indian-born Australian, Peter Jackson, permitted to confront a Caucasian in an American ring. Just as the male ego cannot countenance unisex track races – despite the fact that the gap in times for the respective sexes is closing and, in some long-distance events, the two are expected to converge within the next thirty years – so the white ego could not risk the humiliation of defeat. Jackson's skill and stamina were of the highest order, so much so that he stood toe-to-toe with Gentleman Jim Corbett for sixty-one rounds in 1891, richly meriting his draw. Racial bigotry denied him the chance to advance any further and, according to his biographer, Daniel Wiggins, Jackson's early demise at 40 was largely attributable to a broken heart. Being refused a room on account of his race at the Baldwin Hotel, an establishment he had hitherto frequented, thrust reality home to this naïve character.

Black Americans have been used as dispensable muscle for aeons, from the slaves pitted against each other in bare-knuckle combat by their white owners for betting purposes, to the teenage grunts in Vietnam who gave their lives for no better purpose. Jack Johnson, though, was the first to take something in return. And he paid for the privilege. Not for him the so-called fighting-slave collars that were knotted on his fistic ancestors to prevent them from escaping; he was weighed down by the millstone of white fear and disgust. Fully four decades before Jackie Robinson bejewelled baseball, thirty years before Jesse Owens sped into the Olympic annals, and nearly a score before the Harlem Globetrotters began trotting, Johnson sowed the first seeds of black athletic pride.

In some ways, Johnson can even be considered the prototype black militant. The surge of electricity generated by his Independence Day victory over Jim Jeffries, the former champion who had taken up cudgels on behalf of 'that portion of the white race that has been looking for me to defend its athletic superiority', was incalculable, in all senses. In his biography of the 'Manassa Mauler', *Jack Dempsey*, Randy Roberts contended that, 'Never before had a single event caused such widespread rioting. Not until the assassination of Martin Luther King Jr would another event elicit a similar reaction.' Lives were lost in the nationwide racial skirmishes that ensued. William Shaw, the general secretary of the United Society of Christian Endeavour, implored state governors to ban the film of the fight; in Cincinnati, where black-white tensions were especially taut, Mayor Louis Schwab had little option but to comply. A contemporary song reflected Johnson's galvanic influence, and the extent of his symbolism:

The Yankees hold the play
The white man pulls the trigger;
But it makes no difference what the white man say
The world champion's still a nigger.

Yet, in the eyes of firmer-heeled blacks, intellectuals too, Johnson remained the epitome of the 'bad nigger', not least for marrying outside his race and flaunting his white flirtations. Many other contemporaries were simply ambivalent. His removal, unsurprisingly, soon became a priority for the panic-stricken white community. By 1913, five years since burning Burns, he fled to Europe, escaping the authorities after being found guilty of crossing a state line, and having sex, with a woman other than his wife. In 1915, the unbowed champ returned to the Americas, if only to Havana, where he was counted out against the skyscraping Jess Willard while shielding his eyes from the sun. Jail beckoned, and the resultant uproar tarnished Johnson's legacy beyond repair. His race would spend a long time recovering.

A Negro heavyweight championship had been up and running since 1902, and continued to do so until 1932, which was just as well. Getting a crack at the main throne in the twenty years following Johnson's exit was out of the question, even for worthies such as Sam Langford and Harry Wills, against whom Jack Dempsey steadfastly refused to defend his title despite much exhorting from white observers. In the less turbulent racial climate of the immediate post-Depression era, however, Joe Louis Barrow, one of eight offspring raised with profound difficulty by Lily Reese and Munrow Barrow, an Alabama sharecropper, was able to rise to the heights barred to his forebears. It didn't hurt that the heavyweight division of the 1930s had thus far been short on pure-bred American heroes, what with a German (Schmeling) and an Italian buffoon (Primo 'Satchel-Feet' Carnera) clogging up the air. Even when Carnera was finally found out, it took a flashy Jew (Max Baer) to do the trick.

Helped, if anything, by a speech impediment that enabled managers to limit his utterances, Louis gained equal respect from both sides. Promoted as an antidote to the prevailing ills, within the ring and without, he united black and white behind him. Beige of skin and strikingly handsome, Louis had been taught how to deport himself. He was respectable. His vices, such as they were, extended to voracious gum-chewing and an even more child-like fixation for ice-cream. To smooth his passage, handlers, promoters and the media worked in rare harmony to dilute memories of Johnson and so lower the colour hurdle. Louis epitomised physical power, they informed the public, not black supremacy. His nickname, 'Brown Bomber', suited this emphasis to a T: how many blacks referred to each other as browns back then? A governmental pawn? To a degree Louis was exactly that, not least during the Second World War, yet efforts to paint him as an honorary white were pointless: he stood four-square at the centre of racial debates, and was uniformly perceived as a credit to his race far beyond his retirement in 1949. He was nominated for the Spingarn Medal for his civil rights work, was awarded the Legion of Merit by the army in recognition of his war effort, and was finally laid to rest in Arlington Cemetery. If radicals viewed him as an Uncle Tom, they occupied an extremely sparse minority.

Louis made an indelible mark. 'Save me, Joe Louis, save me, Joe Louis, save me, Joe Louis . . .' were the dying words of the first man in the southern states to be executed by poison gas. When he and Sugar Ray Robinson were ensconced in army training at Camp Sibert in Alabama, and refused to sit in the area reserved for blacks, the outcry brought about a change in policy. Louis opened doors, and many stayed open, yet he cannot be said to have uprooted stereotypes the breadth of America. In the Jim Crow territory below the Mason-Dixon Line, where segregation enveloped the south like a highly flammable blanket, waiting to be torched, economics impelled his acceptance. But a black man in Atlanta or Alabama could no more watch a fight by the side of a white man than get in the ring with him. Two years after Sonny was paroled, in 1954, the US Supreme Court ruled in the case of *Brown v. Board of Education of Topeka (Kansas)* that segregation in the schools of Topeka was unconstitutional. In the estimation of C. Vann Woodward, the verdict merely served to render the south 'more deeply alienated than it has been at any time since 1877'. Even St Louis held a magnetic attraction for a boy from Arkansas.

The boy, though, was approaching manhood in a similarly repressive environment. Missouri State Penitentiary housed 3500 inmates, a third of them coloured. Prison conditions in America at the time were such that cell-mates joined forces in 1954 to stage a nationwide riot. Some $8 million-worth of the jail's property was destroyed, along with a number of lives. For the most part, Sonny kept his nose clean: records show him as having been reprimanded 'for shooting craps' and 'hollering in the line', but there were no problems of a disciplinary nature. He enrolled, if only briefly, in the school programme run by a civilian and otherwise attended by a smattering of the better-behaved clientele. For the remainder of the time, he was assigned to the kitchens and also proved particularly useful down at the docks, lifting and unloading vegetables. Joe Gonzalez, an inmate who later followed Sonny into the ring, dubbed him 'Sonny Boy', thus claiming the credit for his *nom de plume*.

Not that all was sweetness and light. The prisoners, not unnaturally, divided themselves into gangs. Hank Calouris was said to run the West-siders, Nick Baroudi the Italians and someone known as Frankie the East-siders, and these three forged an alliance to victimise the blacks. This, unsurprisingly, did not quite tally with Sonny's concept of fair play. One day, or so the story goes, he walked across the yard, lashed Calouris with the back of his hand and muttered, with quiet but unmistakable menace: 'I'll do that every time I hear you touched a coloured boy. If you don't like it, I'll see you in "The Hole" at 6.' Baroudi and Frankie were given the same ultimatum. The quartet duly convened at the appointed time in 'The Hole', a storage-room beneath the cells where fights could be conducted without fear of disturbance. Sonny emerged five minutes later, leaving behind all three of his adversaries, each staring at the ceiling.

The prison authorities none the less saw Sonny in an affable light. 'He was just a big, stout man,' recalled W.P. Steinhauser, a former assistant-warden. 'His arms were as big around as my legs. He wasn't too much of a mixer. He was a reserved sort of fellow. We had no trouble with him at all.' Bernard Poiry, who also rose to the rank of assistant-warden during his forty-year stint at the institution, has similar memories. 'I was yard-master at the time and I remember being asked to find someone I could trust to carry the dirty clothes to the cleaning-place at the front door of the prison. Yes, I said, I know a solid, reliable bloke: Sonny. He came back to the penitentiary when he became champ and gave a $5 tip to all the inmates . . . Originally, he was put in the old 'A' hall, the segregated section. He was a good, quiet inmate, no kind of bully at all. Never had much to say. I don't think he ever had a violation and, if he did, it was minor. That was very unusual. He was the sort of fellow whose lack of education and intelligence people took advantage of.'

Poiry's duties included organising boxing matches three or four times a year, the odd one open to the denizens of Jefferson City. The talent-spotter, though, was Father Alois Stevens, the Catholic chaplain in charge of the athletic programme (his Protestant counterpart was responsible for showing movies and taking band practice). Taunted, it was said, by a bunch of older inmates, Sonny apparently erupted with rage and initiated a vicious spat, which in turn brought a visit to the chaplain. During their years together, Helen had repeatedly told him to 'cultivate his religion', but despite attending a Methodist church in Arkansas Sonny never really did his mother's bidding. Yet his respect for Father Stevens was automatic and absolute. 'He was religious in most general terms, but I don't think he was ever baptised. He got along pretty well with his fellow-inmates. He was pretty much a big kid when he came in, and he had a lot of kid left in him when he left. He was relaxed with people he trusted, especially children. With some, though, he might give a blank stare. You could see him wondering what the angle was. He loved playing tricks on people. He had a two-headed quarter that he had a lot of fun with. I liked him, so I went to work on the parole board on his behalf. I wanted to give him a chance.'

Father Stevens was quoted as having advised Sonny that outbursts of this nature could only extend his sentence and that, with his physique, he might make a useful acquisition for the prison boxing team. 'We had them boxing and wrestling during the winter and playing baseball in the summer. I was also able to get in some big-time wrestlers to put on a show, boxers too, sometimes. Sonny was the most perfect-looking specimen of manhood. He was 18 or 19 and 202lb, clumsy and awkward but, after a while, he got very good and cleaned up. They always had trouble getting his gloves on when his hands were wrapped. His hands were *so* large. Astonishing. Boxing kept him out of trouble.' It also provided the ideal outlet for all that pent-up anger and frustration. At the same time, there were signs of mellowness when he met Geraldine Chambers at a prison dance. A munitions factory worker, Geraldine already had a daughter, Arletha, by a previous marriage, but that didn't bother Sonny, who took her hand on 29 August 1951.

Penitentiary bouts were held either in the auditorium – which would be rent asunder during the 1954 riots – or the yard. Father Stevens recalls Sonny fighting on eight or ten occasions over the course of two winters as his reputation gathered steam. Poiry soon sat up. 'One inmate suggested we should take notice because of his punch. There was no one to match him. Word got out to St Louis, and they arranged to bring a pro in to take Sonny on. Sonny ripped the headguard off the pro's head.' Father Stevens helped instigate the contest. 'Father McGwire, [a fellow-priest] who was formerly in the newspaper business, was acquainted with Bob Burns, the sports editor of the *St Louis Globe-Democrat*, which had been sponsoring the local Golden Gloves for years. McGwire went with me to see Burns and try and get Sonny into the Golden Gloves. Burns called Monroe Harrison, a school caretaker who effectively ran the Golden Gloves for the paper, and he came down to the prison with a boxer.'

Frank Mitchell, whose family ran the *St Louis Argus*, a black newspaper he himself would later publish, was already managing a stable of fighters. 'I was to be the bankroll man, if this thing [with Sonny] worked out. Bob Burns called Monroe Harrison, Monroe called me. Tony Anderson, a veteran trainer, was consulted. He knew fighters. He could spot them – *snap* – like that! Tony took the best heavyweight in St Louis to Jefferson City for this scouting trip on Liston.' Thurlow Wilson, regarded as no more than 'a journeyman' by Father Stevens, was the nominated slugger. 'Don't make no difference to me,' shrugged Sonny when asked how many rounds he wanted to fight. 'Make it five or six rounds. He won't last that long,' retorted Wilson. Barely two rounds were required – and it was Wilson who wilted. Although Anderson felt Sonny was afraid to use his right 'because of the tremendous power he had', the left jab more than compensated. Spitting out teeth, Wilson withdrew, saying, 'I don't want no more of him.' As one of Joe Louis's one-time sparring partners, Harrison had no difficulty in spotting such palpable talent. 'You've found me a live one,' he congratulated Father Stevens. 'Get him. I can make a champion out of him,' Anderson in turn informed Mitchell.

Due in large part to the unfavourable attitude of the St Louis police, the parole board initially rejected the various entreaties mounted by Father Stevens, Burns, Mitchell and Harrison on Sonny's behalf. In June 1952, however, Sonny was released into the prison farm, a minimum security auxiliary unit about ten miles outside Jefferson City. Finally, on 30 October, less than half-way through his sentence, he was paroled and placed into the care of Mitchell and Harrison. Despite the former's later claims, Burns, who had made a number of contacts at Father Stevens's behest, was most probably responsible. Boxing, the board accepted, would steer Sonny down a righteous path. After all, had it not transformed delinquents such as Archie Moore and Jack Dempsey?

The management team was already in place. Harrison had no capital, so he had brought in Mitchell in a putative two-man operation. They found Sonny a room in the Pine Street YMCA and a job with a steel company. By night he trained religiously, either at the Masonic Temple on Olive Street or at the nearby Ringside Gym, accompanied by Anderson, who would draw 10 per cent of the purses when Sonny turned pro and remained in his corner for seven years. A trainer, in essence, is taxed only when required to convince a hurt or beaten employer to carry on, which presumably explains why Sonny would go through so few. 'I paid the man $1.5

million, which is very good for someone just pouring water, putting in my mouthpiece,' Larry Holmes once said of Mike Tyson's former trainer, Richie Giachetti. 'Sonny wasn't a bad boy,' Anderson assured 'Doc' Young. 'He was badly misused. I could bawl him out in my way of bawling him out, and he'd be all right. But you couldn't push him around like a dog. He was a fight-handler's dream. I only had to push him to get rid of an opponent.'

At this juncture, the style was basic. Left foot planted flat on the canvas, bouncing on the ball of his right, Sonny deployed his strength and reach to sound effect. The left jab, a sacrilegious Excalibur newly unsheathed, was gaining lustre. In February 1953, Mitchell entered him for the eighteenth annual St Louis Golden Gloves at the Kiel Auditorium. In his preview for the *St Louis Globe-Democrat*, Raymond V. Smith wrote: 'Heavyweights, usually the smallest group of the eight weight divisions in the open and novice departments, will be plentiful. Rated top-notch contenders are . . . Charles (Sonny) Liston of the Ringside Gym.' Smith was soon putting flesh on the PR outline: 'Charles (Sonny) Liston, the Big Bertha from the Ringside AC, hardly worked up a good sweat in knocking out Luther Corder, his semi-final opponent, in the second round.' Watched by a crowd of 15,449 on a not-so-unlucky Friday the 13th, Sonny then won a unanimous decision over Lloyd Willis, the All-Army champion. 'He left-handed them all,' remembered Mitchell. On the same page as Smith's account of the final was a one-column photo of a lean-faced, smiling Sonny. He'd learn.

Having thus qualified for the Midwestern Golden Glove Championships in Chicago, Sonny caught the 8.58 a.m. train to the Windy City on 21 February. In his first contest, he expended three rounds fashioning a technical knock-out over Donnie Freeman from Fort Worth, substantiating an early reputation as a sluggish starter. Then he defeated Oklahoma's Carl McClure on points, that very same evening; you wouldn't catch Mr Holyfield and his contemporaries working so hard for millions, let alone for free. Tullos Lee Mead from Memphis, a noted knock-out specialist, was dispatched breezily, Sonny toying with him before unleashing a burst of lefts to the head and rights to the body that compelled the referee to step in midway through round two. Nearly ten years later, Mead looked back in anguish: 'When Liston knocked me down, I made the mistake of getting up.'

The only St Louis representative left in the tourney then outpointed Ben Bankhead of Kansas City in the semi-finals and marched more than a little gingerly into a confrontation with Ed Saunders, the imposing 6ft 4in Olympic champion from LA, whose career and life would soon be simultaneously abbreviated after a bout in Boston. Mitchell was in no doubt about the size of the task, nor his charge's apprehension: 'Sonny was scared to death, but he beat the hell out of him.' This earned Sonny a place in the national Amateur Athletic Union championships in Boston, and he tuned up by adding the Ozark AAU title – without flexing a muscle. Word had spread; all his fellow-contenders defaulted.

At Chicago Stadium in March, Sonny stumbled to the floor in the first round when off-balance, but recovered to beat the highly-touted New Yorker, Julius 'The Hammer' Griffin, and so win the Golden Gloves national heavyweight title, firmly against the odds. The bubble eventually burst in Boston a month later, when he knocked out Detroit's Lou Graff, his first opponent, within a minute of the start of round two, before losing to the canny Philadelphian, Jim McCarter, on points. June brought the *Globe- Democrat*-sponsored International Golden Glove matches, ranging St Louis's Golden Glovers against some of the foremost amateurs from Europe. Yelled on by a throng of 7849, Sonny gave the locals a 5–5 draw courtesy of a first-round TKO over a West German southpaw, Herman Schreibauer. At one point during the fight, he was heard to whistle.

By now, Sonny had also imposed his presence on the professional ranks. While preparing to meet Archie Moore, Nino Valdes, a richly-promising 230-pounder from Cuba, worked out with him. Sonny took a solid right without so much as a blink, then bounced back with a flurry of blows to the body that persuaded Valdes to retreat. The next step was not long in arriving. On 2 September 1953, Sonny made his professional debut at the St Louis Arena in a scheduled four-rounder with Don Smith, and nailed him to the floor in thirty-three seconds with what Mitchell insisted was his very first punch. At the same venue fifteen days later, he decisioned another local lad, Ponce DeLeon, in four rounds.

As well as marking the first full year of Rocky Marciano's heavyweight reign of terror, 1953 also saw the first paperback publication of *The Souls of Black Folk*. In his introduction, W.E. Burghardt DuBois condensed more than half a century of academic endeavour into the condition of his people, piercing the heart of the matter with telling accuracy:

> 'Today I see more clearly than yesterday that back of the
> problem of race and colour lies a greater problem which
> both obscures and implements it: and that is the fact that so
> many civilised persons are willing to live in comfort even if
> the price of this is poverty, ignorance and disease of the
> majority of their fellow-men; that to maintain this privilege
> men have waged war until today war tends to become
> universal and continuous, and the excuse for this continues
> largely to be colour and race.'

On turning professional, Sonny had signed a two-year contract with Mitchell and Harrison, with a two-year renewable option. Unfortunately, although the managers had agreed to pay him $35 a week when he wasn't fighting, or had no job, it was not long before they claimed that they could not afford such a commitment. It was this, according to Mitchell, which led to contractual arrangements being entered into with 'questionable characters'. Like some down-at-heel prostitute, Sonny was in no position to be picky about the subletting of his body. Still, he was grateful for the regular meals. 'In a week, maybe two, they'll make you a star.'

Four

Frankie and Blinky

The big man arrives
Disco dancers greet him
Plain-clothes cops greet him
Big man, small town, fresh lipstick glistening
Sophomore jive
From victims of typewriters
The band sounds like typewriters
The big man he's not listening
His eyes hold Edith
His left hand holds his right
What does that hand desire
That he grips it so tight . . .
. . . Edith and the Kingpin
Each with charm to sway
Are staring eye to eye
They dare not look away
You know they dare not look away

(Joni Mitchell, *Edith and the Kingpin*)

Communism apparently defeated, the American Way affirmed, boxing was regenerated in 1953 as the armed forces flooded back into the lists following the Korean War. Local heroes could now be nurtured again. Clubs reopened, sixteen of them between July and December. In North and South Carolina, whites and blacks were given the go-ahead to occupy the same ring; in New Orleans, blacks were included on the undercard for a white promotion for the first time. The rush to tap the resultant flow of talent was breathless. At the turn of the following year, *The Ring*'s Chicago correspondent,

Lenny Myers, shamelessly transformed his typewriter into a billboard: 'ATTENTION PROMOTERS: your writer represents some of the nation's top crowd-pleasers. Right now available are such pleasing boys as Davey Moore, featherweight, and Dick Powell, featherweight. Contact your writer for boxing events, publicity, and other fistic attractions.' In February 1954, 'Liston, Charley, St Louis, Mo' was listed in *The Ring's* Class 'C' of American boxers.

Nat Fleischer, editor of *The Ring* and perhaps the staunchest keeper of the flame, found it 'gratifying to report that 1953 saw a big drop in scandal reports. Here and there an odd case came up in which the culprits suffered what they deserved. But when one considers the vast number of persons otherwise identified with the sport, boxing in 1953 can well stand on its own feet as a sport that has carried on honestly, with manipulations almost nil, with commissions enacting legislation that kept boxing clean and that, at least in the US, kept deaths and injuries to a new low, despite the world figures [fifty-three], of twenty-one fatalities.' *The Ring* had first begun monitoring mortality rates in 1930, when the number of professional boxers worldwide was rising towards its pre-war peak of 10,000. By 1953, however, that figure had been cut in half, with 3000 of them domiciled in America. Under the auspices of its chairman, Robert K. Christenberry, the New York State Athletic Commission (NYSAC) was setting the pace for ring safety, installing flooring that was said to be injury-proof and experimenting with a glove that would remove thumbing from the repertoire.

The dangers persisted that year, however, threatening by-standers almost as much as performers. In Vienna, Karl Machin disagreed with the referee's verdict, clouted the official on the chin and laid him out cold for three minutes. Four Chuck Davey fans died of heart attacks watching their man being massacred by Kid Gavilan. In Manila, Lim Kee Chan and Little Paras, a pair of slingers from Singapore, failed to turn up for their scheduled bouts: the ring was peppered with bottles and cigarette butts; substitutes were hurried into action only to be summarily knocked out; the manager of one of them threatened to sue the boxing commission because his boy was supposed to be fighting a week later, and doctors now doubted whether he would be in condition for a month at least. The promoter, not unexpectedly, suffered a coronary.

Fleischer appeared less certain of his ground when assessing another thorny issue: 'It has been rumoured that some of our major fighters are owned in part by undesirables, but no proof has ever been submitted . . . many of those who were in this field have quit due to fear of prosecution.' But the arrival, via television, of a captive, potentially huge audience, had raised the stakes. Other vultures were hovering over the carcass, sufficiently insulated to peck away at their leisure without fear of detection. Sonny would benefit, and suffer, from this. The trade-off, ultimately, did not prove ideal.

Proving that underworld figures wielded a sizeable stick in boxing circles was a longstanding *cause célèbre*. During Prohibition, Al Capone, Owney Madden, Lucky Luciano, Frenchy Demange and Legs Diamond all drank heartily from their well of fistic investments, unfettered by federal concern. To the authorities, bootlegging and murder were greater priorities. But in the wake of Jake La Motta's alleged dealings in 1947 with 'The Boss', Joseph Di Carlo, those authorities delved deeper, which was tangible acknowledgement that a new orgy of organised crime had been brought on largely by the public desire for material compensation in the aftermath of the war effort. La Motta oiled the wheels of justice, complaining that his refusal to co-operate with Di Carlo and his brethren had retarded his pursuit of the middleweight crown. A purge was only partially accomplished through the Kefauver hearings and other congressional show-pieces in the late 1950s and early 1960s. Although the transcripts of these filled in blanks that had hitherto gaped like holes in a hull, La Motta's own connections included, the case remained leaky thanks to the Fifth Amendment.

To unravel this maze of intrigue, it seems pertinent to delve into the catalytic role of television. 'Will You Pay For TV Shows Soon?' asked *The Ring*'s *TV Fights* annual for 1954, underlining the inescapable fact that a new powerbroker had muscled into the fray.

In 1948, the sixty-odd television stations in operation across the States commanded an audience of around 1.75 million; by 1950, this figure had swollen by 3000 per cent. The burgeoning popularity of boxing telecasts was indisputable: the night before the second Jersey Joe Walcott-Joe Louis match in 1948, the Hotel New Yorker had reported complete bookings for rooms furnished with sets. No other roof in the world at that time covered as many cathode tubes – 150 – as the New Yorker. Twelve months later, 16,500 bars and restaurants in the Big Apple alone were said to have screened at least one televised fight. In 1952, fights were beamed almost every night of the week to some 5 million homes, 31 per cent of the market; within three years, the audience had soared to 8.5 million. Even *I Love Lucy* failed to outpull boxing in the ratings. This accessibility signified that boxing had left intimacy behind and was ready to benefit from a vast multitude of fresh disciples. Local bouts now gained a regional and sometimes national audience, live gates became less important, and gamblers began buzzing hungrily around the enlarged honey pot. Needless to say, the incentive for the less scrupulous to help themselves increased correspondingly.

In a bid to head off the threats of piracy and reduced profits, the broadcasters sought to prevent public screening of fights without authorisation. Concern was expressed over the financial viability of Madison Square Garden, the Vatican of fisticuffs: the passing in 1947 of that earl of entrepreneurs, Mike Jacobs, had heralded a drop in the venue's boxing revenue which, by 1950, would reach almost 50 per cent – thanks, in the main, to television. Shortly before the Louis-Walcott duel was held at the Garden, lawsuits were heard and injunctions were obtained: the New York Supreme Court granted temporary blocks to an amalgam of promoters, broadcasters, boxers and sponsors involved in the presentation, preventing a local cinema and a Boston charity from charging money to view. Since it was considered that non-news broadcasts on radio and TV were protected by property rights legislation, promoters and broadcasters were deemed to have quasi-property rights over sporting events.

In order to secure a slice of this prospectively huge pie, and thus safeguard his future, Louis had been persuaded to form Joe Louis Enterprises Inc., the brainchild, according to the historian, Barney Nagel, of one Harry Mendel, a press agent-cum-promoter who had formed a friendship with the 'Brown Bomber'. A fortunate, highly controversial victory over Walcott first time round had convinced the champion that retirement was close at hand. Joe Louis Enterprises would hereafter sell the contracts for the four leading heavyweight contenders – Walcott, Ezzard Charles, Lee Savold and either Gus Lesnevich or Joey Maxim – to anyone able to pay to promote title fights. The winner of the initial bout would then put his prize on the line against the next man in the queue, with Louis holding all radio, film and television rights, as well as a 51 per cent stockholding. The other 49 per cent was earmarked for Harry Voiler, who owned a hotel in Florida and had connections within the Hearst empire. But when Voiler failed to stump up the sum agreed, $100,000, Louis urged Truman K. Gibson, a close black associate and former prominent War Department aide (who claimed that the so-called Mendel Plan was, in fact, his baby), to elicit support from David Charnay. Charnay was one of several partners in Tournament of Champions Inc., a promotional subsidiary of the TV company CBS which had been assembled in 1947 to capitalise on boxing as a means of developing the television market. In the end, Charnay resisted involvement, so Mendel suggested approaching James Norris, a Madison Square Garden stockholder and heir to the Chicago Stadium Corporation, a considerable empire founded on property, booze, grain speculation and indoor stadia, together with his partner, Arthur Wirtz.

Louis, Gibson and Mendel met Norris on a golf course in Florida, and the International Boxing Club (IBC) of New York sprang from the loins of their discussions. Norris and Wirtz paid Louis $150,000 in cash (as opposed to the requested $250,000), and gave him 20 per cent of the stock and a contract of employment. Louis subsequently assigned his promotional rights to the four contenders to IBC and vacated the scene, leaving Gibson in his stead. In 1949, Mendel played his trump: Abe Greene, a firm friend who just happened to be the president of the National Boxing Association, agreed to recognise as the heavyweight title-holder the winner of IBC's forthcoming first championship promotion. In March of that year, Norris advised the Madison Square Garden officials that it would be for the greater good for everyone to 'work together now and keep the events for our buildings and not create a competitive situation that would be harmful to us all'. For, in a forlorn attempt to reactivate its cash tills, the Garden had purchased all of Mike Jacobs's interests, a shopping list that included leases on prime boxing venues such as Yankee Stadium and St Nicholas Arena. Norris's message, though, was clearly understood; these assets, in turn, were transferred to IBC, which thus assumed control of virtually half the championship boxing in America.

'The Octopus', as IBC became known, now extended its tentacles. In May 1949, Norris, whose fortune was estimated to lie between $50 million and $400 million, bought out Tournament of Champions, which then enjoyed, among other things, an exclusive arrangement with New York's Polo Grounds, another prestigious fight venue, as well as a remunerative Wednesday night boxing slot on CBS TV. IBC also acquired control of promotion for the heavyweight, middleweight and welterweight divisions, whose aspirants were contracted to grant sole promotional rights, for a three- to five-year period, to any championship bill IBC put on. Norris then increased his stake in Madison Square Garden to a controlling interest, enabling him to dictate policy. Then he became president of the Garden, just as he was already president of IBC's two arms, in New York and Illinois, and its parent company, the Chicago Stadium Corporation. He and Wirtz were now directors of all four concerns. In this life-size game of Monopoly, IBC had landed on a vacant lot in Mayfair with money to burn.

Standing on the corner, however, was the Boxing Managers' Guild of New York, a veritable rogues' gallery formed in 1944, ostensibly as a social club and benevolent protective union comprising managers and matchmakers. The underlying function, not unexpectedly, was to maximise returns from live gates and broadcasts. A strike at the Guild's offices in April 1949 forced IBC to turn over a $1000 share for any fighter participating in an event shown on TV – in addition, of course, to the purse. Further strikes followed, much to the exasperation of IBC. Worn down, Norris and Truman Gibson arranged to pay the Guild $135,000 over the next three years via two of the latter's leading lights, 'Tex' Pelte and Jack Dempsey's erstwhile manager, Jack 'Doc' Kearns, a man once described as having 'no ethics or morality'. Gibson would later insist that all that these payments were intended to purchase was a halt to the strikes, but the stench of protection money was unmistakable.

Meanwhile, the IBC payroll was soon accommodating one Viola Masters, whose husband-to-be was none other than John Paul 'Frankie' Carbo, the so-called Czar of boxing, a distinctly shady manipulator who 'controlled' the majority of the members of the Guild. When later cross-examined by a Senate investigating committee, Gibson would attest that Miss Masters was given a position 'to counterbalance or to negate any possible ill effect' from the deal with Kearns and Pelte; Carbo and Kearns, he explained, were 'deadly enemies'. Yet at the same investigation, known officially as *United States v. International Boxing Club 1960*, but more commonly dubbed the 'Carbo Hearings', it transpired that Carbo had attended at least one boxing-oriented meeting, with James Norris, at Kearns's home.

Norris, for his part, would concede under oath that the hiring of Miss Masters was nothing but a pay-off to Carbo, whom IBC needed to keep the Guild off its back even though it could not be seen to be associating with such a disreputable character. Mind you, of all the epithets used to convey Carbo's lifestyle, 'disreputable' was probably the kindest. A New Yorker born in 1904, his police record revealed seventeen indictments, on counts ranging from vagrancy and suspicious character to grand larceny and murder, although he virtually always skirted conviction. He spent a year in Sing-Sing for killing a cab driver in 1924, and was tried in 1939, along with 'Bugsy' Siegel, 'Lepke' Buchalter and other such undesirables, for his part in the infamous Thanksgiving Day murder of Harry Schacter, a member of Murder Inc. Testimony indicted

Carbo as one of the hitmen but, when the chief prosecution witness fell mysteriously to his death from a hotel window on Coney Island, the case collapsed. Among Carbo's other cohorts, meanwhile, numbered one Joseph Di Carlo.

In 1947, Carbo had come clean (sort of) when he admitted controlling Mike Jacobs and hence the New York boxing market. The fact that the NYSAC fined the puppets, Jacobs's Twentieth Century Club, a cursory $2500, simply underscored Carbo's authority and sphere of influence. Jake La Motta only agreed to fight Sugar Ray Robinson in a 1951 IBC promotion after consulting Carbo; when IBC set up a showdown between Marciano and Walcott the following year, it was Carbo who set the terms. Walcott's manager, Felix Bocchicchio, subsequently held out for a larger purse before agreeing to a rematch; again, Carbo's negotiating acumen was called upon, and ultimately prevailed. He then began using his influence to arrange for four illustrious names – Carmen Basilio, Willie Pep, Tony DeMarco and La Motta – to participate in IBC-organised fights. He was also said to use Billy Brown, a matchmaker for IBC undercards, as a means of fixing up fights in New York; soon there were managers complaining that Carbo's say-so was needed before they could engage their charges there. Come 1955, averred Aaron Kohn, the managing director of the New Orleans Crime Commission, Carbo was running IBC (which was now creaming off $90,000 a week from TV alone) and, in effect, professional boxing in the United States. Kohn recounted a visit by Carbo and Blaize D'Antoni, a New Orleans businessman, to Norris's New York office, wherein Frankie divvied up the territory. 'Jim, from now on you got the upstairs. Dan's [D'Antoni] got the downstairs,' he pronounced, running a finger across the breadth of a wall map of the USA.

The NYSAC, it should be explained, was handicapped in the Twentieth Century Club case by the ease with which someone, anyone, could become a manager, since a licence was not considered necessary at the time. Any old frontman with powerful acquaintances could handle a fighter. Despite the inexhaustible zeal of Frank Hogan, the Elliot Ness of sports gambling, Carbo could not be touched, still less curbed. Later in 1947, the New York State Assembly belatedly ruled it illegal to act as manager, promoter or second without a licence. Unfortunately, the penalty – a year in jail supplemented by a $5000 fine – scarcely constituted the strongest of deterrents. In any event, the simplicity with which one obtained a licence was laughable. Take Frankie 'Blinky' Palermo. Reputed to be the numbers king of Philadelphia, his closest associates included Mickey Cohen, a racketeer from the West Coast, John Vitale, the Satanic Majesty of the St Louis underworld – and Carbo.

To be fair, the NYSAC, along with other athletic commissions, was also guilty of acquiescence. When Julius Helfland, the former King's County assistant-District Attorney and renowned 'racket-buster', was appointed NYSAC chairman by Governor Averill Harriman in 1955, his brief was to bring an end to 'the bowing-under of the commission to threats' by promoters to take fights out of the state, and so flush out boxing's criminal limescale. He succeeded in gaining indictments against the Boxing Managers' Guild, effectively ending its manipulative reign, but he also colluded, albeit indirectly, with Norris and Carbo.

In 1957, Helfland received word that a welterweight elimination bout between two of Carbo's boys, Virgil Akins and Isaac Logart – one arranged by Norris and Carbo in the wake of Carmen Basilio's step up to middleweight – was set to take place outside New York, in Denver, where the Colorado State Athletic Commission was prepared to recognise the winner as champion. According to Norris, Helfland's instructions were loud and clear: 'Now I expect you to bring that match to New York. The match belongs in New York and, dammit, you had better bring that match to New York.' This edict spurred Norris into convening a pow-wow with, among others, Carbo and Herman 'Hymie The Mink' Wallman, a furrier-cum-manager who was allegedly permitted a free rein by Carbo in return for paying officials to smile benignly on his fighters. This enabled Wallman to provide Carbo with the inside dope he needed in order to place his bets with confidence. Agreement was reached, and the Akins-Logart contest proceeded to New York. It was surely not beyond Helfland's powers of perception to foresee the means by which his order would be obeyed. Helfland claimed he had had Carbo under surveillance for some eleven years, but only when Frank Hogan finally obtained court orders for wire-taps in 1958 were his suspicions confirmed. The bugging revealed that Wallman and Bernie Glickman, Akins's manager of record, had taken orders from Carbo, so too Norris.

Palermo's character was to come under fire during the Kefauver hearings in 1960. Ike Williams, who dominated lightweight boxing from 1947 to 1951, testified that he had been blacklisted by the Boxing Managers' Guild in 1946. Informed that he would not pull the gloves on in earnest again until he took on Palermo as his manager, Williams chose the sensible option. Under the new regime, Williams claimed, Palermo deprived him of $65,000 in purses due, and relayed countless bribes. Before a fight against Freddy Dawson in 1948, Williams alleged, he was told that the officials were rooting for his opponent. When word reached them that he had warned the press he would 'have a story' to report after the contest, the officials backed down. Williams subsequently beat Dawson – and was fined $500 for casting doubt on the officials' integrity. The chairman of the Pennsylvania State Athletic Commission that levied the fine, funnily enough, was Leo Raines, one of Palermo's buddies. The pair had previously travelled to California together in order to watch – yes, Williams. La Motta stoked the fire even more vigorously when he stepped into the ring with Kefauver. Prior to his meeting with Billy Fox in 1947, La Motta alleged, his manager and brother, Joey, who declined to testify, had communicated an offer to take a dive. The bribe, Jake said, emanated jointly from William Daly, one of Carbo's henchmen, and Fox's manager of record – Blinky Palermo. Pride dictated La Motta's refusal but, when Thomas Milo, the Mob's New York money-man, advised Jake that compliance would ensure a shot at that elusive middleweight title, he submitted. He also let the world in on the pact, or at least tried to, willingly sustaining a hiding in a contest devoid of any shred of credibility.

Carbo and Palermo were finally brought to book in February 1961. Although Carbo had been indicted in New York three years previously for his unlicensed matchmaking and managing pursuits, Frank Hogan had contrived to win only a misdemeanour conviction, and even that would have been impossible in many other states, Hogan himself having badgered the New York authorities into punishing non-licence-holders in the first place. 'The name of Frankie Carbo symbolises the degeneration of professional boxing into a racket,' railed the assistant-DA, Alfred J. Scotti, but Carbo escaped with a two-year sentence that sent him to Riker's Island, and he continued to tempt providence. Eventually, inevitably, his past caught up with him.

In October 1957, Jackie Leonard, IBC's West Coast promoter, had called on Carbo to help him pay Kid Gavilan (yet another of Frankie's puppets) the $12,000 which he had promised the spent force following his meeting with Gaspar Ortega. Although Gavilan received barely half his due, Carbo now had a useful debtor. A friend of Leonard's, Donald Nesseth, a manager himself, then begged the promoter to use his influence to obtain a nationally-televised fight for Nesseth's would-be welterweight wonder, Don Jordan. Leonard obliged, and Truman Gibson arranged a bout with the then leading contender, Isaac Logart, which Jordan won on points. Three wins later, Gibson guaranteed Jordan a match-up with the champion, Virgil Akins, like Logart one of Carbo's boys. Not long after this, Palermo allegedly called Leonard to dot the i's and cross the t's, stipulating that 'we are in for half [your] fighter, or there won't be any fight'. Gibson, who was with Leonard at the time of the call, insisted that he would 'take care of everything' and persuaded Leonard to accept the terms. But Nesseth, a more defiant sort, was wary of being seen to double-cross the under-world. In any case, he distrusted Gibson, and he subsequently declined the deal on Jordan's behalf. Leonard and Gibson none the less convinced Palermo that his (i.e., Carbo's) demands would be honoured. Jordan beat Akins in December 1958, and again the following April, in a pre-arranged rematch in St Louis, after which Palermo and Carbo were due to be handed their agreed share. Nesseth, though, maintained his defiance. On 28 April, Carbo called Leonard, and threatened to have his eyes gouged out.

Carbo's warning, Leonard recalled, was unequivocal: 'We are going to meet at the crossroads . . . You will never get away with it. I have had that title twenty-five years, and no punks like you are going to take it away from me . . . You are going to be dead . . . We will have somebody out there to take care of you.'

Anxious to find a back door for Nesseth and Leonard, Gibson and Palermo proposed that Jordan take on another of Carbo's fighters, Sugar Hart. Blinky, allegedly, offered Leonard a financial sweetener for winning round Nesseth, but the manager felt that Jordan's title would be at risk and demurred. Palermo and Carbo then ordered one of their assistants, Joe Sica, an LA promoter, to tell Leonard that the only way he could avoid the 'noose' was 'to grab hold of Nesseth and make him take the fight'. Nesseth asked Gibson to get in touch with James Norris in the hope that the IBC president would simmer Carbo down. Norris refused. On 4 May, another Carbo strongarm, Louis Dragna, a clothing-store owner more commonly referred to as the 'triggerman' for Murder Inc., dropped in on Leonard and Nesseth. Twenty-four hours later, the Los Angeles Police Department tapped Leonard's phone and concealed a microphone in his office, and duly gathered the evidence to confirm that Gibson had tried to bribe Leonard to activate the Hart-Jordan bout.

On 11 May, William Daly was allegedly invited to LA by Gibson, who had arranged a meeting with Leonard. Sensing Daly's presence to be for the purposes of intimidation, Leonard wore a microphone that allowed the police to record the ensuing conversation. Gibson, according to Daly, had said that he had been betrayed by Leonard's part in the removal of the welterweight title from IBC hands, and that he and Carbo had resolved to rub out both Nesseth and the promoter. Daly, meanwhile, spelt out the depth of Carbo's fury and related the case of Ray Arcell as a means of depicting the consequences for continued stubbornness. Arcell was a promoter/manager under Carbo's wing who had handled many of Joe Louis's victims and who survived to be still active at 81 as Roberto Duran's co-trainer. Choosing not to co-operate with the Czar's wishes, he had had his skull fractured. Explaining the tactics used on Arcell,

Daly employed a fiendish attention to detail: 'They use a water pipe
. . . lead pipe . . . and they just get an ordinary piece of newspaper,
see, newspaper don't show fingerprints . . . and you sitting in a
crowd . . . they whack you twice and split you – fracture your skull.
And knock you unconscious, and they just drop it . . . and after they
drop it – the law – they're protected by the law. They have to have
witnesses.' The fearful Leonard, wary of the fact that the law might
offer him little protection, reported all this to the California State
Athletic Commission, for which folly he was allegedly bludgeoned in
the same manner as Arcell, although an investigation – surprise,
surprise – failed to identify the assailants.

The US Attorney's office hastened the case to the grand jury
early in 1961, and Carbo, Palermo, Sica, Dragna and Gibson were
indicted for 'extortion affecting commerce and conspiracy to extort
in violation of the Hobbs Act, for interstate transmission of threats,
and conspiracy to transmit an offense against the United States.'
Along with Carbo, Palermo was further charged with extorting
$1725 via physical threats to Leonard and, together with Sica, of
attempting by similarly subtle means to coerce Nesseth into
relinquishing control over Jordan. Frankie and Blinky were charged
on five more counts with regard to interstate transmission of
injurious threats to Leonard and Nesseth. 'Boxing smells to high
heaven,' lambasted Governor Edmund G. Brown, as calls for the
industry to be brought under federal control mounted with hitherto
unseen intensity amid the outcry that succeeded the revelation of
the charges. Within a day of Brown's tirade, the Senate Sub-
committee on Antitrust and Monopoly had begun its investigation
into monopolistic practices prevalent in professional boxing,
although the main issue soon turned out to be organised crime – a
particular obsession for the chairman of the sub-committee,
Senator Estes Kefauver, and one that had started to vex the Senate
a couple of years earlier.

A New York pow-wow between the underworld overlords in 1957
had emphasised how much power the mobsters enjoyed, prompting
the Senate to embark on an investigation into labour racketeering.
When John Kennedy was elected President in 1960, he installed

his brother at the head of the Justice Department, and it was Robert who pursued the union leader, Jimmy Hoffa, with a view to a kill. The middle Kennedy brother also now threw his weight behind the prosecution of Carbo and his cohorts, and linked his proposed national crime commission to the setting up of a federal boxing commission. However, when Kennedy moved up to Attorney-General, he argued that an extension of the FBI's powers would be sufficient. His consequent lack of full-throated support for the various Kefauver bills boded ill and, when the senator himself died in August 1963, the call for federal control subsided. There was scant consolation a year later when Title XVIII of the United States Code was amended, prohibiting 'schemes in interstate or foreign commerce to influence by bribing the outcome of sporting contests', the penalty for which went as far as a $4000 fine and ten years in jail.

None the less, in February 1961, Frankie was fined $20,000 and sentenced to twenty-five years' imprisonment. He failed to last the course. Blinky received a fifteen-year term and an identical fine, but was paroled in 1971. Sica was sentenced to twenty years, but Dragna was acquitted on appeal. Gibson, who claimed to have been framed by Leonard and Daly, not to mention being tried prejudicially, had his ten-year sentence suspended by a judge who acknowledged his dutiful and impressive career in government and legal circles. Placed on probation, he tried to clear his name in 1963, but failed. Arguably, this was foreseeable from the moment Gibson informed Senator Kefauver that IBC dealt with the underworld 'to maintain a free flow of fighters without interference, without strikes, without sudden illnesses, without sudden postponements'. Asked whether he was aware of what certain suspicious characters might do on his behalf, Gibson retorted, 'Not completely, no,' and so left his inquisitors to come to the conclusion that the assistance could very well have sprung from dens of iniquity, Carbo's for instance. It was this connection that brought down Gibson. IBC, by now forcibly dependent on its splinter organisations, sank with him.

Back in 1954, though, IBC was repelling all boarders. The state's war against the monopolists had paved the way for a suit brought by the Justice Department in 1952, citing Norris, Wirtz, IBC and the Madison Square Garden Corporation as co-defendants. After eighteen months, however, the charges were dismissed in the space of forty-five minutes by Judge Gregory T. Noonan, who based his decision on the Supreme Court rulings of 1922 (*Federal Baseball Club v. National League*) and 1951 (*Toolson v. New York Yankees*), wherein baseball was exempted from the prevailing antitrust laws. Why, Noonan argued, should boxing be treated any differently to baseball? The plaintiffs contended that broadcasting rights had altered the scenario, but Noonan pointed out that baseball, too, had benefited from this new source of income. The aim of the Sherman Antitrust Act of 1890, the mother of all monopoly legislation, had been to safeguard trade and commerce; it now seemed that courts were content merely to seek 'unreasonable' restraint of trade. As for sport, that most honourable, heroic of occupations, being coupled with business, the very idea remained utterly repugnant.

All of which brings us back to Sonny's predicament at the outset of 1954. Frank Mitchell had to find a way of financing his quarry's future. No stranger to the St Louis police himself, Mitchell had a lengthy history of arrests without conviction. That he should turn to Carbo's compadre, John Vitale, whose strike rate against Missouri law enforcers amounted to a healthy fifty-five acquittals from fifty-eight arrests, hence contained a degree of inevitability. Mitchell later denied having made any direct overtures: 'I'm no associate of Vitale. I know him just as everybody else in St Louis knows him. I met him on a golf course in a foursome – not by invitation. He was introduced to me. I, of all people, couldn't afford to discriminate. I learned that he was interested in boxing and boxers. I told him about Sonny and my hardships. Vitale said he'd give Sonny and another of my fighters, Jesse Bowdry, jobs at his concrete manufacturing company at $65 a week. This was good money. This was my association with Vitale. I don't think I did anything wrong. I had to get him [Sonny] out of my pocket.'

To the naked eye, Vitale was no more than the president of the Anthony Novelty Company. In reality, he presided over union

activities in St Louis with a hefty stick, and he hired Sonny primarily
to maintain order among black labourers. Following the death of
two local union officials in 1952, the finger of suspicion had picked
out Vitale, yet no hard evidence was forthcoming, and he wriggled
free. Witnesses for the prosecution were remarkably reticent.

□WORLD HEAVYWEIGHT CHAMPIONSHIP□

15 ROUNDS

SONNY
LISTON
VS
FLOYD
PATTERSON

CHAMPION   FORMER CHAMPION

PLACE   **DATE**

MIAMI BEACH CONVENTION HALL   **THURSDAY EVENING**
1700 Washington Avenue   8:30 P. M.
MIAMI BEACH, FLORIDA   APRIL 4, 1963

NO HOME OR THEATER TV
IN MIAMI AREA

Dear Sir:

The price scale for the Sonny Liston - Floyd Patterson World's Heavyweight Championship bout
to be held at Miami Beach Convention Hall on the evening of April 4, 1963, is as follows:

RINGSIDE $100.00	GRANDSTAND	$20.00
RINGSIDE ARENA $50.00	ARENA and GRANDSTAND	$10.00
	End Arena and GRANDSTAND	$5.00
(Prices Include Tax)	*(All Seats Reserved)*	

For your convenience, an order blank is attached hereto. All ticket orders must be accompanied
by check or money order payable to Championship Sports, Inc., Miami Beach Convention Hall, Miami
Beach, Florida. Tickets will be forwarded promptly by registered mail.

Very Truly Yours,
CHAMPIONSHIP SPORTS, INC.
Al Bolan, General Manager

Gentlemen:

Herewith enclosed please find my check/money order for $_____ in payment of_____
tickets at _____ for the LISTON-PATTERSON FIGHT ON APRIL 4, 1963.

NAME _____

ADDRESS _____

CITY AND STATE _____
(KINDLY PRINT CLEARLY)

**PLEASE DIRECT ALL COMMUNICATIONS TO: CHAMPIONSHIP SPORTS, INC.
MIAMI BEACH CONVENTION HALL, 1700 Washington Avenue, Miami Beach, Florida**

Five
Bear Growls

*It's hard being black. You ever been black? I was black once –
when I was poor.*

(Larry Holmes, *On Boxing*)

'Maybe Father Time is the only one with the style to beat Rocky Marciano after all.' Writing in *The Ring* after the Brockton Blockbuster had kayoed Ezzard Charles in September 1954, Ted Carroll echoed the sentiments of the entire boxing industry. His scepticism as to the likelihood of any mere mortal doing the job was well-founded. Marciano had now successfully defended his world heavyweight title on four occasions. The leading contender was none other than the tall Cuban, Nino Valdes, the first 'foreigner' to occupy such a position in fifteen years and the same aspirant whom Sonny had forced to back-pedal in the gym before turning pro. Indeed, not until Marciano abdicated in 1956 did a new line of succession shuffle humbly, almost apologetically, into place.

Not that the majority of Americans desperately minded the status quo. Not since Jim Braddock stunned Max Baer in 1935 had a Caucasian American ruled the roost, and not since Rocky has anyone repeated the feat. Precious few are the boxing legends who retire and stay retired; the descent into the pit of (relative) anonymity must have looked horribly steep to Joe Louis, Muhammad Ali, Larry Holmes, George Foreman and Sugar Ray Leonard. Even fewer are those who leave the limelight unbowed. In heavyweight terms, make that one: Rocky Marciano.

Having taken his place in the queue, Sonny, meanwhile, had just experienced his first brush with ring mortality. Up to now, his initiation had been less than arduous. After he had earned a six-round points verdict against Benny Thomas the previous November, January 1954 saw him twice level Martin Lee of New Orleans with right cuffs to the cranium, also in the sixth round and also under the St Louis Arena lights, to earn that early, if modest, ranking in *The Ring*. Stan Howlett, a former sparring partner whose left eye Sonny had cut during a work-out in his amateur days, was outpointed over six rounds in March, bringing Sonny his first out-of-town date, against the highly-touted Johnny Summerlin, in Detroit three months later. Frank Mitchell, who had decided that Sonny needed more strenuous competition, played matchmaker. 'The trainer [Tony Anderson] was working on Liston's right hand. His left hand was almost perfect. In Detroit, there was talk that Summerlin would knock Liston out in two or three rounds. But when people saw Liston in the gym, the odds began dropping.' *En route* to an eight-round points win, Sonny proved to his handlers that he could take a punch. In the sixth, in Mitchell's words, 'he got a little careless and got hit. Real good. But he took all Summerlin could give him.' The victory drew critical acclaim, *The Ring* naming Sonny its heavyweight-prospect-of-the-month. When the pair were rematched in August, Sonny again earned the nod from the Detroit officials, this time by a wider margin. Nobody was calling him Charles any more.

However, Sonny's budding popularity in the Motor City received a set-back when he fell foul of Marty Marshall on 7 September. As early as round two, he had Marshall primed for ejection but refrained from applying the *coup de grâce* in the interests of giving the crowd their money's worth, as requested. 'I was told to take it easy for a coupla rounds. Marshall's a clown – they told me – who'd bounce around and flick punches from all sides. I was standing there, kinda wondering, when all of a sudden he lets out a yell and, with my mouth wide open, gaping, he slugged me right on the jaw. It didn't hurt, but I couldn't close my mouth. I had to fight the last six rounds with my mouth open. After a while, it hurt real bad.' The jaw, in fact, was broken. Marshall, who subsequently became a stock-checker for a paint company, was offended by Sonny's account: '[It was] A right cross. It's not true that I jumped in the air and whooped and that we were laughing it up all through the fight.'

Whatever happened – whether Sonny's mouth was open because he was laughing, as some ringsiders asserted, or he really was pausing in the middle of a fight to take in the scenery – he did not become aware of the extent of the injury until afterwards, and ploughed on in ignorance before losing on points. When he returned to St Louis, the jaw was wired, putting him out of action for six months. Mitchell, who had said that his duties at the *St Louis Argus* took precedence, copped a barrowload of flak for not being there. Sonny was hurt and angry in every possible sense. Mitchell, in turn, was not best pleased when Sonny presented him with a dentist's bill for $20. The operation on the jaw cost the St Louis Athletic Commission $400. Nice to know one's boss is the generous, caring sort.

It was then, while Sonny was recuperating, that the financial situation deteriorated to an insufferable degree for Monroe Harrison and Mitchell. No fights for six months meant that they had to find that $35 every week, with no prospect of anything in return that would slake the thirst of their supposedly dehydrated coffers. Mitchell bought out Harrison for $600 and sold his share on to a local drugstore owner, Eddie Yawitz. Enter John Vitale. 'It was hard to keep Sonny in a job after it got out that he was an ex-con,' Mitchell rationalised. 'That stigma. It was all on me. I needed some help.'

The come-back began on the familiar stomping ground of the St Louis Arena the following March, in 1955, when Neil Welch was the conquest on points over eight rounds. April saw a return with Marshall, this time on home turf. According to our troublesome friend, revenge, via a sixth-round knock-out, was only bitter-sweet. In 1962, Marshall would again attempt to puncture the Liston legend, insisting to the *Detroit Free Press* that he had knocked Sonny down during the course of that second contest, a feat no other foe managed until Ali. 'He hurts when he breathes on you,' Marshall would relate during the build-up to Sonny's challenge to Floyd Patterson. 'But I can't understand why he insists he was never knocked down. I remember every little thing about it. I wish it had never happened. It was the fourth round. I knew I had to stay away from him, because if he hits you . . . but Liston has a fault. He drags that right hand. I mean, he carries it too low. He came in with that left of his, and I crossed over with my right to his jaw. He went down. I don't know whether he was down for an eight count because he needed it, or because the rules required it. But he was down.'

From his vantage point in Sonny's corner, Tony Anderson begged to differ: 'Marshall landed a punch on Liston's glove, and Liston had his feet so tied up he fell. The referee started to count. I told him it wasn't a knock-down.' Whether or not we accept his version, Marshall paid for his temerity. 'He hit me after that like . . . nobody should be hit like that. I think about it now and I hurt. He came after me in the fifth round. He hit me with a right hand on my ear. It didn't knock me out and it didn't knock me down. But it hurt so much, I just had to go down anyway. The next round he knocked me down three times. I've got two parts of me that remember Sonny Liston – that ear he hit, and my stomach. He hit me in the stomach with a left hand in the sixth. That wasn't a knock-down, either. It couldn't be. I was paralysed. I just couldn't move. I didn't move enough to fall down. But he didn't know I was hurt, because I was doubled over and his head was above me. He couldn't see my face to know I was in pain. It didn't matter. He knocked me down three times later in the round, and that was it. But the thing that gets me is his not remembering the time I knocked him down. Everybody remembers. It was in the papers.'

The debate, though, was irrelevant. Maybe Sonny could be toppled from the vertical, but he was beginning to introduce his opponents to the canvas with such regularity that the odd momentary reversal could be brushed off with the nonchalance of a wildebeest flicking midges from its hide. The midges came and fell, Marshall merely the first to be dispatched in a run of five consecutive KOs whose comprehensive authority disguised the hectic nature of Sonny's schedule. In Pittsburgh on 5 May 1955, he levelled Emil Brtko in the fifth; back in St Louis less than three weeks later, Calvin Butler was prone by the second; in Indianapolis on 13 September, Johnny Gray contrived to stay upright until the sixth; and Larry Watson lasted into the fourth in East St Louis on 13 December.

It was just prior to the rubber match with Marshall in Pittsburgh on 6 March 1956, in which Sonny would outpoint his quasi-nemesis over ten rounds, that Frank Mitchell met Tom Tannas, the erstwhile manager of Ezzard Charles. 'I approached Tannas and I told him, "I've got the next heavyweight champion of the world. Can you move him for me?" ' Tannas agreed to take a 50 per cent stake, the share apparently vacated by Eddie Yawitz's mysterious disappearance from the scene. Pausing briefly in his efforts to talk Charles into retirement, Tannas wrote a letter to Nat Fleischer who, it seems, had forgotten the prospect-of-the-month of two years ago: 'I have a heavyweight prospect who might have it all. His name is Sonny Liston. I'm having trouble getting him fights, and maybe a plug would help. Don't worry about him standing up.' The outlook was certainly promising, but gloom soon consumed the horizon as of old, convincing Tannas to change his mind.

On 5 May 1956, Sonny and Geraldine attended a party thrown by some friends on North Taylor Avenue, St Louis. Accounts of what transpired varied extravagantly, but the upshot was the same: Sonny was charged with beating up a police officer and leaving him unconscious behind 2818 North Taylor Avenue, the law enforcer in question being hospitalised with a smashed knee and a seven-stitch gash over his left eye. 'I was making my relief corner and passed an alley,' reported Patrolman Thomas Mellow. 'A cab was parked in it with the parking lights on. From the entrance to the alley I asked who the driver was. The driver came down, said his name was Patterson. I told him he could get a ticket, but I was going to let him move the cab. Then Liston came down. "You can't give him no ticket," he said, real rough like. "The hell I can't," I said. I took out my ticket book and flashlight to get the city sticker number off the cab. As I started over, Liston came over and gave me a bear hug from the front, lifting me clear off the ground.' Mellow then related how Sonny and the cabbie allegedly dragged him to the rear of the alley where, he claimed, Sonny grabbed his gun and Patterson told Sonny to 'shoot the white son of a bitch'. Then, Mellow stated, 'Liston releases me and points the gun at my head. I'm pushing up on the barrel with both hands to keep from looking down the muzzle. They were walking all over me. I hollered, "Don't shoot me." Liston let up and then he hit me over the eye – with either his fists or the gun. Then they ran up the alley.' Mellow, according to the official police report, was 'found lying in the alley, badly beaten, with his uniform torn, his badge ripped off, and his revolver missing.'

Sonny painted a backdrop of a rather different hue: 'I saw the cab pull into the alleyway, and I hurried out of the house. Meanwhile, a cop came up and told the cabbie he was going to give him a ticket. I said, "How come you going to give the cab a ticket? He's just doing his business." The cop turns on me and says, "You're a smart nigger," and when I say, "I'm not smart," he reaches for his gun and tries to take it out of his holster, but I take it away from him. Later, the cop said I was drunk. Now, how could a drunk handle a sober cop trained to make arrests and to pull his gun?' In his statement to the St Louis police, Sonny also alleged that Mellow had insulted Geraldine. Knowing Sonny's (literal) distaste for alcohol at that stage of his life, a friend dismissed the possibility of his having been inebriated: 'He gets as sick as a dog. Whatever happened in that alley, it wasn't drinking that caused it.' In fact, Frank Mitchell, who pleaded with the authorities for leniency upon hearing Sonny's side of the saga, claimed the obverse was true. 'Sonny told me this cop called him a black son of a bitch. He said the cop said, "Take care of your own business or I'll lock you up." The truth of the matter is, the policeman had been drinking. When the cop called him this name, Sonny just grabbed him, hugged him, took the pistol away from him, and the cop fell on his leg and broke it. He'd been in the hospital before because of his leg. Sonny got excited. Not knowing what to do he ran. He went to his sister's.' Mitchell, though, was relying on second-hand information, since he was out of town at the time. Although Patterson denied any involvement, the police elicited a statement from the cabbie saying that he had waited at the entrance to the alley and then driven Sonny to 15th Street, where his sister lived. At one point in the journey, Patterson recalled, Sonny showed him a .38 revolver and told him that he had taken it from Mellow. The gun was indeed recovered at 15th Street.

Sonny was duly incarcerated for nine months in the city workhouse, and released in seven. The sentence itself was perhaps the most perplexing, not to say suspicious, element of this affair. Nine months for beating up a cop, if that is what Sonny did, was a piffling slap on the wrist when compared with the punishments generally doled out for offences of that ilk. St Louis, furthermore, was not a city then renowned for its concept of racial equality. A black ex-jailbird duffs up a policeman, nicks his gun and runs. Surely this was a cue for the full wrath of the system to hail down? There were other, lesser anomalies. Why didn't Mellow simply put a ticket on the cab windshield and be done with it? The officer later said he entered the house on North Taylor Avenue at one point, a statement at odds with his earlier evidence – but why? Could he not have stated his purpose at the door? In March 1956, Martin Luther King had vowed that the civil rights campaign would rely on 'passive resistance and the weapon of love', an assertion made in the wake of the arrest of the 115 blacks who had participated in a bus boycott in Montgomery, Alabama. This must have sounded a shade idealistic to Sonny. The whiff of racial victimisation saturated the whole rancid business, and continued to besiege him wherever he turned. Suspended from boxing by the Missouri State Athletic Commissioner, Charles W. Pian, Sonny was arrested on four further occasions while awaiting his December trial date: on 14 June, he was pulled up for speeding; a week later, he was picked up as a suspected thief and released; on 14 August, he was had up for failing to answer the speeding summons; and on 14 October, he was again suspected of being a thief, again without sufficient grounds. The consistency of the dates, naturally, was purely coincidental.

'A pattern was beginning,' Pete Hamill later observed in the *New York Post*. 'The St Louis police force apparently had declared war on Sonny Liston.' When Sonny left the workhouse in the summer of 1957, the automatic fire resumed with even greater systematic intensity. 'We wanted to break up Liston's associations with hoodlums. Every time we could jump Liston up, find him, we did,' one officer volunteered. 'Every time he fights, half the hoodlums in the country turn up in St Louis,' contended another. Captain John A. Doherty, who had a weakness for boxing, ordered his staff to 'arrest all known gangsters on sight. If they don't belong in St Louis and if you haven't got anything on them, run them out of town.' When Sonny fought at the Arena, plain-clothes cops were scattered throughout the aisles and entrances.

Sonny rolled with the punches. 'Some night you'll wind up dead,' a local sportswriter warned him, but that 'didn't seem to move him at all'. Indeed, Sonny would glance back at his predicament with surprising, if distinctly black, humour: 'There was nothing they didn't pick me up for. If I went into a store and asked for a stick of gum, they'd say it was a stick-up.' In a serialised, ghosted autobiography in the *Chicago-American*, however, Sonny strove to analyse the situation, and why neither Joe Louis nor Floyd Patterson ever encountered such overt attention. 'In the first place, I probably came from a worse environment than they did. They were raised in the north, in Detroit and New York, where people are at least aware of the juvenile problem. I was raised in the south, which is just now tackling the problem. I'm sure I would have been better had I been fortunate enough to meet a [Cus] D'Amato . . . You know what I often wonder about? Where were all those people who claim they were interested in juvenile delinquents when I was coming along as a kid?'

Commissioner Pian none the less deemed Sonny worthy of a reprieve. 'After a series of arrests, Liston came to me and asked for another chance. I talked to Captain Doherty, who was then head of the hoodlum squad, and to several sportswriters, and they agreed he might merit another chance, if gotten away from hoodlums.' Thus it was that Pian obtained approval to lift Sonny's suspension. Not that that was much use. The prospect of having their every move scrutinised by the law deterred opponents from venturing to St Louis. Yet another spoke in a wheel that seemed to be coming off.

Others, though, were in motion by the time Sonny re-emerged via two knock-outs in Chicago in early 1958, Bill Hunter the first victim inside two rounds on 29 January, and Ben Wise enduring twice as long before succumbing on 11 March. That same evening, Sonny signed a five-year contract, to all intents and purposes with – Blinky Palermo. Frank Mitchell, John Vitale and Sonny had driven to the Windy City for the Sugar Ray Robinson-Gene Fullmer fight the previous January, where they met up with Blinky. Sonny, trumpeted Mitchell, was no less than 'the next heavyweight champion', a boast he repeated when he bumped into Truman Gibson and Joe Louis in Detroit. 'He [Palermo] asked me the same question I had been asking myself,' Mitchell recalled. 'Why waste Liston when he was ready for the big time?' Palermo advised Mitchell that, although he could not possibly take over the managerial reins himself, he could 'get somebody to help you'. That somebody was Joseph 'Pep' Barone, a Philadelphia matchmaker who also operated the Pep Athletic Club in Allentown. Barone rang Mitchell upon the latter's return to St Louis following the Hunter fight, and the pair, along with Vitale, reconvened in Chicago, where Barone informed Mitchell that he was taking over as the manager of record and would bring Sonny back to Philly with him. Barone obtained a 24 per cent stake in Sonny's future, Vitale and Palermo 12 per cent apiece, and Frankie Carbo, naturally, the controlling 52 per cent.

The motivation for Carbo and his chums was transparent. The heavyweight title was now in the clutches of Floyd Patterson, and hence Cus D'Amato, his feisty and fiercely protective manager-cum-Svengali. Fearful of giving out his address in case the Mob came a-knocking, D'Amato slept in the back room of his New York gym on East 14th Street, his only companions a police dog and, so legend has it, a revolver under the pillow. His dedication and paranoia were equally well encapsulated by his sleeping habits prior to Patterson's tussle with Archie Moore in 1956 for the hot seat vacated by Marciano's retirement. So certain was Cus that the Mob would send its goons to hurt his boy, he bedded down outside Floyd's bedroom door for the last few weeks of training – in a cot. In the learned opinion of the Mob, Cus was 'crazy', an epithet generally conferred on prominent members of their hit list. The reason was simple: Cus was repelled by organised crime and refused to bow and scrape. Acutely aware of the identities of those at the source of the IBC monopoly, he battled James Norris at every turn. And while Patterson was champion, he could dictate the terms. Sonny was coming to be regarded as the Mob's avenging angel.

All the wheeling and dealing, however, was subsequent to an odd little episode that began around the turn of the year. A supposedly reputable Chicago businessman who 'dabbled in the fight game as a hobby' (but whose name Mitchell preferred to keep anonymous) had informed the manager that he thought he would be able to 'get some fights here for Sonny'. In another letter to Fleischer, Tom Tannas, though well out of the picture, had underscored the difficulties in getting fights for Sonny anywhere: 'Liston can fight like hell, and those in boxing know it. That is one of the principal reasons he can't get fights. He's too good. No one wants any part of him these days.' Now, however, all of a sudden, there was even talk of a television sponsor on a local or regional basis. On 3 February, a week after hunting down Hunter, Sonny apparently signed a three-year contract whereby he would be entitled to 50 per cent of all future purses, with Mitchell and 'the Chicagoan' sharing the other half and paying all expenses incurred. Once Sonny had got the better of Wise, though, this deal became inoperative for some reason, even though the St Louis attorney responsible for drawing it up insisted that it was 'completely legal'. According to the erratic Mitchell, when Pep Barone first contacted him, he 'assumed' our chap from Chicago was behind it all. But, when Mitchell and his unidentified acquaintance met up after Sonny had left town, the latter said he had played no part in the new arrangement because 'some of the boys in the fight mob came up to me one night and said they were taking Sonny east'. The plot, as ever, remained thick with loose ends, not to mention thieves.

For Frank Mitchell, after he had sold his interest to Vitale, this was effectively the end of the line. When the Senate hearings commenced in 1960, he would claim that he had been forced to pawn jewellery in order to pay his legal fees, and that Sonny still owed him $2000. Yet the way Mitchell told it, the parting of the ways seemed amicable, if illusory. 'I asked Sonny, "Is this OK?" Sonny said, "Yes, I want to leave St Louis. The police are bothering me." Barone said that, when Sonny was made, I'd be "in". From then on, I was practically out of the picture.' Mitchell nevertheless retained a keen affection for Sonny, and expressed as much to 'Doc' Young: 'He's playful, he's jolly. He likes to kid all the time. He has a great sense of humour. But I think that, had he had an education, he wouldn't have been a professional man. To my knowledge, he doesn't drink. He's really good at heart. He likes children. He has a lot of sympathy for underprivileged people. When he first came to me he couldn't write his name. He had to draw it. I tried to get him to go to school – night-school – but he wouldn't. I tried to teach him to write at the office – but he became impatient. It lasted about a week or so. When he first came to St Louis he ran with rough kids around North and O'Fallon and Franklin, down in that area. It was just a beehive of activity in juvenile crime. It was a hell-hole . . . a ghetto, a slum area . . . poor housing, wobbly steps, broken windows, filth!'

It should be said that Mitchell's recollection might best be accompanied by a sizeable cellar of salt. By his own admission, he would take the Fifth Amendment when summoned to the Kefauver hearings, because 'I couldn't remember accurately the whole story – I was afraid I'd subject myself to perjury.' But if Mitchell now began to fade into the background, Sonny, in contrast, was firmly in the foreground, and far from the filth of yore. Home was now an apartment in the Hamilton Court Hotel, Philadelphia – where Palermo owned a restaurant – complete with rent, food, clothing and the use of a car, evidently at Palermo's expense. Documentary proof, in the form of a $300 restaurant receipt and a hotel bill, both

Sonny's, was discovered in the briefcase which Blinky was carrying when he was arrested in June 1959 in the course of watching Virgil Akins at the St Louis Arena. This, though, was not known at the time. What mattered was that Sonny now had the launching-pad his ring skills deserved. This game of pass-the-parcel was beginning to run his way, even if he was the one being lobbed from hand to hand.

Six

The Chase

*Martin Luther King took us to the mountain top; I want to
take us to the bank. I'm not fighting the Civil War, I'm
fighting the poverty war.*

(Don King)

There are many who contend that the day the music died was 24
March 1958, the day Elvis Presley reported to the Memphis draft
board to have his locks lopped off. For Sonny, however, it was
merely the overture that was over. The exposition started in St
Louis ten days later when he outpointed the obdurate veteran, Bert
Whitehurst, over ten rounds. Next up was Chicago and Julio
Mederos, whom he knocked out in three while Mitchell and Barone
hovered in the wings, haggling over his future. 'He hurt me with his
jab,' mumbled Mederos afterwards, scarcely able to credit the
source of his fate. Chicago was also the venue for a nationally
televised bout on 6 August against the powerful Wayne Bethea,
who was expected to provide Sonny with his first truly rigorous
examination. The test lasted precisely fifty-six seconds, Bethea
losing seven teeth as well as face in a skirmish that catapulted
Philadelphia's most conspicuous 210lb resident into the wider
public consciousness. Truman Gibson said he would offer Floyd
Patterson $250,000 to fight Sonny, but the gauntlet was treated
with silent disdain. Cus D'Amato, after all, was at loggerheads with
Gibson and his IBC brethren, although some were already
beginning to suspect that the adroit manager was merely thinking of
his champion's health.

The stop-go pattern of his career thus far had left Sonny with a surfeit of energy and a liberal dose of determination. Now, at last, it was time to turn on the tap. Frankie Daniels prolonged their argument at Miami Beach on 7 October with barely more conviction than Bethea, hitting the floor in the first round and manfully resisting any urge to rise. Less than three weeks later came another scrap with the wily Whitehurst, in what would prove to be Sonny's last fight in St Louis for eleven long years. Again they went the distance, and again it was 'The Bear' whose paw was raised. Sonny's eighth and final bout of an industrious year then saw him return to Miami Beach on 18 November and call in Ernie Cab's number inside eight rounds. Three rousing appearances on national television were enough to secure a No.7 rating in *The Ring*'s end-of-year poll to discover the country's most popular fighters.

The real ground-breaker came the following February. Pitted against the Syracuse-based Mike De John in Miami, Sonny, now ranked for the first time among the ten leading contenders for Patterson's title, captivated another nationwide audience by bringing proceedings to a close in the sixth. The left put De John down for a count of eight then, as he rose, the right bounced him back to earth. 'He can't fight,' attested De John, who had previously shaken Sonny in the third. Rocky Marciano, no less, was in profound disagreement. Sonny, he predicted, would be ready for Patterson within a year if he crouched a little lower and moved his hands more rapidly.

Marciano also felt that the left jab needed sharpening, although that comment may have been a tad tongue-in-cheek. 'His left jab is the best of any fighter I've seen since Louis. This fellow gets real force into his jabs like Joe used to do. He's great, just great. The left jab set up De John. Then Liston cut him down with body punches. To me, he appeared a more effective body puncher than [Ezzard] Charles. I would have to say Ez was a better boxer. I thought Liston looped his punches more than he should. He should shorten 'em up more. He can move faster than Jersey Joe [Walcott]. I'd rank Liston No.2, right behind the Swede [Ingemar Johansson].' But could Sonny take a punch? 'I don't know,' conceded Marciano. 'He really didn't have to, fighting De John. A couple of upper-cuts shook him. His legs wobbled, but he came right again.' Would the Rock fancy taking on Sonny himself? 'No thanks.'

Not that Sonny was growing fat on the proceeds of his labours. For the De John fight, he was entitled to the TV receipts plus half the gate, but his more highly rated victim had been guaranteed $20,000. This, Sonny claimed, virtually stripped the cupboard bare once Barone and company had taken their quota. This inequable arrangement would be repeated as reluctant foes started to demand their danger money. Palermo, meanwhile, received his share for handing control over Sonny's TV appearances to IBC. Jim Norris's desperation was transparent: Patterson was out of reach, and Ingemar Johansson, about to be the new champion, was similarly untouchable. On 26 June 1959, the 4–1 underdog from Gothenburg knocked Patterson down with his celebrated, self-styled 'Hammer of Thor' right hand in the third round of their meeting at Yankee Stadium. There were six further counts before referee Ruby Goldstein called a halt, a throw-back to Dempsey's demolition of Luis Firpo thirty-six years earlier.

While bent on garnishing Sonny's reputation by matching him with predominantly inferior opponents in front of the armchair masses, Norris had turned his attention to Johansson some time before he overturned Patterson. The man who apparently controlled the Swede, a youthful promoter, William P. Rosensohn, was duly installed as president of Worldwide Boxing Promotions Inc., a new company assembled by Truman Gibson. Here again, though, the machinations were greasier than they appeared. When Gibson met up with Johansson and his adviser, Edwin Ahlqvist, he became aware that Rosensohn Enterprises was largely under the auspices of the infamous Tony 'Fats' Salerno and a low-life bookie, Charley Black. Norris accordingly ditched the impotent Rosensohn and made a beeline for the champion, but Johansson, a shrewd, spirited man, refused to play ball. In a series of magazine interviews he revealed that Salerno, in fact, had garnered his one-third share for helping persuade Cus D'Amato to agree to Patterson defending his title against him, while Black, a friend of Cus's, had extracted his for enlisting Salerno's support in the first place. Thus had Johansson been compelled to take on Rosensohn as his American manager. Rosensohn was consequently divested of his match-making and promoter's licences by the NYSAC, at which point Roy Cohn entered the picture. Having previously earned notoriety as Joe McCarthy's counsel, Cohn together with his partner, Bill Fugazy, took over Rosensohn Enterprises and then formed Feature Sports Inc., under which guise they promoted the first two Patterson-Johansson encounters.

In the meantime, the battle to denude the IBC continued to rumble. In January 1955, less than a year after he had affirmed boxing's exemption from the anti-monopoly regulations imposed by the Sherman Act, Judge Noonan had been overruled by the Supreme Court. Replenished with evidence supplied by the NYSAC, the Justice Department demonstrated how 'The Octopus' was dipping into pots far beyond the nearest state line. As a measure of the predator's potential, the prosecution revealed that 25 per cent of current IBC earnings came through sales of transmission rights, and forecast that technological advances would swell that quota considerably (in one particularly fruitful year, as it transpired, IBC revenue peaked at $8.5 million, with telecasts the principal benefactor). IBC clung to the 1922 ruling in *Federal Baseball Club v. National League* as a sinking man would a raft, but the Supreme Court, in defiance of all logic, reinforced baseball's uniquely hallowed place in the national consciousness by deciding that, since all sports were not created equal, only the national pastime was exempt from antitrust legislation.

The upshot was that IBC embarked on a diet, shedding all of its most obvious monopolist trappings. The leases on St Nicholas Arena, the Polo Grounds and Yankee Stadium were relinquished, the contract with Joe Louis allowed to lapse, all exclusive contracts shelved. This, however, made little impression on the scales of justice. On 2 July 1957, the district court for the Southern District of New York found James Norris, his partner Arthur Wirtz, the International Boxing Clubs for New York and Illinois, and the Madison Square Garden Corporation guilty of violating the

Sherman Act. Judge Sylvester J. Ryan ordered the two men to dissolve the IBC and to sell all their stock in the Garden within five years (which ultimately had the somewhat ironic effect of more than doubling their initial investment of $1.7 million). Unlikely support for IBC came from hitherto hostile commentators such as Arthur Daley of the *New York Times*, who was adamant that the end of IBC would 'create a vacuum with nothing but chaos on its fringes'. IBC, he argued, was the cement that bonded boxing's 'diverse fragments' – in other words, it was a necessary evil. To Daley and public alike, what mattered was the bill of fare, not the chefs and restaurants. With IBC blending the ingredients, boxing had been served by a conveyor belt stocked with crowd-pleasing talent. Their pockets bulging, broadcasters and advertisers were happy, too. But IBC profited most, of course, and the Supreme Court, equally naturally, decided it had 'an odorous monopoly background'.

Appeals ensued. The onus was now on Congress to rephrase the strictures of the Sherman Act, but this political football, predictably, was punted straight back to the Supreme Court, which to this day has yet to bring baseball, now prospering under the extensive umbrella of Major League Baseball, into line with other sports. Baseball had long since recovered from the 'Black Sox' scandal of 1919, when Charlie Comiskey, the owner of the Chicago White Sox, paid his pennant-winning team such a pittance that eight of their number accepted bribes to throw that year's World Series, thus providing Scott Fitzgerald with the inspiration for Meyer Wolfsheim and his molar cuff buttons ('A dentist?' 'No, he's the man who fixed the World's Series'). Now, however, the sport was felt to symbolise America at its squeaky-cleanest. On the other hand, IBC, which staged 99 per cent of all championship fights between 1949 and 1959, was associated with boxing, one of the most pus-ful zits on the nation's self-image. Yet, in rejecting IBC's entreaties, the Supreme Court overlooked one gaping loophole: the IBC's parent companies, the Chicago Stadium Corporation and the Madison Square Garden Corporation, could simply sprout new arms to promote their boxing activities. Thus were National Boxing

Enterprises and Title Promotions Inc. born, both allegedly under the direction of Truman Gibson. By such means did Norris, who by this time had ostensibly passed control to Gibson anyway, mount his bid to wrest the heavyweight crown from outside clutches.

This mission was rendered all the more imperative by the decline of boxing on the small screen. In 1952, some 31 per cent of viewers had tuned in to boxing broadcasts; by 1959, the programme schedules were vastly more varied and that figure had been slashed to 10.6 per cent, persuading sponsors that prize-fight promotions promised a limited source of revenue. Indeed, NBC dropped its coverage the following year, provoking a backlash that harangued television for deserting a ship it had itself done so much to sink. In the view of the NYSAC's James Farley Jnr, most of boxing's recent ills 'have stemmed from the control of television through the auspices of Jim Norris, the IBC, and their associates'.

Not that any of this tempered Sonny's hunger in the early part of 1959. 'Now we want only rated fighters,' Pep Barone had declared after Sonny decked De John. 'We want to fight the best and we feel public opinion will force a match with whoever is champion after Floyd Patterson fights Ingemar Johansson.' Cleveland 'The Big Cat' Williams, who would challenge Muhammad Ali eight years later when well past his prime, fitted the bill admirably. Though hailed by Sonny as the hardest hitter in the division, Williams had precious little time to inflict any damage when the pair locked horns in Miami in April, being up-ended in the third round. In August, by which time Johansson had unseated Patterson (and Carbo, Palermo, Sica, Dragna and Gibson had been rounded up by the FBI), Sonny was reunited in Chicago with Nino Valdes, an even more hazardous obstacle. The Cuban may have scotched his chances of fighting Marciano – 'his manager didn't want Rocky to fight me, so he came to see me and asked me to fight Rocky for nothing; I picked up a chair and threatened to throw it at him' – yet he remained a redoubtable proposition. Once again, though, it was all over by the end of the third. First came a left to the stomach, then a left hook to the head that staggered Valdes and forced him to drop his guard, then a right cross to complete the job. The year ended with a technical knock-out over Willi Besmanoff in Cleveland on 9 December, Besmanoff failing to answer the bell for the seventh after sustaining heavy cuts over both eyes. (Two years later, by way of comparison, a voluble young whipper-snapper by the name of Cassius Clay would knock out Besmanoff in seven rounds.) More encouraging still, D'Amato's part in the Johansson-Patterson fracas had cost him his licences as manager and second within the jurisdiction of the NYSAC. That set in train his gradual divorce from Patterson, although he continued to advise the ex-champ and receive a third share of the purses for the duration of his suspension.

Sonny and Geraldine were finally in the process of obtaining a home of their own, a two-storey house, No. 5785 Dunlap Street, Philadelphia, to be exact. The outlook seemed rosier than ever. It was clouded, however, by Sonny's first run-in with the Philly constabulary. Upon arriving at the scene of a car accident, Patrolman David E. Knox reported finding Sonny grappling with the inappropriately-named John Polite. Knox stated that, when he questioned the pair, they became loud and unruly. For his part, Sonny claimed he had been slugged from behind, though by whom he did not know. There was no arrest, but the signs were familiar. Sonny's exploits in St Louis had accompanied him like a tattoo. To the local police, he had beaten up a fellow-officer, and this supposedly gave them *carte blanche* to harass him at every conceivable turn. Little did he know that his photo was taped to the sun visor of every squad car in the city.

For the moment, mind, this incident appeared to be no more than a speck of dandruff. Since the wins over De John, Williams, Valdes and Besmanoff had all been televised to a nationwide audience, it was less than surprising when Sonny was elevated to the summit of *The Ring*'s fan poll. Other, more dispassionate, observers concurred. 'Who would you pick to lick him?' wondered Teddy Brenner, the Madison Square Garden matchmaker, who shook his head with pity at the prospect. 'I wouldn't bet on a grizzly bear against Liston,' proffered Davey Moore's trainer, Teddy Bentham. Sugar Ray Robinson's trainer, Harry Wiley, was more circumspect: 'A very powerful man, but a little slow. A fellow who can move and stick would have a good chance against him.' Charley Rose, the veteran manager, merely issued a warning: 'Wait until they really turn him loose, if they ever do.'

In the January issue of *The Ring* came a more pragmatic view from Ted Carroll, who wondered whether Sonny was destined for frustration: 'Is he fated to join the late Sam Langford and Harry Wills as the third member of a trio who, due to conditions over which they had no control, never got the chances they deserved?' Carroll stressed Sonny's credentials, while outlining the quandary he presented. 'Managers do a disappearing act when Liston's name is brought up as an opponent for their lads, even in these TV times of scant selectivity. Sportswriters, disturbed by his "connections" and personal history, are hesitant in penning the panegyrics which would ordinarily be his, and commissioners are nervously awaiting the time when some decision will have to be made as to his fitness to assume the No.1 contendership which, purely from the standpoint of ability, seems inevitable . . . Under the argument of rehabilitation, and having paid his debt to society, the imperfections in his past may be waived as they were in the case of Rocky Graziano and others. But Liston's reported patrons provide a puzzler since the elimination of undesirable influences in boxing management are most difficult to bring about. No real solution to the setting up of a "front man" has been found, even if Frankie Carbo has been jailed.'

The inevitable crept inexorably closer when the 1960s opened, a landmark quickly followed by the death of another sporting outsider who favoured violence as an absurd gesture of intellectual despair – Albert Camus, the Algerian goal-keeper who gave Sartre a run for his money as the custodian of French literature. Returning to Miami on 23 February, Sonny gained his sixth successive knock-out victory at the expense of Howard King, who had taken a cruel left to the solar plexus and was being counted out by referee Jimmy Peerless when the bell went to end the seventh. Sense prevailed, and King was forced to abdicate before the start of the eighth. Cleveland Williams's claws were blunted even more comprehensively than they had been in Miami when he and Sonny were rematched in Houston four weeks later: this time, he failed to survive the second.

Sonny was now firmly installed as the official No. 1 contender ahead of Patterson, who had signed to fight Johansson again at the Polo Grounds in June. Not that he harboured any illusions about the significance of this: 'I could be No. 1 for a long time,' he told reporters, more than a little ruefully. Then came the braggadocio, as Sonny wrily pronounced himself willing and able to take on Patterson and Johansson simultaneously. One equally playful writer asked him what would happen if one of them got behind him. 'That's what the ropes and corners are for. They can't get behind me there.' Occupying his corner now was Willie Reddish, a 43-year-old ex-heavyweight from Philly who had been driving a truck and training young pugs for the Police Athletic League in his spare time when Sonny plucked him from obscurity to be his trainer a year earlier.

Sonny remained in Houston to reinforce that ranking in April against the local hero, Roy Harris, the ex-teacher from Cut'n'Shoot, Texas, who had floored Patterson in August 1958 before his tilt at the world title was terminated in the twelfth. Harris had comprised the white half of the first ever mixed-race bout in the Lone Star state, in April 1957, an encounter recalled in *Time* magazine by his opponent, Bob Baker, a man whose flair for decorative yarns far outweighed his fistic ability. 'I knew I was going to lose. I was fighting a white boy, and no coloured man is going to beat a white boy in Texas. I hit him and he went down, and I thought, "Why, this boy can't fight at all." But I can hear the crowd, and they're counting on this boy. So I said, "Kid, please get up." I know that, if he didn't get up, they weren't going to let me out of that town alive. I love my wife and I love my kids, and most of all I love me. And I told the kid to get up, and I'm thankful that he did. And after that I was careful not to hit him. So he won.'

If Sonny was beset by similar concerns he did his best not to show it. Still rated among the world's top half-dozen despite a general suspicion within the trade that he had never been anything more than a 'ham-and-egger', Harris weighed in 17½lb behind Sonny's 212½ and soon felt the difference. In the first round, Sonny uncorked a stunning left hook to propel Harris under the ropes for a count of nine. Shaking his head in an effort to silence the clanging bells, Harris rose momentarily, only to be sent right back whence he came courtesy of another withering hook. Another nine count. Again Harris staggered upward, again the left hook reversed his flight path. Since three knock-downs in a round constituted an automatic TKO under NBA rules, that was it. 'He's a better puncher than Patterson,' commented Harris, after what was only the second loss in his thirty-two-fight career.

The merry-go-round continued apace. On 22 June, Patterson laid out Johansson in round five, the Swede's left foot fluttering in the breeze as the rest of his body froze. Any lingering doubts about Sonny's right to be the next challenger were then erased with similar finality against men whom the renascent champion had studiously avoided. The first 'Fancy Dan' Sonny had ever encountered, the skilful Zora Folley, was conceding 14lb when he entered the Denver ring armed with a record of ten consecutive wins. The gambling fraternity and critics alike envisaged this as Sonny's most searching task yet, favouring the boxer ahead of the slugger. So much for expert opinion. Midway through the second round, Sonny had put Folley down for two counts of nine. Folley recovered to back Sonny across the canvas, only to walk slap-bang into a left hook followed crisply by a right to the head that clubbed him to the floor. The bell intervened to save Folley as he rose without enthusiasm. At the outset of the third, he attempted to dance out toward Sonny, but his legs dragged and his eyes were as misty as a Loch Lomond dawn. Sonny feinted with his left as Folley tried to shake his marbles back into place, then landed a conclusive right-left combination. Only six minutes and twenty-eight seconds had been required for that left hook to supply the denouement for the ninth time running.

Next on the chopping-block, in an official elimination contest, was Eddie Machen, a cagey, clever fighter who had no intention of knocking off early. For a Seattle gathering numbering 7682, not forgetting a nationwide TV throng, the result was eminently unspectacular. Adopting negative run-and-hold tactics, Machen spent most of the evening retreating from Sonny's left jab. One moment grabbing Sonny in a sprawling embrace, the next twisting from side to side to avoid right crosses, he even stooped to turning his back and simply running. The clinches clinched it. 'I had no respect for him,' Machen would later recall during Sonny's penultimate work-out for his first meeting with the then Cassius Clay. Indeed, he sparked a flare-up in the process by claiming that Sonny was disinclined to fight him again, shrewdly concealing the fact that he himself had ducked the challenge when offered a guaranteed $25,000. 'I kept asking him, "Where's that big punch?" and calling him names. He isn't used to being called names, and no one can calm him down either. The trainers can't say, "Look, Sonny, cool it", because he won't listen to them. I cursed him every time I got a chance. It kept him confused. It kept him from concentrating. He ain't the smartest guy in the world, you know.'

Bothered and bewildered, if not exactly bewitched, Sonny occasionally lost his temper, pushing and shoving and even wrestling with Machen. The catcalls flew: 'Get a bicycle . . . Use your right . . .' He turned his attention to Machen's ribs, and referee Whitey Rowstad twice docked points as the crowd snorted in response to a couple of suspiciously low blows. Not that the odd point was of any consequence. Machen had already won his solitary round when a barrage to the body dropped him to his knees in the eleventh. Rowstad picked up the count, then unaccountably stopped to give Machen a rest in the corner. The twelfth came and went, leaving Sonny a resounding winner on points. Stymied he may have been, and by a man whom Johansson had kayoed inside a round, but here, surely, was invaluable evidence that he had staying power.

Yet still the prevaricating persisted. For a while, it looked as if Patterson-Johansson III would be postponed but, even then, it was Henry Cooper, the British and Empire champion, and not Sonny, who was deemed the likelier opponent for Patterson, this owing much to D'Amato's friendship with Harry Levene, the London promoter. 'Is Patterson afraid of Liston?' asked John Hunter of Iowa State University in a letter to *The Ring*. 'Of course, Patterson is using the fact that some of Liston's associates are racketeers as an excuse.' Pride pricked by innumerable accusations of that ilk, Patterson rebelled, asserting his intention to fight Sonny should he defeat Johansson in Miami. When that latter promotion was finally put together and scheduled for March 1961, the parties responsible were Patterson and Roy Cohn's partner, Bill Fugazy, a link that pointed strongly to a rift between D'Amato and Patterson, one that could only work to Sonny's advantage.

While Sonny was in Seattle for the Machen fight, the spectre of Patrolman Thomas Mellow surfaced once more under the guise of a $90,000 suit for damages. Ten days later, it was reported that Sonny had filed a petition with the county clerk, Norman R. Riddell, requesting that, since the parties were residents of different states, the suit be removed from the state court to a federal one. If any settlement ensued, the details were never published. As with so many other episodes in Sonny's life, the truth sneaked out the back door, never to be seen again.

THE CHAMPION   THE CHALLENGER

HEAVYWEIGHT CHAMPIONSHIP OF THE WORLD

PRESS HEADQUARTERS
46 Beacon Street
Boston, Mass.

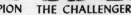

Seven

'I'd rather be a lamppost in Denver'

Now you swear and kick and beg us
That you're not a gambling man
Then you find you're back in Vegas
With a handle in your hand
Your black cards can make you money
So you hide them when you're able
In the land of milk and honey
You must put them on the table
You go back, Jack, do it again
Wheel turning round and round . . .

(Donald Fagen & Walter Becker, *Do It Again*)

Perhaps it was the chivalrous spirit engendered by John F. Kennedy's Arthurian ascent to the presidency? Most likely, it was the widespread acceptance that boxing would continue to lose credibility so long as the rightful challenger was denied the opportunity he so blatantly deserved. Whatever the reason, the NBA, together with Nat Fleischer and his fellow-scribes, were virtually unanimous in their support of Sonny after Patterson had downed Johansson in the sixth round of their third and final duel at Miami's Convention Hall on 13 March 1961. Scrutinised by Marciano, Schmeling and Louis, Sonny had again knocked out Howard King, a late substitute for the optimistically-dubbed Young Jack Johnson, in the eighth round of their clash at Miami Beach a couple of weeks earlier, this despite being decidedly overweight at 219½lb. Fleischer was especially voluble, urging Cus D'Amato to give Sonny 'his merited chance'.

Sonny then decided to take matters into his own hands, startling D'Amato by walking into his office and asking him why he wouldn't let Patterson fight him. The answer ran along the lines of 'you know what you have to do', one in keeping with D'Amato's oft-publicised demands that Sonny cleanse himself by bidding adieu to his questionable backers. 'I won't get the chance because of Cus D'Amato,' Sonny concluded. Instead, Edwin Ahlqvist offered to deposit $125,000 in an American bank to tempt Sonny into a bout with Johansson, to be staged in Sweden in September, even though his charge had also blacklisted Sonny during his tenure as champion because of the latter's management set-up. The worms were turning. Pep Barone's initial reaction was positive: 'We'd be delighted to take such a match. In fact, we'd like to fight Johansson and Patterson the same night.' This cockiness soon turned to caution. Ahlqvist, after all, was talking big. The fight would take place in a 63,000-capacity stadium and generate gate receipts in excess of $¾ million, with the winner going on to face Patterson the following June. Barone backtracked: 'You don't go into a thing like this before finding out how solid the offer is. I still need to be convinced Ahlqvist means business.' He may well have done, but subsequent events would supersede his plans.

Sonny was quickly reminded of the extent of the face-lift that was required. On 1 April, Dr Dan O. Kilroy, the chairman of the California State Athletic Commission, vowed that Sonny would never be permitted to fight within the state boundaries under his present management. 'From what we have learned,' Kilroy declared, 'Joseph Barone, who is Liston's manager of record, is no manager at all. Liston is managed by underworld figures who are hidden.' Sonny, he continued, had to prove 'he has rid himself of his underworld ties. And I just don't see how Liston can do that without a machine gun.' Influenced, it was rumoured, by Joe Louis, Sonny promptly announced he was asking Barone to give up his contract with two years still to run, 'so I can get a title fight', and resolved to quit the ring if he was refused.

On 19 April, in the Allentown offices of Eugene J. Gorman, the brother-in-law of the federal judge, J. Cullen Ganey, Sonny duly bought Barone out, agreeing to pay him out of the next two years' earnings. 'I don't see how Patterson will be able to walk down the street now, unless he gives me a fight,' Sonny reasoned. 'Is my house clean enough now for him to give me a fight, or was he only looking for an excuse to duck me when he told the world he wouldn't fight me until I cleaned house?' While denying any links with Carbo and Palermo, Barone claimed to have been offered $150,000 but was taking half that 'because I don't want to deprive him [Sonny] of a heavyweight title fight'. How considerate – although Barone, it can be safely presumed, was well looked after by his bosses. Senator Estes Kefauver, who was due to interrogate Sonny in two weeks' time, proclaimed that, provided the sale was valid, 'it will be a big boost to clean professional boxing'. D'Amato, typically, did not budge an inch. 'Whatever plans Patterson may have, already have been made. He [Sonny] is not included in these plans. He should have done this a long time ago. Anyone who may try to impose Liston upon Patterson, I will take to court.' The champion himself, besieged by tax problems and reputed to be lining up an unrated opponent to ensure a ruffle-free pay-day, assumed the posture of a self-appointed deity, reiterating his manager's insistence that Sonny get shot of his unscrupulous financiers. '[Sonny] will have to show me that he is free of all harmful outside influences. When he does that, he will be entitled to his chance.'

The next step along that path was to find a new manager, a task Sonny approached with characteristic irony. 'I'll ask Senator Kefauver to investigate him and make sure he's OK,' was one gem; 'I got to get me a manager that's not hot – like Estes Kefauver,' was another. Among the genuine claimants were Frank Rice, a 71-year-old Montreal resident, and Marciano, who said that an acquaintance of his, the dog-track owner, Russ Murray, was prepared to shell out $150,000 for a management contract. The man eventually chosen was George Katz, who had previously managed the unheralded Gil Turner and was now in for a relatively, not to say suspiciously, paltry share of 10 per cent of Sonny's purses (the usual managerial take was 33 per cent). 'Ten per cent of

$10 million isn't bad,' he countered when this discrepancy was queried. 'Besides, the circumstances are not ordinary. I'm taking over a fighter who's already the No. 1 contender.'

The announcement was made on 10 May 1961, in the Philadelphia restaurant owned by the former boxer, Lew Tendler. This drew a positive reaction from Kefauver: 'If my bill is enacted, the first act of the commission on boxing in my opinion should be to examine Mr Liston's new management with a fine tooth-comb and, if cleared, he should obtain a championship bout.' In approving the contractual arrangements, the Pennsylvania State Athletic Commission not only found Katz's record free of warts and recommended that the NBA ratify its actions, but also offered to handle all the fiscal details of the Barone sale and place the funds 'directly in Barone's hands' when due. Of far greater import was the commission's decision finally to grant Sonny a licence to fight in Philadelphia. This was the cue for Johansson, who was quoted in Geneva as saying he thought he could 'lick' Sonny and suggested a match-up before the year was out. The bottom line was certainly tempting: a guaranteed $200,000, plus $10,000 expenses. Ahlqvist was still thinking big. In Washington, meanwhile, a group of senators were clamouring for an inquiry to be held into the Barone deal. The $75,000 price tag, in their estimation, was simply too much of a bargain to be credible.

Even less credible were some of the characters summoned to appear before Kefauver and his cronies, hence the decision of many to scurry beneath the skirts of the Fifth Amendment. Among these reticent witnesses was Frank Mitchell who, according to Robert Turley, one of the sub-committee's investigators, nevertheless furnished the hearing with one of its more intriguing revelations, namely that he was still receiving 25 per cent of the manager's share from Sonny's purses despite having supposedly departed the scene three years previously. In spite of an understandable reluctance to come forward – he declined to answer eleven questions – Blinky Palermo was named as Sonny's undercover manager and Carbo's right hand, with Truman Gibson acknowledging that a cheque had been paid for Blinky's services in securing

Sonny for IBC. Asked whether he was aware that Palermo had a stake in Sonny's future, Gibson answered in the affirmative, citing Palermo himself as the source. 'Is that the first time you learned that Palermo had an undercover financial interest in Sonny Liston?' prodded investigator John Bonomi. 'Well, you refer to "undercover"; there was no such thing in Illinois, Mr Bonomi, as an undercover piece of a fighter. It was undisclosed, but there is no law in Illinois that requires the disclosure of an interest in a fighter.' Indeed, Palermo had been issued with a managerial licence by the Illinois authorities, also by those in Pennsylvania and other influential states, this after having his New York licence revoked. Only when Blinky came under police scrutiny did the other state athletic commissions follow suit.

Gibson's testimony was invaluable, but there remained a strong streak of sympathy for him within boxing circles and without. This, after all, was a man who had been a member of President Truman's committee on morals, character development and religion in the armed forces. Did he profit from his association with Carbo and Palermo, or was he a victim of a Frankensteinian system he had no part in creating? A letter Gibson wrote to Arthur Wirtz on 6 March 1962 would prove illuminating: 'What measure do you put on a man's life? Was your shrewd bargain, when we last met, your determination? I could not help but think then and now that I never knew Carbo before the organization of the IBC. I never cleared championships with him. I talked with him most infrequently. I certainly did not clear the Akins-Jordan fight with him. Someone did, and the fact that I didn't indicates who put me in the soup. While you are remembering things in the past, please also recollect that I didn't collect any of the profits (nor did Joe Louis, despite his agreement) from the split-up IBC operations from behind a nice insulated shield.'

Back at the Senate hearings, Herman Wallman piled more grist on the mill, testifying to the close association between Frankie Carbo and James Norris, and stating that a manager could make rapid progress once he employed one of Carbo's men as a representative or paid direct tribute to the mobsters. Some notable names endorsed Senate Bill 1474: Marciano said he favoured a national boxing commissioner, as did Louis, who asserted that boxing was in a disgraceful state and that gangsters had taken an unshakeable grip. Kefauver would do little to loosen it.

Sonny acquitted himself well when it was his turn to be hauled before the beak, to the extent that Kefauver concluded that it would be 'unconscionable' for his championship aspirations to be thwarted. A year earlier, when Kefauver had warned him to 'shake off' Palermo, John Vitale and company if he wanted a crack at the heavyweight title, the response had been a plaintive cry of, 'What was I to do, starve to death?' Sonny's testimony now was seared with the same sense of impotence. 'A lawyer can get you sent away to jail for twenty years but he still gets paid,' he reasoned at one juncture. 'A doctor can kill you but he still gets paid. Them guys can't lose. If I had to do it all over again, I would never be a fighter.' This mood was doused by splashes of humour, most of it self-deprecating. Following Palermo on to the stand, he was shown a slip of paper with Blinky's telephone number scrawled on it, evidence the police claimed to have found in Sonny's pocket. Was this his doing? Of course not: 'I don't write.'

After advising the investigation that he currently had $30,000 in the bank, Sonny indicated that his remuneration had not always been all it might (he claimed taking home a cursory $600 out of a purse of $6600 from the first fight against Howard King in Miami). Frank Burns, a St Louis police lieutenant, testified that Sonny had confessed to making the occasional collect call to Vitale to find out 'how everything was in St Louis', but this was shrugged off. Sonny had merely told the police 'what they wanted me to say' in order to rid himself of 'their constant harassment'. Explaining the genesis of his relationship with Barone, Sonny was innocence personified: 'Frank Mitchell told me when I left St Louis that it would be a man by the name of Pep Barone to come up with the contract and for you to sign it, and he will get you east where you can get sparring partners and more fights, a better trainer.' Questioned repeatedly about his associates, Sonny made another characteristic crack: 'I'd have to make $1 million a month to take care of all these people.' On a more serious note, he alleged that some of the ex-fighters now working for the St Louis police department 'wanted the captain [Doherty] to let them take me down to the basement. I said, "Okay – you guys think you're tough." But the captain didn't let them.'

What, though, of those murky faces behind the scenes? 'Pep Barone handles me,' reiterated Sonny. If that statement indicated his confusion over the state of affairs following the management buy-out, he still denied any knowledge of Carbo and Palermo's majority stakeholding. 'Before you can convict anybody for murder you have to come up with a body. Before you can convict me you got to come up with one of those guys as my manager. You can't do it.' 'Do you think that people like [Carbo and Palermo] ought to remain in the sport of boxing?' quizzed Kefauver. 'I wouldn't pass judgement on no one,' Sonny replied. 'I haven't been perfect myself.'

That much was indisputable. Sonny's problem was that his imperfections continued to be seized upon with such inordinate, relentless relish. The Philadelphia police were as determined as their St Louis brethren to bring him to heel, so much so that, in the midst of the hearings, he was arrested for the heinous crime of lounging on a street corner, setting in train a sequence of events that would ultimately prompt Sonny to leave town with the unforgettable parting shot, 'I'd rather be a lamppost in Denver than Mayor of Philadelphia.'

On 17 May, Patrolman James Best reported going to check on complaints about men congregating on a corner close to Sonny's home. When he found Sonny there with another man, he asked them to move. Sonny apparently refused, saying, 'Why not arrest me?' Best obliged. Four hours later, Sonny was released with nothing more than a reprimand in the wake of a special hearing conducted by Magistrate Harry Ellick. The other side of the tale came from his lawyer, Morton Witkin, who had previously served at various times as a majority and minority leader in the Pennsylvania House of Representatives. Sonny had been signing an autograph when Best, who somehow failed to recognise him, or at least said he didn't, ordered him to move on. When Sonny declined to do so he was taken to the police station, where the desk sergeant recognised him, listened to his story and dismissed the incident as a misunderstanding. 'Sonny,' Witkin explained, 'who can be strong-willed to a fault, wanted a lift back. "The red car brought me here," he said. "Let the red car take me back." That was the remark they locked him up for.'

That little escapade was merely the hors d'oeuvres. Sonny was known for his pranks, on one occasion turning off his headlights while doing 70 m.p.h. along the New Jersey Turnpike, on another pretending his car was out of gas while on a deserted stretch of road *en route* from New York to Philadelphia. His usual idea of fun, apart from the two-headed coin he still had from his prison days, was to recite dialogues, complete with sound effects, from the routines of black comedians such as Red Foxx and Pigmeat 'Here Comes The Judge' Markham. 'He could imitate what he heard down to creaking doors and women's voices,' recalled Jack McKinney of the *Philadelphia Daily News*, a regular companion and confidant. 'It was hilarious hearing him do falsetto.' Having fun at the expense of law enforcers was another matter, however, particularly when the law enforcers in question were lining up to catch him out.

On 12 June, the merry prankster went too far. At 3 a.m., John Warburton, a guard at Fairmount Park (through which Sonny had to drive to get home from the gym), noted the presence of two cars parked beside each other on Lansdowne Drive. When he approached the vehicles, he allegedly espied two men racing into one of them and then speeding away with the headlights out. The other car was driven by one Dolores Ellis, who apparently told Warburton that the men had flagged her over and pretended to be officers. For his part, Sonny assured Detective Richard Edwards that he had stopped the car because he thought he knew Mrs Ellis. Sonny and Isaac Cooper, whom George Katz testified as having accompanied his man on some road-work that night, were both consequently charged with impersonating an officer. Mrs Ellis testified that a spotlight had been shone in her face when Sonny's car pulled alongside hers, and that she had twice been instructed to get out of her seat. Sonny, she said, had remained at his wheel and she at hers, although Warburton stuck to his story about having seen *two* men run back to Sonny's car. Magistrate E. David Keiser ruled that the pair had been guilty solely of errors of judgement and ordered them to apologise to Mrs Ellis in court. Charges pertaining to disorderly conduct and resisting arrest were also dismissed. Sonny even found time for a quip, leaning over to Katz and saying, 'If I get time, you're entitled to 10 per cent of it.'

That, unfortunately, was not the half of it. Before the protagonists went to court, the Pennsylvania State Athletic Commission resolved to suspend Sonny's newly-granted licence were he convicted of any of the charges. The District Attorney's office launched an investigation and, lo and behold, despite Magistrate Keiser's dismissal of the case, the licence was suspended indefinitely on 14 July. The PSAC's rationale was plain to see: Sonny's two arrests constituted actions 'detrimental to boxing and the public'. Sonny threw himself on the mercy of Commissioners James H. Crowley, Alfred M. Klein and Paul Sullivan who, after an hour's deliberation, submitted their verdict to the seventy-five-strong throng that had congregated in a small office in the state building. The suspension would be effective throughout the NBA's member states 'until such time as you have rehabilitated yourself and demonstrated a respect for the law'. Sullivan maintained that Sonny had enormous physical and moral potential and that the commission had no intention of ruining his career. That No. 1 ranking nevertheless evaporated at a stroke.

A brief typed statement was issued on Sonny's behalf: 'I regret I have caused the Pennsylvania State Athletic Commission any embarrassment by reason of my indiscreet behaviour. I can assure the committee that, from now on in, I shall so conduct myself as to creditably merit the confidence you have imposed on me by granting me a boxer's licence. I place myself in your hands.' In the meantime, Philly was ablaze with rumour. One story had it that Mrs Ellis's lawyer had been paid $2500 to ensure a meek prosecution. District Attorney James C. Crumlish then claimed to have received an anonymous letter from, of all places, New Jersey, tipping him off that a $5000 pay-off, split between Mrs Ellis and her lawyer,

Harvey N. Schmidt, had procured Sonny's freedom. Crumlish ordered the immediate rearrest of Sonny and Cooper. Recently sworn in as the only black member of the city's voter registration commission, Schmidt rebutted the pay-off allegations and threatened to sue Dan Parker for an article the latter had written for the *New York Mirror* stating otherwise. 'I could not say these men did anything criminally wrong in respect of my client,' Schmidt said. 'That is the only reason why I agreed to allow my client to drop the matter.' Like any self-preserving journalist, Parker refused to name his purportedly irrefutable source and, at the hearing on 2 August, Sonny was released on $500 bail. In dismissing the charge of resisting arrest, Judge Victor Blanc was of the opinion that the case had been blown way out of proportion.

Even so, Sonny was still held on a charge of extinguishing his car lights in order to avoid identification. He appeared before Joseph Scanlon, the commissioner of jury trials, protested his innocence and requested trial by jury. This was duly set for 28 September, and Sonny was speedily acquitted. Joseph Gold, the presiding judge, averred that if it had not involved Sonny, the case 'would have been disposed of in the magistrate's court'. Sweating profusely and looking extremely overweight (he hadn't trained since March), Sonny denied fleeing the scene and insisted he had knocked the light switch by accident when in the process of disengaging the handbrake. 'I think Mr Liston is a very foolish man who has juvenile tendencies that will be knocked out of him one of these days,' suggested Gold. Sonny mopped his brow after the verdict: 'It's great. It's great.' Was he bothered by all this? 'Why should I be? I didn't do anything wrong, and no crime was committed. Just like my manager said, it was a mistake.' 'He'll never make another mistake,' vowed Katz. 'Now we'll show the world he's a real, worthwhile champion. Patterson is going to fight us.'

Not just yet he wasn't. Without a licence, Sonny was no threat to anyone, least of all Patterson. The newspaper and magazine reports Geraldine read to him made for distinctly uneasy listening. Writing in *The Ring*, Lester Bromberg noted a similarity between

Sonny and Joey Giardello, who was the leading middleweight contender at the time of his arrest in 1954, along with two accomplices, for six charges resulting from 'a riotous assault' at a Philadelphia gas station. 'Joe,' commented the baffled magistrate, Elias Myers, 'I never saw anyone who threw away a million dollars before.' 'I wish I could put my head on Sonny's shoulders,' offered Giardello. In a letter to Bromberg, Lew Jenkins, a lean Texan who had been world lightweight champion in 1940, supplied a cautionary tale: 'If you ever talk to Sonny Liston, tell him to quit trying, nobody is ever going to waste as many chances as Lew Jenkins. I was the all-time champ.'

A heavy drinker, Jenkins had lost his title shortly after breaking a rib and injuring his neck in a motor-bike crash. 'I wound up with no money. I chased myself out of the big time before I could appreciate it. I was plain stupid. I hope Sonny Liston will be smarter.' Bromberg's own viewpoint was more balanced than most: 'Where fun ends and calculated mischief begins, who really can tell until it's too late. And he [Sonny] skirts that thin line almost by habit. It is typical of personality contradictions that, once in the gym, Liston does not horse around. He'll box round after round, seemingly enjoying it. The only fighter of recent years with his addiction to the grind was Hurricane Jackson, an eccentric.' The summation was difficult to gainsay: 'But when there isn't the ultimate in tragedy, there still is failure and later regret. It is up to Sonny Liston, strictly, to decide which path he chooses to tread.'

'Doc' Young contrived to round up a smattering of folk prepared to muster a more benign appraisal. 'How much more can they do to him?' wondered Skinny Davidson, trainer of the world light-heavyweight champion, Harold Johnson. Davidson recalled Georgie Gibbs, a blind ex-fighter and trainer to whom Sonny was in the habit of giving '$10, $15, $25' after a fight. 'Anybody who's handicapped that Sonny sees, he goes right to helping them. As for what's happened to him in Philly, I think he's being harassed. The law has made Liston what he is by harassing him.'

Sonny's own trainer, Willie Reddish, also focused on his generosity. 'Few people know Sonny – really know him. He's never, for instance, passed a beggar, white or coloured, on the street without giving him something. He didn't do it for effect. He never knew I even noticed, but I did. I'd watch him out of the corner of my eye. I've also noticed how Sonny takes care of his wife and mother. Any man who cares for his wife and mother like he does has his heart in the right place.' Katz referred to Sonny having 'a complex about being with people. He thinks he only belongs with guys like himself.' It was hardly surprising, therefore, to discover that Sonny was chary of socialising with his neighbours. That said, Georgianna Myer regarded him with a certain affection: 'Few of us got to know him personally, but we all got used to seeing him come up and wave a cheery hello to us. It's a pleasure to have a neighbour like that. He was so inconspicuous and quiet that we wondered whether the guy ever talked.'

John Saunders, then secretary of the PSAC, had befriended Sonny upon meeting him in Pittsburgh after his second tussle with Marty Marshall in 1956, and frequently glimpsed a sensitive nature. 'I recall he told me several times that he was hurt by the articles that were appearing in the papers. He said he was going to leave the city and asked me what I thought of the idea. "Sonny, do you feel like you're a bum, a hoodlum?" I asked him. "No," was the reply. "I think I've paid for whatever I did wrong. I just want people to forget and let me forget, but they don't seem to want to let me." Sonny's no hardened criminal. I've seen the guy break down and cry in my office. He felt the treatment he was getting was totally unjustified.' When Sonny told Saunders of his intention to attempt 'rehabilitation', the secretary asked him where he had got such a word from. Sonny explained that whenever he came across a word he didn't know, he would ask someone what it meant and then use it when the opportunity arose.

There were opportunities aplenty over the subsequent months of enforced idleness. While training in Denver for the Folley fight, Sonny had met Father Edward Murphy, a Jesuit priest from the local St Ignatius Loyola church. Sonny expressed an interest in Catholicism and joining the church, and the pair conversed at length. Once the Fairmount Park *brouhaha* was over, he returned to Denver and placed himself under Father Murphy's direction in an educational rehabilitation programme. At last he was heeding the advice of Father Stevens, who had repeatedly sought to impress upon Sonny the importance of education and who had resumed contact when Sonny rang him during the Kefauver hearings seeking advice. In Father Stevens's opinion, Sonny was 'illiterate, not dumb. In fact, he was pretty smart. I told him he had to write and read because, as I used to tell him, "if you get famous you want to read about yourself". I arranged for him to go to school in St Louis on Saturdays, with a girl, but he missed most of the lessons. Mitchell didn't encourage him. Fortunately, his interests became romantic and he met Geraldine. She was probably the best thing that ever happened to him. He worshipped the ground she walked on. She would write his letters for him, read to him, organise his money, or at least as far as she was allowed to. He was pretty articulate, although he was never very talkative. We stayed in touch until he went to Philadelphia, where his handlers probably didn't want me to be in contact, and until the Kefauver hearings he never rang me. He wasn't used to the telephone because he grew up without one.'

The Denver venture was accompanied by a welter of publicity and more than a few cynical jibes. Father Murphy, for instance, was lampooned as 'the house priest'. Sonny stayed in the rectory with his new-found spiritual counsellor-cum-teacher for three weeks, then moved into a nearby house when Geraldine came to join him. Sonny continued doing road-work and generally kept himself in trim, but the majority of his time was spent with Father Murphy and the Reverend William Wade, a member of the St Louis University, who homed in on four specific subjects: reading, writing, humility and understanding. According to Father Thomas Kelly, a close friend of Father Murphy, there was another area that was ripe for improvement. 'Murph tried to get him to stop drinking. That was his biggest problem. You could smell him in the mornings. Oh, poor Sonny. He was just an accident waiting to happen. Murph used to say, "Pray for the poor bastard." '

Since neither friends, managers nor Fathers Stevens or Murphy ever referred publicly to any alcoholic attachment – indeed, there were those who still maintained that Sonny had a physical revulsion for the demon drink – Father Kelly's recollections may well have been a trifle hyperbolic. What cannot be disputed is the replenishing effect of those four months. 'I feel like a new person,' announced Sonny, playing up the situation for all its worth. 'I feel I have found a true friend for the first time. I am learning for the first time how to live, how people should treat each other. I got into a lot of trouble [as a kid] because I hardly knew right from wrong.' Writing in *Ebony* magazine a year later, Allan Morrison suggested that in Father Murphy Sonny may have found 'the Freudian father-figure his childhood lacked. The first had been Father Alois Stevens. Both were gentle, understanding men who convinced him that he had a sound future. The presence of a fatherly symbol is important to Liston's well-being. His attorney and main adviser, Morton Witkin, a courtly, shrewd and amiable man, currently comes closer to filling the role. Like his two Jesuit predecessors, Witkin is white and totally unlike Sonny's father in manner and attitude. He treats Liston with the respect he needs so desperately.'

Other sections of the media needed convincing. Questioned by a New York reporter as to the precise nature of what he had learned in Denver, Sonny launched into a familiar diatribe. 'The newspapers always put me down as a bad guy. You can't live it down. They always bring it up. When I got in the last trouble, they had big headlines. When I was cleared, they had this much [he indicated the amount by cocking his hand and bringing together his thumb and forefinger until they almost touched]. Whatever there was is over, but will people believe it? Will they believe me?' Father Murphy was asked if he felt Sonny had 'rehabilitated' himself. 'I don't like that word. Reorientation is better.' Not unexpectedly, the biggest doubters were the St Louis police. 'Down there, I guess he was a tough guy,' Father Murphy rationalised. 'He wants to be champion. Joe Louis is Sonny's idol. He wants to be like Joe. He doesn't smoke or drink. Out here, he was on his own. He won the respect of everyone. He is fond of children, and the kids are crazy about him. I want to get him into the fight against juvenile delinquency. He did a good job when he spoke to the boys at the home. He told them they can't make it if they didn't behave themselves. They listened to him.'

Purge or put-on? No one was entirely sure, although it did seem that scepticism would have greeted whatever efforts Sonny might have made to redeem himself. If he had sequestered himself in a monastery belonging to a silent order, the tongues would have wagged with no less intensity. There was little evidence, certainly, of any advance in his reading or writing abilities. The upshot was that the Sonny who checked out of his Denver dry-out clinic held out no more hope for public redemption than the one who checked in.

At this point, money – what else – took a hand. Patterson was due to fight Tom McNeeley in Toronto on 4 December, and plans for a TV double-header were set in motion. Who better to open proceedings than the champion's *bête noire* (Henry Cooper had assumed Sonny's No. 1 ranking when the suspension was imposed, but the pulling power of a Brit with eggshell eyebrows was not up to much)? And where better to do so than on his Philadelphian stomping-ground? To facilitate this, however, Sonny had to become *persona grata* again. No worries. At the start of the year, Al Klein, the chairman of the PSAC, had responded to Sonny's licence application by decreeing that he 'would have to be clean before he could fight in Pennsylvania'. Evidently, Sonny had bathed well. 'It has never been the purpose of the commission to destroy the career of Liston or any other athlete,' Klein now declared. 'The unique circumstances of the programme projected for 4 December present to Liston an opportunity which, if now denied to him, could well accomplish irreparable damage to him, both as a championship contender and as a man. The commission is not prepared to be the instrument of such damage.' How touching. 'That's good, that's good,' retorted Sonny when he learned of his reinstatement. 'Now I won't have to knock off that Britisher to get to that title. Maybe I don't have to fight Cooper now to show who's who.' (There had been talk of a meeting with Cooper, but there was never any likelihood of it actually happening. According to Jim

Wicks, 'Enery's minder of a manager, 'We don't want to meet this geezer Liston walking down the street, let alone in the ring.')

Thus it was that Sonny at last saw action again, nigh-on nine months since defeating Howard King. Making his bow in front of a Philadelphia congregation, he made short work of the unrated Albert Westphal, a 5ft 7½in baker, knocking him out inside two minutes with a left jab-right hand combination. Asked, somewhat needlessly, if he fancied a rematch, Westphal sensibly declined. Still clad in his trade-mark white robe ('no sense changing clothes; I didn't even work up a sweat'), Sonny proceeded to the press room under the stand at the Municipal Auditorium and sipped orange juice as he watched Patterson pulverise the inexperienced, if game, McNeeley, who had already paid ten visits to the canvas when a left jab put him away for good in round four. Up to that point, Sonny had been firing sarcastic broadsides at the televised image of his elusive quarry throughout the transmission. Now he stopped, albeit hardly out of respect: 'I don't want to blow my chance,' he explained. One luminary felt he should have had it that very night, JFK himself remarking that both fights were mismatches and that Sonny should have been in that Toronto ring with Patterson instead of McNeeley. Cus D'Amato, as ever, contradicted this with his customary cryptic stubbornness. 'Liston knows what he must do to get a fight with Patterson. If he does it, he knows he can sign for the fight tomorrow.' With Carbo on Riker's Island and Palermo on his way to jail, no one was quite sure what this alluded to. Patterson wasn't letting on. 'I would definitely give Liston a chance. There are no obstacles to me, but my manager says there are pretty serious ones.'

More than thirty years on, Patterson claims that D'Amato never once expanded on these 'serious' obstacles. 'Cus didn't want me to fight Sonny just yet, but he never gave me a reason.' Really? Now living on a twenty-five-acre property in up-state New York, Floyd manages his adopted son, Tracy, a young featherweight 'who had hung around camp since he was 11, seven days a week. He was very shy and reminded me so much of myself that I fell in love with him.' In 1992, Tracy stopped the Frenchman, Thierry Jacob, in Albany to win the WBC super-bantamweight title.

One story in circulation at the time had it that the President conveyed to Patterson his dismay at the flat fare provided by the double-header and urged him to do the right thing, leaving Floyd with little option but to give his word that he would do just that. 'There was no truth in that at all,' Patterson counters. 'The President simply asked me who my next fight was going to be against, and I said, "Between you and I, Liston".' Sonny was convinced that it was this incident that finally persuaded Patterson to shelve his objections: 'Frankly, I don't think Patterson would have fought me if he hadn't promised the President.'

Contrary to the prevailing interpretation, Patterson is adamant that the accusations of cowardice that pursued him throughout this period had no bearing on his eventual decision to go against D'Amato's wishes. Indeed, D'Amato actively encouraged fear, believing that fighters should not aspire to as hopeless a goal as fearlessness, but instead employ dread to their advantage. The 17-year-old Patterson, albeit unwittingly, had followed that doctrine to the letter in his inaugural professional outing shortly after returning from Helsinki as Olympic middleweight champion in 1952. 'They wanted to fill out the card one night, and so they moved me up to the heavyweight match [against Julius Griffin]. I was scared. Oh, I was scared. I remember climbing into the ring and looking across at this guy and I was never so scared in all my life. He had tremendous muscles all over him. He looked like a great tree-trunk. And, when that bell rang, I was so scared I just ran straight out to him . . . and I knocked him out right then.'

Far from being propelled by pride, Patterson maintains that his motives for taking on Sonny were altruistic. 'I felt very sorry for Sonny so I gave him his chance. I'm glad I did; he deserved it. I resented the way the press treated him. They were always making fun of him. People can change, but they need the chance to change. It wasn't a colour thing. I had a bad past because I ran away from home and played hooky from school, but I got sympathy because I got myself out of a hole. Sonny was different because he beat up a cop, but all he may have done is fight back, just as I did. When I was 13, a cop hit me over the head with an empty crate after I'd stolen something, so I hit him back. I remember going back to my apartment one night when a lady I knew tried to surprise me. Instinctively, I threw up my right hand and caught her with it, causing her to fall. We're all capable of it. I think Sonny's career would have lasted a lot longer if he had had people on his side. The people he did have were there for the wrong reasons. I found out that my victories were based on people. If no one cared, I wouldn't have. When I lost I went into hiding: I was ashamed because I'd let people down. I've never been ashamed of feeling ashamed.'

D'Amato saw the situation rather differently. 'I wanted the fight,' he assured Norman Mailer. 'Floyd came up to me and said, "Cus, you got to make this fight. Liston's going around saying I'm too yellow to fight him. I don't care if a fighter says he can beat me, but no man can say I'm yellow." Then Floyd said, "Cus, if this fight isn't made, I'll be scared to go out. I'll be afraid to go into a restaurant and see Liston eating. Because if I see him I'll have a fight with him right there in the restaurant, and I'll kill him." I wouldn't try to keep Floyd from having a fight after he says something like that.'

Ernie Terrell, who would learn all about being a subject of contempt when he stepped into the ring with Ali in 1967, sparred with Sonny before the Westphal fight then met him in a four-round exhibition match in Chicago shortly afterwards, an engagement that compelled Sonny to go cap-in-hand to the Illinois State Athletic Commission beforehand in order to renew his licence there. Terrell was left in no doubt about the enormity of the task awaiting Patterson, if and when the match was made. 'What I admire about Sonny is that he has a fighter's attitude. This separates him from the boys – separates him from every other fighter I know. He's in the ring to "kill" you, not just to beat you or knock you out – but to kill you.'

Sonny was a tad more scientific, though no less brutal, when analysing his tactical thought-processes. 'The middle of a fighter's forehead is like a dog's tail. Cut off the tail, and the dog goes all which-way 'cause he ain't got no more balance. It's the same with a fighter's forehead.' Pressing his knuckles together, he would elaborate on his distinctly un-Freudian theory of the unconscious. 'See, the different parts of the brain set in little cups like this. When you get hit a terrible shot – pop! – the brain flops out of them cups, and you're knocked out. Then the brain settles back in the cups, and you come to. But after this happens enough times, or sometimes even once if the shot's hard enough, the brain don't settle back right in them cups, and that's when you start needing other people to help you get around.' If Sonny had his way, Floyd Patterson would soon be needing others to help him get around.

Eight

The Punk versus the Bad Nigger

Hard as hurdle arms, with a broth of goldish flue
Breathed round; the rack of ribs; the scooped flank; lank
Rope-over thigh; knee-nave; and barrelled shank . . .
. . . Churlsgrace, too, child of Amansstrength . . .

(Gerard Manley Hopkins, *Harry Ploughman*)

Nino Valdes was livid. Sitting bolt upright in his room at the Broadway Medical Centre in New York's Washington Heights, where he had registered under his given name, Ramos, he rolled up his shirt-sleeve to reveal that once devastating right arm, the same muscle-bound limb that had put the fear of God into Rocky Marciano's manager nearly forty years earlier and might well have brought Cuba its first heavyweight championship had his own manager, Bobby Gleason, not incurred the wrath of Jim Norris. Now, though, that arm was littered with enough needle-punctures to sate an over-zealous acupuncturist. For someone with a non-existent command of Spanish such as myself, his frantic, furious gibbering was virtually unintelligible. Occasionally, he would intersperse his native ululations with a smattering of English. When I asked him about Sonny, the answer sounded like 'hard man'. One word, however, was eminently decipherable. 'Insulin,' hollered Nino, with sufficient force to alert the attendant nurses, who suggested it might be better for all concerned if I left. Jabbing his right forearm repeatedly with a meaty index finger, he continued to indicate the source of his distress. '*Demasiado* [too much] insulin. Like being hit by Liston.' Any visions I may have had of obtaining the in-depth recollections of one of Sonny's victims were suddenly engulfed in a permanent fog.

Around the corner, directly opposite the Columbia Presbyterian Hospital, the Audubon Ballroom stretches for half a block. Staring out from over the unusually, if respectfully, graffiti-free entrance are the solemn, piercing eyes of Malcolm X, black America's antidote to Doctor T.J. Eckleburg. 'Malcolm X lives,' proclaims an adjacent sign, but it was here that the one-time Black Muslim leader was murdered. Yet, for all the fear and loathing engendered by the son of the Reverend Earl Little during the early 1960s, it would be no exaggeration to suggest that the twenty-fourth of Tobe Liston's twenty-five offspring struck a similar shaft of terror into the heart of white America. The press even went so far as to dub Sonny 'Malcolm X'. The difference was that the real McCoy managed to attract vastly more support from his own people.

As negotiations for the showdown embarked on their tortuous route, the proposed confrontation between Patterson and Sonny was depicted as a battle royal betwixt good and evil, between 'the punk' and 'the bad nigger'. Since ridding himself of Johansson (no great shakes himself), Patterson had earned a handsome living wiping out bums, but now, arguably for the first time since Marciano fought Ezzard Charles in 1954, here was a heavyweight match-up worthy of its billing. For once, there was no need for hype. 'I'm the bad guy,' Sonny whispered to 'Doc' Young. 'Okay, peoples want to think that, let them. Only – bad guys are supposed to lose. I change that. I win.' Patterson, on the other hand, was almost an honorary white, a diligent, modest, church-going man who found favour with establishment figures such as Eleanor Roosevelt and made the ultimate statement of integration by marrying a white woman. A veritable Mr Clean, he was sufficiently respectable to warrant an audience with the President. Rose Parks's refusal in 1955 to give up her seat on an Alabama bus to a white passenger, a courageous action widely deemed to have been the catalyst for black militancy, seemingly meant little to Patterson, whose concept of a radical gesture, apparently, was to drink from a whites-only water fountain and announce that the water tasted much the same. As time wore on, the halo he donned after becoming the youngest man to win the heavyweight title lost much of its lustre among working-class and radical blacks alike, who came to regard him as an ingratiating 'Uncle Tom' figure. A war had to be won before black could befriend white.

That Patterson should turn to the sanctuary offered by white liberal America was only to be expected. To the growing army of middle-class blacks he remained a symbol of possibility, whereas Sonny supplied an unwanted reminder of the downtrodden past they were striving to consign to history. A product of Brooklyn's murderous Bedford-Stuyvestant slums, the same unforgiving breeding-ground that would soon sire a behemoth named Mike Tyson, Patterson, now 27, was living proof that an impoverished black man could better himself and win universal esteem *and* be secure. Before he was 30 he would be able to rely on investments alone for an annual income of $35,000 over the next twenty-five years. Few could have forecast such a climb for a child whose shyness led him to walk along the subway tracks in Brooklyn and hide himself in a workers' cubby-hole situated no more than three feet off the rails, pulling the iron door over him just to make sure of concealment. A thief from an early age ('I was about 8 . . . I stole to survive'), a kindly spinster had helped steer him back toward the straight and narrow via a 'special' school. As a teenager he had begged a friend to accompany him on dates with his 13-year-old bride-to-be as a means of breaking the silence. He later converted to Catholicism and renounced hatred. He bought a dictionary, and demonstrated his expanding vocabulary at every opportunity. When he regained the title from Johansson, wrote Gay Talese, 'he was the Great Black Hope of the Urban League'. The Great Black Hope had nevertheless taken a set of fake whiskers and moustache with him to the fight, this to enable a swift, anonymous exit in the event of defeat.

'I have hated only one fighter,' Patterson claimed. 'And that was Ingemar in the second fight. Not because he beat me in the first fight, but because of what he did after. It was all that boasting in public. And I'd be home watching him on television, and *hating* him.

It is a miserable feeling, hate. When a man hates, he can't have any peace of mind. And, for one solid year, I hated him because, after he took everything away from me, deprived me of everything I was, he rubbed it in.' Those closest to Floyd had difficulty equating the man with the job. 'I can't get used to my kid brother being a name fighter,' his brother, Frank, told Lester Bromberg. 'I remember him as the boy who would cry if I hit him too hard when we boxed in the gym. When he was a young pro he once refused to watch his next opponent spar at Midtown Gym, Chicago, because he considered he would be taking an unfair advantage.'

But Patterson was never more than a handy chisel to white America. He had his uses. Here was someone who crossed the colour line without lighting a fuse. No marches, no strikes, no inflammatory speeches, no odd religious habits. See. It can be done. But Patterson was still black, and he was still rejected. When he moved into a white neighbourhood in Yonkers, New York, he was greeted with open hostility. The other kids on the block called his children 'niggers'; one neighbour trained his dog to deface the Patterson home; another erected a fence to hide the unwanted outsiders from sight. 'I tried, it just didn't work,' he lamented. What did he expect?

In 1962, though, Patterson was 'the Hope of the Civilised World', as Joseph D. O'Brien would put it in *The Ring* a quarter of a century later. 'John F. Kennedy was counting on him. Eleanor Roosevelt was counting on him. Every parlour liberal who ever attended a Pete Seeger concert or voted for Adlai Stevenson was counting on him. Every middle-class black who figured Sonny Liston would give the race a bad name was counting on him.' 'I knew about that but I didn't believe it,' Patterson now claims. 'I remember being told, I can't recall who by, that it was up to me to beat Sonny because I stood for this and that. But I felt pressure only from myself. I always admired Martin Luther King's approach, not Muhammad Ali's. He [King] changed things by being peaceful. I had to be a good champ, to respect people, to treat them as you'd like to be treated. People may have thought Sonny wasn't a very good representative of black people because of all his bitterness and anger. But that was his response to the press. They gave him nothing.'

Mailer elaborated. 'There was one reason beyond any other for picking Patterson . . . [he] was the champion of every lonely adolescent and every man who had been forced to live alone . . . he was the man who could not forgive himself if he gave less than his best chance for perfection. And so he aroused a powerful passion in those lonely people who wanted him to win. He was champion, he was a millionaire, but he was still an archetype of the underdog, an impoverished prince. And Liston was looking to be king. Liston came from that world where you had no dream but making it, where you trusted no one because your knowledge of evil was too quick to its presence in everyone . . . Liston was voodoo, Liston was magic . . . Liston was Faust . . . He was the hero of . . . anyone who was fixed on power.'

One man who stood firmly against Patterson was Malcolm X. To him, boxing exploited blacks, and promoters only allowed them to progress 'if they were going to make money for him'. In common with other black militants, he had come to the conclusion that sport had no bearing whatsoever on social injustice and the civil rights movement, that the battle would be won on the streets, not in the stadiums or on the track. These sentiments were endorsed by the experiences of Jesse Owens, who returned from the Berlin Olympics expecting his lifestyle to improve drastically, only to find himself cantering alongside horses and working as a janitor in order to pay the rent. For all the respect and idolatry accorded Joe Louis, the 'Brown Bomber' still had to take up professional wrestling in order to wipe out a huge tax debt to the same government whose cause he had served so stoutly during the Second World War. Yet Malcolm X took a keen interest in Patterson's fights. Floyd had enraged him by insulting the Nation of Islam in the press, although he was sure that this had been done at the behest of the white man. As a consequence, Malcolm X was rooting for Sonny to 'shake Patterson up'. The National Association for the Advancement of Coloured People, in contrast, pleaded with Patterson not to go ahead with the fight. 'Hell, let's stop kidding,' admitted Percy

Sutton, the president of the body's Manhattan branch, when it became clear that the efforts would come to naught. 'I'm for Patterson because he represents us better than Liston ever could or would.' In making its plea, the NAACP merely joined the massing ranks of those who acknowledged the truth. Patterson – good, honest, God-fearin' Floyd – amounted to no more than the leanest, tastiest slab of raw meat thus far thrown into Sonny's cage. Reason had blunted his edge.

Mind you, as yet, the lip-smacking was a little on the premature side. Indeed, the debate surrounding Sonny's entitlement to occupy a championship ring remained intense. The ludicrous argument that he would bring disgrace to the boxing industry, that notable bastion of honest chivalry and human decency, was trotted out *ad nauseam*. In his book *Defeat of the Great Black Hope*, Maurice Berube summed up the consensus view by characterising Sonny as the 'stereotypical nightmare of the bad nigger, the juvenile delinquent grown up'. Thankfully, in some quarters at least, a sense of objectivity prevailed. 'If he's not in prison at the moment, he must currently be legally straight,' reasoned Sir David Harrington Angus Douglas, the twelfth Marquis of Queensberry, in a poll conducted by *Sports Illustrated*, the magazine's own pompous conclusion being that, 'In this day and age we cannot afford an American heavyweight champion with Liston's unsavoury record'. 'If he's a very good boxer he must be entitled to a fight with Patterson,' the Marquis countered. 'You might as well say I won't fight somebody because he's not a Christian or not white . . . your efficiency as a boxer, swimmer or runner is not terribly related to how nice a chap you are.' Writing in the *New York Herald-Tribune*, the immortal Red Smith cut through the hypocrisy of the endless red tape. 'Should a man with a record of violent crime be given a chance to become champion of the world? Is America less sinful today than in 1853, when John Morrissey, a saloon brawler and political head-breaker out of Troy, NY, fought Yankee Sullivan, lammister from the Australian penal colony in Botany Bay? In our time, hoodlums have held championships with distinction. Boxing may be purer since their departure; it is not healthier.'

It seems apposite at this point to inject a wider perspective into the debate. The very notion that we can blithely shove athletes on to stratospheric plinths and expect them to behave like performing paragons is downright silly, not to mention grossly unfair. Consider, if you will, the job description. Position: role model. Qualifications: physical prowess and, ideally, a photogenic face. Hours: endless. Pay: plenty, albeit only from subsidiary channels. Benefits: regular ego massages. Retirement: when jealousy finally turns gossip into scandal. Pension: none.

For the privilege of playing games for a living, no vice can be tolerated, no weakness allowed. Since they are activities that entwine so inextricably with victory and defeat, time limits and adjudicators, fixed boundaries and prescribed penalties, athletic contests give us that replenishing air of certainty that reality stifles. Thus it is that we aspire to be winners, to be perfect. Yet winners, for the most part, are only winners because of their single-mindedness, a devotion that cannot be expected to set equal store by the responsibility of setting an example, of compensating for the inadequacies of others. Nice guys, after all, rarely finish first: for every Gary Lineker, history has celebrated a dozen successful scoundrels. We demand honesty, yet when we get it we scorn it. The holier-than-thou attitude that crucified John McEnroe whenever he scolded himself or challenged an umpire is nothing more than sanctimonious tosh. Is it not enough that he entertained us so regally? Michael Jordan's profoundest fear is to risk the slurs that puncture images with the suddenness of a pin-prick. 'I've spent a life building something positive,' he informed Sam Smith in *The Jordan Rules*, 'and I know any mistake I make could damage that for the rest of my life. People look to their role models to be almost flawless . . . It's hard to live up to something like that . . . harder than basketball.'

The adoption of role models *per se* is an act of communal self-deception induced by the ruling classes and catered to by the entertainment industry, the star factory. Nothing, moreover, suits the white establishment better than to portray the heavyweight champion as a role model, and this was particularly true in 1962.

The heavyweight champ, after all, tended to be black and poor and, as such, a highly effective, all-purpose tailor's dummy. 'The heavyweight championship,' observed Robert Lipsyte of the *New York Times*, 'was a way for the white establishment to say to black America: "You should channel your rage and energy into going out and being someone who fights to entertain us . . . You can go out, get drunk, get laid, do whatever you want as long as you stay within the parameters of what a member of the underclass is. Choke down your rage at how your people are getting screwed over, work very hard, make millions of dollars, ultimately self-destruct, and keep our stereotypes in order." '

The New York authorities, however, persisted in spurning Sonny as role-model fodder. The Patterson bout was originally scheduled for the spring, in the Big Apple, a venue that had hitherto been about as far from Sonny's reach as a life membership of the Ku Klux Klan. On 17 April, he applied for a licence to fight in New York State, having been assured by the NYSAC chairman, Major-General Melvin L. Krulewitch, the man appointed by Governor Nelson Rockefeller to clean up boxing, that the commission 'would make no decision based on his record alone'. If Sonny was otherwise qualified, Krulewitch continued, 'we would consider his application on its merits. I repeated that we had frequently licensed boxers with records, and that sometimes the sport helped them come back. Within the hour, the FBI informed me that there was nothing.' By 'nothing', it may be assumed that Krulewitch meant there was nothing to stop Sonny fighting in New York, although he would later contradict this. While Sonny's case was being examined, Krulewitch refused Teddy Brenner permission to introduce the challenger to the crowd before a fight at the Garden. 'To permit Sonny, in the midst of our investigation, to appear at the Garden would have indicated advocacy on his behalf,' Krulewitch explained. Around this time, the *New York Post* ran a story about a trip to the West Coast purportedly made by Patterson's lawyer, Julius November, in order to pursue an offer to hold the fight in Los Angeles. Apparently, November then flew to New York to discuss holding it at Yankee Stadium. Given the income and prestige the bout was certain to generate, the pressure on the NYSAC to approve Sonny was enormous.

After nine days' humming and hawing, however, the application was turned down – a brave decision indeed. To Krulewitch and his cohorts, Sonny's relationship with Katz was highly suspect, and they concluded that the latter's paltry 10 per cent share marked him down as no more than a front man for other, less salubrious investors. 'The history of the Barone-Liston contract is of interest,' the press statement noted. 'In 1961, it was dissolved for a consideration of $75,000 to be paid by Sonny Liston within two years to Pep Barone. A portion of these monies was paid to Barone out of the December 1961 Liston-Westphal bout, leaving a balance still due to Barone of some $57,000. George Katz subsequently entered into an agreement with Liston as manager, under which the division between manager and boxer was 10 per cent:90 per cent, a most unusual distribution. Out of the Westphal fight, Katz received some $7500. In the present proceeding before this commission, George Katz, the manager under the contract dated 24 April 1961 between Katz and Liston, does not appear either as manager or in any other capacity, although his name is mentioned.'

Then we got down to the nitty-gritty. 'A child of circumstances, without schooling and without direction or leadership, he [Liston] has been the victim of those with whom he has surrounded himself,' the statement continued. 'The history of Liston's past associations provides a pattern of suspicion. His association with Vitale, Palermo, Mitchell, and others is a factor which can be detrimental to the best interests of professional boxing and to the public interest as well. We cannot ignore the possibility that these long-time associations continue to this day. The wrong people do not disengage easily. There would be more than a calculated risk in this issuance of a licence on this application. The commission unanimously disapproves the application and denies the licence to Sonny Liston.' Morton Witkin described the decision as 'unfair, unjust and un-American'. In public, Sonny appeared unruffled. 'I'm not concerned. I will continue to train as if nothing had happened.' Deep down, he must have felt as if his legs had been chopped off at the knees.

Writing in *The Ring* in 1971, Krulewitch, who once remarked that 'Iwo Jima was never like this' when discussing his strenuous efforts to root out boxing's undesirables, delved deeper into the thinking behind the NYSAC ruling. 'Liston gained his unenviable *sui generis* position because *he was not good for boxing* [my italics]; he had been associating with persons whose reputations did not recommend them as citizens; and in the opinion of our commission, he could not be trusted with the world title if he achieved it . . . It [the verdict] was not discussed with me by Governor Nelson A. Rockefeller or Attorney General Louis Lefkowitz. It was based on evidence collected not only by our commission, but by the commission of Philadelphia and the FBI . . . he [Sonny] was bad. But who was responsible? We all were, I suppose. Even Father Stevens, Liston's priest friend in prison who helped him to a parole, unwittingly led him astray . . . Sonny was a single human life, no better, no worse than the capricious and fickle angles of life permit.'

Powered by a gust of self-righteous wind, Senator Estes Kefauver veered even closer to running aground on the treacherous banks of sympathy. In an article for the mass-circulation *Family Week* headlined 'Will Gangsters Be The Real Winners?', he expressed his distaste for the prospect of Sonny becoming champion in customary chest-thumping fashion. 'As matters now stand, no one can be sure whether Liston will keep all, or substantially all, of his purse – or whether it will go to racketeers. This doubt exists because there is no way to compel such disclosures. The only effective guarantee is provided in my Senate Bill 1474, the Federal Boxing Control Bill, which is pending on the Senate.

'In 1960 and 1961, the Senate sub-committee, of which I am chairman, held hearings which proved that boxing was monopolistically controlled by a group of criminals. Investigation revealed that the power structure was built like a pyramid. At the bottom, or the working level, were fighters like Liston. Above them were the legally listed managers, "front men" chosen because of their relative freedom from criminal records. In the next tier of the hierarchy were the regional chiefs, such as Frankie (Blinky) Palermo, who made most of the decisions for Liston and other Mob-controlled fighters. At the very top was Frank Carbo, Czar of professional boxing in America, now in Alcatraz. This able and evil man for years held absolute sway . . . he decided whether important bouts were to be held and secretly acted as manager for one or the other – or sometimes both – of the principals. Some persons have asked me if I was not being unduly harsh on Liston. I have nothing but goodwill toward this unfortunate man . . . Those who heard him that day [at the hearings] must carry with them the haunting memory of a tragic story.'

Neither Kefauver nor the NYSAC, it should be said, were too wide of the mark. When Palermo was incarcerated at the Lewisburg Penitentiary, Pennsylvania, the store was left in the hands of Sam Margolis, his partner in a Philly restaurant. Margolis's duties extended to assuming Blinky's role as Sonny's invisible adviser and keeper; the Mob's desire to grab hold of that heavyweight title was as fervent as ever. Only a few months before the NYSAC hearing, Margolis introduced Sonny to the Nilon brothers, Robert, James and Jack, childhood buddies from Leeperville, Pennsylvania, now concessionaires and security service contractors for sporting and other entertainment events. The meeting led to Robert and James entering into an agreement with Sonny to form Inter-Continental Promotions Inc., a deal that involved Sonny taking 50 per cent of the stock and fighting exclusively for the corporation. On 16 December 1961, Sonny transferred 275 of his 500 shares as some kind of *ex gratia* payment to Margolis, who in turn deposited fifty of them with his lawyer, Salvatore Avena. It may be assumed that at least some of the remainder found their way into the clutches of the men Margolis was fronting for, namely Carbo and Palermo.

Although George Katz was still officially Sonny's manager, he did not act on his behalf in the build-up to the title challenge. This may have been attributable to Sonny's fears that other athletic commissions would follow the New York line, but there were other contributory factors. Sonny had been upset by Katz's failure to contact him during his sojourn with Father Murphy and generally found him to be a source of annoyance, complaining that Katz would 'get on edge when I got on edge'. Jack Nilon offered a further insight into Katz's character by alleging that, given the choice, the latter would prefer his picture in the paper to a $1000 bill. Although it would be another year before Sonny severed all ties with Katz and took on Jack Nilon (for the regular one-third share), the latter was now to all intents and purposes installed as manager. Not that this made a jot of difference to Cus D'Amato, ever one for a snappy quote: 'There's no change – whether it's Nilon, rayon, cotton or silk.' Nilon, apparently, was an observant Catholic, a revelation that drew some cussing from Cus: 'I don't give a damn if he was the Pope.'

The state of Washington was prepared to accede to Sonny's request for a licence, so too Florida. The quest for a venue finally ended in Chicago, a city whose underworld links would have rendered any unwillingness laughable, not to say duplicitous in the extreme. 'I'm a firm believer in rehabilitation,' announced Joe Triner, the chairman of the Illinois SAC. The rendezvous was set for 25 September 1962 and, after everything that had gone before, the choice of Comiskey Park as the stage had something of a poetic ring about it. This was the home of the Chicago White Sox, the team involved in baseball's – and therefore sporting America's – darkest hour.

The financial details of the fight were a battlefield all of their own. At first, Sonny, so eager for the fray that fiscal considerations were of secondary import, undertook to hold over a substantial portion of the purse for a return match and fight the first under any promoter selected by Patterson. The company nominated, Championship Sports Inc. (CSI), took due advantage and offered Sonny 12½ per cent of the live gate plus 10 per cent of the ancillary rights, having earlier turned down the Liston camp's request for a 12½/12½ take on top of a guaranteed $200,000. 'It's ridiculous,' Sonny exclaimed. 'It appears they are trying to rob me blind. The others got 20 per cent. Why not me?' The customary champion-challenger split was indeed 40–20, but there had been exceptions, such as the 12½ per cent Gene Fullmer had received for fighting Sugar Ray Robinson in 1957. It was speculated (wrongly) that Sonny would gross $425,000 from aggregate gate receipts of $4 million; his previous best pay-day (before deductions, natch) had been the $75,000 he earned for whupping Westphal. Sonny ultimately resolved to take whatever he could get, recalling the barmy days when he accepted such humiliation merely to obtain opponents, when he could receive $4000 for beating Mike De John while his victim made off with $12,000.

Compromise eventually won out. Patterson was to receive 55 per cent of the ancillary proceeds plus 45 per cent of the gate; Sonny would get that 12½/12½ deal after all, plus the $200,000 guarantee, while CSI would rake in 42½ per cent of the live gate and 32½ per cent of the ancillary rights. Sonny's training expenses, according to Jack Nilon, amounted to a piffling $25,000. The contract also provided that, in the event of Sonny winning, the return would take place by 30 September 1963 at the latest, the new champion's quota being fixed at 30 per cent of both the gate and the ancillary rights.

Patterson trained in Elgin, Illinois, at a camp littered with tiny white bungalows and infested, as Norman Mailer put it, with a 'humourless' atmosphere. Shortly after the deal was inked, his autobiography, *Victory Over Myself*, was published, a worthy tome brimful of words such as 'introspection', 'obligation' and 'responsibility', hardly the words of a man intent on beating another to a pulp. Interviewed on television by an inquisitor with a Ph.D., he strove with little conviction to project himself as a man-eater, vowing to 'go back and train hard to get *vicious*'.

Sonny, of course, needed no such training. Incorporating bouts of rope-skipping to the beat of Duke Ellington's *Night Train* (performed, observed Mailer, with 'hypnotic, suspended rage'), he worked out at the disused Aurora Downs trotting racetrack with Willie Reddish. Stories quickly metamorphosed into legends, shaking barstools the breadth of America. Speed bags, it was said, were yanked from their hinges, heavy bags relieved of their stuffing by a pair of fists belonging, depending on each media narrator's chosen phraseology, to either 'a gorilla', 'a latter-day caveman' or 'a jungle beast'. 'Nobody hit those bags like Sonny,' confirmed Johnny Tocco, a trainer who linked up with Sonny at the beginning and end of his career. 'He tore bags up. He could turn that hook, put everything behind it. Turn and snap. Bam! I saw him knock out guys with a straight jab. Bam! In the ring, Sonny was a killing machine.'

Not surprisingly, Sonny's distrust of the press verged on the paranoiac. With few exceptions, he refused to talk to white journalists individually. Reddish was often deputed to stave off the swarm of reporters who converged on the respective camps in the weeks leading up to the fight. Press agents were under strict instructions from Sonny as to who and who not to admit to the work-outs. 'Sonny will fool you,' asserted Ben Bentley, who would be employed by Sonny in a PR capacity for the rematch with Patterson. 'I guarantee you he knows the face of everybody in the first three rows of the audience, and he knows the name of every newspaperman on the stage. He makes a point of asking me.'

The interview process was not dissimilar to putting a reluctant patient into a dentist's chair and charging admission to see the show. If Sonny was reluctant, his verbal assailants endured every excruciating moment with him. Peter Wilson of the *Daily Mirror*, a.k.a. 'The Man They Can't Gag', found the experience a painful if absorbing one: 'The answers came, if they came at all, like someone spitting pebbles . . . Sometimes he takes so long to answer a question, and has so much difficulty in finding the word he wants to use, that it's rather like a long-distance telephone call in a foreign language. But the man is fascinating. While his scarred face is immobile and his enormous painted-saucer eyes have the fixed glare of an octopus, his hands compel attention. The palms are soft and white, like the inside of a banana skin. His fingers are the unpeeled bananas. Instead of the talon you expect to see sprouting from such massive engines of destruction, they were perfectly tended, varnished nails. It is as though the hangman had had a manicure before going to work.'

Unlike most hangmen, however, Sonny was not above the odd

wisecrack, even if these rarely surfaced in one-to-one situations. This, after all, was his chance to be Pigmeat Markham, to be Red Foxx, to have an audience hanging on every last syllable. 'He should be locked up for impersonating a fighter,' he retorted – bringing the house down in the process – when a Swedish reporter asked him for his view of Ingemar Johansson. Having boxed only four competitive rounds in the past two years, was he not worried that ring-rustiness might have set in? 'No. In future, as champion, I'll only want to box ten or more rounds in the next twenty years. The fights will last thirty, forty, fifty seconds.' Whether he was using questions as a means of heightening suspense, or turning them into set-up lines, confidence did not so much ooze as gush from every pore.

When *Esquire* dispatched Robert Riger for an in-depth tête-à-tête, the writer somehow failed to identify Sonny, who duly pointed him in the direction of Reddish. Riger should have guessed he was being thrown a line when he shook hands with the burly presence at the bar, an experience he likened to patting a mattress: 'I couldn't feel the edge of his hand anywhere.' 'Sonny follows orders good,' Reddish informed Riger. 'He does what he's supposed to do. He is very alert . . . and calm under pressure. He's very calm in the dressing-room before a fight. He is not moody. Sometimes things annoy him, like bad weather or newspapermen, but he's a regular guy. He jokes and plays ball and, when it comes time to work, and Joe Pollino, his cut man, tapes his hands, he gets more serious. He moves fair for a heavyweight. He has to go get everybody. With the exception of [Cleveland] Williams in their first fight, I never seen anyone move in on him. He has the best jab of any heavyweight since Joe Louis. There is no question about that. His combinations are short and snappy. His elbows are in close. His powerful shoulders give him great short impact, not the deliberate round-house arms of Marciano.' Reddish acclaimed the right hand which Sonny connected with Westphal's cheek at the Municipal Auditorium as 'the hardest single punch [he] ever threw. Westphal went down hard. I thought he was hurt real bad. He just lay there still, with blood coming out of his ear.'

There is a telling scene in that marvellous baseball movie *Bull Durham* wherein Kevin Costner's wily catcher instructs the club's promising young pitcher, 'Nuke' Laloosh, to 'learn your clichés' in readiness for the media assault to come. Riger must have felt as if Sonny had been given the same advice. There was certainly no eye-to-eye contact: 'I got the feeling that when he *had* looked me in the eye as I walked across that room he had found out all he wanted to know.' Did Sonny like fighting, or would he rather be a foreman, or perhaps a clerk? 'Fighting's OK.' Did he use his jab to set opponents up? 'I jab to hurt, that's all.' If Patterson fights in a crouch, will his jab be less effective? 'I jab wherever his head is.' Did he have a good upper-cut? 'Yeah.' Sonny relented, eventually. Did he use his upper-cut when he was in trouble, or out in the centre of the ring? 'In the centre of the ring. I don't believe in waiting until I get into trouble. I fight to keep out of trouble and I fight to get out of trouble. I fight my own fight. I always fight my own fight. Never mind what style he has. If he is big like [Nino] Valdes or if he is fast and jumps around a lot, it does not make any difference. It doesn't matter what the crowd is like, whether they're for me or not for me. I don't pay any attention to the crowd. I just go in and fight my fight.' Had his victories stemmed from the enemy's mistakes? 'His only mistake was getting in the ring with me.'

As Sonny spoke, Riger noticed the incessant thumping of a boot heel, 'like an impatient hunter pounding the butt of his rifle on the floor of the lodge, anxious to get on with the hunt'. 'The worst person in the world to fight,' Sonny declared, 'is a scary [as in scared] person. It's hard to hit him. In the first place, he's not going to give you a shot at him. The best kind of a man to fight is a man who wants to fight, who comes to fight. That way it won't be laggin' along. Either he'll knock me out or I'll knock him out. The guy that hits and runs is not so tough – you can tame him.' The musings of the existential boxer *par excellence*. What, then, of the guy of the moment? 'I saw Patterson fight Johansson the first fight on TV. I was there for the second and there for the third. 'Cause I have seen Patterson fight a lot doesn't mean it will be easier. It is always easier to fight a man you never seen, a man you know nothing about. Then you don't have any plan. If you know too much about a man and you got a plan and your plan don't work, it may tie you up.' In a transparent allusion to Sonny himself, Riger asked whether he felt that his idol, Joe Louis, benefited from facing fearful opponents. This prompted a hearty laugh as Sonny extended his arms out along the top of the sofa, threw back his head and bared his Persiled teeth. 'They were scared because they knew he was going to kill them. Yes indeed. That's why they were scared.'

If Patterson was scared he did his manful best to disguise it, curtly dismissing the unflattering comparison between his and Sonny's performances against Roy Harris (the only opponent they had in common). 'I would say that that Harris fight was my worst fight to date. It came after a long year's lay-off,' he told Riger. 'All these reporters ask me if I'm going to change my style. If I'm going to crouch more to avoid the jab, or stand up and bring my hands up on my face, or hold them lower so I could get a punch off faster. Look, the hands have nothing to do with it – well, I mean that it is not so important . . . I *know* there are times when a man can be hit . . . it's all in the mind.' The visuals *Esquire* used to accompany Riger's article were arresting, if a little too stagey. 'Last Man In The Ring: Sonny Liston And Floyd Patterson Talk About Being Tough And Scared', ran the cover line over a photo of a black boxer lying, as if counted out, on the canvas against a backcloth of empty seats. Embellishing the text inside was a shot of Sonny clad in a white sweater and sitting down, chin resting moodily on that colossal left fist, hair cropped with characteristic disregard for the shampoo industry, wrist encircled by a gleaming watch, possibly a Rolex, a symbol of his approach toward the gates of prosperity. The camera, so they say, never lies, but rarely can a pose have been more deceptive.

Sonny's mood fluctuations and commensurate ability to impose his will were crystallised in an odd incident at the eve-of-fight press conference. His new gloves weighed in at a shade over the regulation 8oz, prompting an outburst from Jack Nilon. 'Don't give me none of that,' the putative manager screamed, simultaneously venting his fury at Nick Florio (the brother of Patterson's trainer, Dan), Joe Triner of the Illinois SAC, and Cus D'Amato who, in what was presumably a ruse designed to rile the easily-provoked contender, had objected to Sonny's plan to wear foam rubber-padded gloves on the grounds that they would allow his knuckles to punch closer to the surface. 'How do I know what kind of scale you use?' ranted Nilon. 'What do we want to cheat you on a quarter of an ounce for?' reasoned Triner. 'Just to get Sonny upset, just to get Sonny upset, that's all,' Nilon snapped. If that was the intention, it worked a treat. 'What the hell's going on?' growled Sonny in a disdainful tone that reminded Mailer of the ageing Clark Gable's 'genial, rum squire's voice, the indulgent "I've been around" voice'. As the matter was explained, Sonny nodded impatiently, only half-listening. His expression, noted Mailer, 'seemed to say, "Which one of these bullshit artists is most full of it right now?" '. Pulling on one of the gloves, he reached into its innermost recesses and worked his fist about, testing it for comfort, then ripped it off and slammed it on the adjacent table. 'It still don't fit,' he fumed, enigmatically.

Darting around the room from face to face as if in search of the culprit, Sonny's eyes, to Mailer's surprise, far from being a cross between 'reptile and sleepy leopard', contained shards of beauty. 'They had the dark, brimming, eloquent, reproachful look one sees sometimes in the eyes of beautiful coloured children, 3- or 4-years-old . . . Liston was near to beautiful . . . One cannot think of more than a few men who have beauty. Charles Chaplin has it across a room, Krishna Menon across a table, Stephen Spender used to have it, Burt Lancaster oddly enough used to have it . . . they say Orson Welles had it years ago, and President Eisenhower in person, believe it or not. At any rate, Liston had it. You did not feel you were looking at someone attractive, yet felt you were looking at a creation. And this creation looked like it was building into a temper which would tear up the clubhouse at Aurora Downs.'

'Let's see that glove,' Sonny ordered, 'let's weigh it again.' As the gloves were hurriedly put back on to the scales, he squatted, scowling in exaggerated fashion at the numbers as if ignorant of their meaning. 'He's not going in the ring with gloves over regulation weight,' yelled Sonny's cut man, Joe Pollino, a wiry Italian with a gnarled face. 'Well, this scale isn't the official scale,' D'Amato observed quietly. 'What do you call the official scale?' snarled Pollino. 'There is no official scale. I'll bet you a thousand dollars they're more than 8oz.' Nilon, stationed on Sonny's other flank, picked up the angry chorus of disapproval, directing his venom toward the officials. 'Why do you bother my fighter with this? Why don't you go over to Patterson's camp and bother him the day before the fight? What's he doing? Sleeping? He doesn't have a hundred reporters looking down his throat.' Sonny's patience was apparently wearing thin. 'I don't want to stand much more of this. This is the sort of thing that gives reporters the chance to ask stupid questions. Just stupid questions, that's all.' Suddenly, tapping the gloves on the table, he pricked the grim bubble enveloping the room. 'Oh, they're all right. Let's use them.' Cue a deep, reverberating chuckle. 'I'm going to hit him so hard [there] isn't gonna be any more than just an extra quarter of an ounce he's being hit with.'

The conference appeared to be at an end when Sonny abruptly held up a hand as if answering a question in class. Clearly revelling in his new-found status as Holy Roman Emperor, he glowered at the officials, heaping volte-face on volte-face. 'I don't want to wear these gloves. I've changed my mind. We've had a special pair made for me. Bring the new gloves over.' At this, two courtiers marched in carrying an enormous white glove. As the paparazzi gathered round, Sonny took the glove and studied it, his mouth now a huge grin. 'Very unusual fellow,' D'Amato confided to Mailer. 'He's more intelligent than I thought. Good sense of humour.'

Interest in the fight, although considerable outside the city limits, was muted in Chicago itself. Training stories were buried in the papers, and ticket sales for what was arguably the most talked-about fistic duel since the second Louis-Schmeling bout nearly thirty years earlier were sluggish; only 18,894 seats of Comiskey Park's 50,000 capacity were ultimately used up as ringside pews went for $100 a throw. Patterson did his bit by splashing out

$10,000 to seat his mother, Annabelle, wife Sandra and dozens of friends. The ballpark authorities had spent $50,000 on converting the diamond into a boxing arena for the venue's third heavyweight title contest, Louis having begun his reign by knocking out James Braddock in a ring sited over second base in 1937, and Ezzard Charles outpointing Jersey Joe Walcott on the same spot twelve years later. The record number of 800 writers from forty-nine states and twelve countries waiting to pass judgement included Ben Hecht, Budd Schulberg, James Baldwin and Mailer; Louis, Marciano, Charles and Johansson (who would cover proceedings for Swedish radio) were among the boxing luminaries scheduled to attend.

The Sky Above The Mud Below, a movie playing many theatres that week, seemed an apt metaphor for the significance of the evening. According to bookies and reporters alike, Sonny's prospects of raising himself from the swamp and scaling the heights were good. Patterson's speed was such that Henry Cooper rated his hands quicker than Ali's; his determination such that, even when floored for the seventh time by Johansson, he somehow clambered to his feet. The general view, though, was that, just as the tide of change would sweep along James H. Meredith, the black student currently attempting to register at the still-segregated (in defiance of Supreme Court instructions) University of Mississippi, it could not thwart someone with Sonny's power, still less the Mob. 'Liston will move out of his corner dead set on annihilation,' predicted Marsh Smith in *Life* magazine, 'his eyes filled with evil, his powerful legs conditioned by girlish skipping, his meanness fortified by raw meat. Ringside will be no place for the squeamish, the moralistic or the faint of heart. And in the ring it will take all of the champion's courage and skill to survive.' With Sonny outweighing the shorter Patterson by 212lb to 187, and outreaching him by 13in, the vital statistics reinforced those sentiments.

On the day of reckoning, the Windy City was true to type, overcoats the obligatory uniform. Goodfellas populated the seats behind Sonny's corner, noted Mailer, 'like birds and beasts coming in to feed. Heavy types, bouncers, plug-uglies, flatteners, one or two speedy, swishing, Negro ex-boxers, for example, now blown up to the size of fat middleweights, slinky in their walk, eyes fulfilling the operative definition of razor slits, murder coming off them like scent comes off a skunk. You could feel death as they passed. It came wafting off. And the rest of the beasts as well – the strong-arm men, the head-kickers, the limb-breakers, the groin-stompers. If a clam had a muscle as large as a man, and the muscle grew eyes, you would get the mood. Those were the beasts. They were all orderly, they were all trained, they were all dead to humour . . . the orders came from the birds.' To Mailer, these characters brought to mind the shifty shyster portrayed with such vivid viperishness by George C. Scott in *The Hustler*: 'Their aura was succinct. It said, "If you spit on my shoes you're dead." It was a shock to realise that the Mob, in the flesh, was even more impressive than in the motion pictures . . . In their mind, Patterson was a freak, some sort of vegetarian.'

There was a disconcerting scene following the weigh-in, as a bevy of bystanders hemmed Sonny in and, to his chagrin, reached out to touch him. Half-way down the flight of stairs leading to the dressing-room, he appealed to Nilon. 'This is no damn good. Too many people around. Everybody touching me. I could have got stuck by somebody up there. Going out to the fight tonight I gotta have a crowd around me. No one gets near me, you hear.' Nilon nodded, but with insufficient conviction to mollify Sonny. 'If you guys have to carry me on your hands over your heads, then that's what you do.' Turning to an old man standing nearby, Sonny softened. 'That's the way we did it in the old days, wasn't it, poppa?'

Nilon lightened Sonny's mood further by telling him that the commission had assured him that the celebrities would all be introduced before he took the ring. 'I know what we'll do,' Sonny suggested. 'We'll get two robes and we'll dress the Moose [Nilon] here up in the one with Sonny Liston on the back and let him get into the ring with a towel over his head. Then, when they're ready, I'll come in. Right, Moose?' 'Sure, Sonny, sure,' concurred Nilon. 'Anything you say.' Anything for a quiet life.

As it transpired, the Trojan Horse was felt unnecessary. Looking every inch the carnivore, Sonny entered the ring clad in a white hooded robe and white shorts. As his feet pawed the canvas in one corner, the bare-headed Patterson embarked on a series of knee-bends in the other. When the champion's name was announced, cheering rent the arena. When Sonny's name was announced, the crowd booed, invoking an atmosphere more suited to a Punch and Judy show. 'They presumed that it was their right to boo,' wrote 'Doc' Young, 'and they did, like a convention of fog-horn blowers. The fans had established Liston as a solid betting favourite . . . they had, in other words, bet their money on Evil. Now they were paying lip-service to Good.' Sonny glared down at Patterson with those reddish-brown saucers of his when the pair were conjoined in the centre of the ring. Patterson stared at the floor, unable or unwilling to challenge those fiendish irises. The psychological duel was as one-sided as it was decisive. During *The Star-Spangled Banner*, sung by Patterson's friend, Mickey Alan, himself a former boxer, Cus D'Amato's countenance was as pale as his white sweater, hand placed over a pounding, fearful heart as if praying for divine intervention. If that was the case, atheism beckoned.

When the bell went, Patterson charged from his corner and thrust a left hook toward Sonny's head, only to miss by some distance. Advancing slowly, the 7–5 favourite then grasped the initiative, tattooing Patterson's head with a series of left jabs, and missing with equal alacrity. As Patterson endeavoured to work his way inside the jab, ducking, weaving and clinching by turn, three lefts peppered his kidneys and ribs like blunt stilettos, stinging darts but no more. Then came a left hook to the body, followed by another fusillade of shots directed at the rib cage, some of which Patterson absorbed, some of which he dodged. One ferocious hook would have ripped his head off had he not evaded it. At last, Patterson managed to break through with a jarring blow of his own, but Sonny dismissed it unblinkingly, bounding back with a right upper-cut that briefly shook its target as if it were a sapling buffeted by a stiff breeze. Still, Patterson did not appear to have been hurt over-much when, suddenly, standing up out of his crouch for the first time, his back about a foot from the ropes, he appeared to glance upwards as if struck, in Mailer's words, 'by some transcendent bolt'. Just as he did this, Sonny unleashed a left hook that ploughed him back into the ropes, knees a-buckle.

For an instant, as his left glove became entangled in the uppermost roped and his eyes pleaded for mercy, Patterson's plight foreshadowed Benny Paret's final moments of consciousness at Madison Square Garden six months later. The impotence, the sense of impending tragedy, and the futility of the occasion were all present and unnervingly, horribly correct, just as they would be when Paret collapsed in a comatose heap under the vituperative, vengeful pounding meted out by Emile Griffith, never to recover. Wading in with a left-right combination to the body, imperfectly timed but more than enough to double Patterson up, Sonny then drove in a left hook to the jaw. It was the first punch of genuine quality, and the last. Patterson sank like a stone, helped on his way by a chopping right, to land on all fours. 'Get up, get up,' yelled Mailer and James Baldwin in unison as they jumped to their feet. When the count reached three, Patterson shook his bewildered, ringing head, his expression one of confusion rather than pain. As the count reached nine, he had one glove off the canvas, but all resistance had drained away, spirit battered as much as flesh. He recovered to prop himself up on one knee but, by then, Mike Murphy, the knock-down timekeeper, had tolled that fatal count of ten. The whole shebang had encompassed just two minutes and six seconds, making it the third shortest heavyweight title fight on record, behind Tommy Burns's eighty-eight-second roasting of Jem Roche in 1908 and Louis's 124-second destruction of Schmeling in 1938. Sonny had treated his task with utter disdain, chewing Patterson up and spitting him out as a pernickety lion would a lamb with a surfeit of gristle. The awed silence that greeted the last rites had the air of a noteless requiem, a requiem for the triumph of so-called Evil over so-called Good, of Might over Right.

Sonny, looking decidedly bemused, was promptly embraced by Jack Nilon. As his arm was raised, a welter of well-wishers, ushers and policemen swarmed into the ring. Scores of hands reached out to slap him on the back and tug him every which-way, to his evident annoyance. He offered Patterson a consoling pat and thanked him for giving him his chance. The ex-champ lay his head on D'Amato's shoulder. 'What happened, Floyd?' asked the 54-year-old manager, the man whose wisdom Patterson had discarded to his cost in order to assert his independence and manhood. Apparently, he had seen all the punches coming, save the decisive one. Patterson also found solace in the arms of his mother, then returned to his quarters and remained in seclusion for half an hour. The longest sentence he uttered to the press was characteristically gallant: 'I think Sonny has inner qualities that are good; I think the public should give him a chance.'

The humiliation continued when Patterson attempted to avoid the crowd by departing through the ushers' room, only to find himself locked inside along with his family and friends. Efforts were made to force the padlock on the back door with a hammer, then an old metal pipe, neither of which succeeded. Eventually, they managed to cut it with a hacksaw. All the while, Patterson stood stock-still, holding his head. Donning his stage whiskers and beard he drove back to New York, only to be stopped *en route* by a policeman who demanded to see his licence. 'You an actor or sumpin'?' queried the officer as Patterson flapped, having left the document elsewhere. He never was ashamed of feeling ashamed.

In hindsight, Patterson attributes the cause of this particular shame to a combination of flawed tactics and marital strife. 'This is no excuse but, at that particular time, I was doing battle in the divorce courts with my first wife, over visitational rights and the like. That lasted for two years, and my mind was diverted. I was prepared to a certain extent, but not to the extent I should have been. I also adopted the wrong tactics. I should have boxed him, toe-to-toe. I should have moved, jabbed, tried to outbox him, not outslug him. The press had built him up as this enormously strong slugger, but I felt my hands were faster, and my punches equally strong. I knew that I had to move a lot, and force him to box, but I never had the chance to put that plan into action. Ali did, though. He frustrated him, made him think.'

1. Handyman: Sonny shows off the tools he used to extricate himself from a life of petty crime – and to claim the world heavyweight crown for the Mob.

2. The one constant: Geraldine holds Sonny's hand; Father Murphy (*left centre*), the man who taught him to write his name, bears witness. Circa 1961.

3. Wayne's whirl:
Sonny flattens Wayne
Bethea after just sixty-
nine seconds of their
Chicago shindig.
Bethea rose but was
prevented from
continuing. August,
1958.

4. (*above left*) Handler rejoices as Albert Westphal is knocked out; victor wonders whether that world title shot will ever happen. Next stop was, indeed, Floyd Patterson. December, 1961. **5.** (*above right*) 'Lissen, I got dis *great* line in sports jackets. Maybe Sonny and Floyd can model 'em?' Jack Nilon deep in negotiations. January, 1962.

6. (*below left*) The king of boxing rides Prince the horse through the Newcastle throng en route to St James's Hall for an exhibition bout. January, 1963. **7.** (*below right*) The last laugh: Sonny conveys the joy of victory a few moments after dispatching Patterson in Las Vegas. Jack Nilon (*left*) appears more concerned about what lurks around the corner. July, 1963.

8. Lost Wages? Sonny on the money as his right cross (*top*) sends Floyd Patterson crashing down and (*middle*) out in the first round of their second brief encounter in Las Vegas. Finally (*bottom*), the pair embrace: an odd custom. July, 1963.

9. *(left)* Danger, man: Sonny, outwardly confident, inwardly confused, takes a break from training shortly before facing Cassius Clay (as he then was) in Miami. Warning signs were never far away. January, 1964. **10.** *(right)* If I can't knock him out I'll squeeze him to death: Sonny contemplates a new tactical strategy as Clay beckons. February, 1964.

11. Mind games: a bemused Sonny looks on as Clay moulds the weigh-in into psychological performance art. February, 1964.

12. Catch me if you can: Sonny narrowly misses Clay's chin with a left hook in Miami. February, 1964.

13. Eyes of a (beaten) tiger: Sonny looks for the nearest exit after surrendering his crown in Miami. February, 1964.

14. Before the fall – and after: how the newspapers saw Liston–Clay I. February, 1964.

15. The party's over: Sonny crouches, Ali is about to strike, but the damage has already been done. A frantic Jersey Joe Walcott moves in to end the Lewiston lunacy. The recipient of the most hotly debated punch in boxing history, Sonny had already been counted out. May, 1965.

16. A disfigured Gerhard Zech raises Sonny's arm after being knocked out in the seventh round of the latter's 'comeback' fight in Stockholm. In fact, it was his fifth outing in as many years. June, 1966.

17. Give 'em enough rope: time to earn the 'eating money' as Sonny, still plugging the Thunderbird, demonstrates his skipping prowess before a rapt crowd of 20,000 in Stockholm. August, 1966.

Sonny retired to his box of a dressing-room and held court. Sporting his 'I Love Sonny' badge with distinct pride, Father Stevens popped in. 'Whenever people at Comiskey saw me, a man of the cloth, wearing that badge, they'd say, "You're for that bum?" as if I'd committed some kind of crime. I said hello and congrats to Sonny but I didn't stay long. Everyone was crammed into that small room and hollering.' Did the man of the cloth not have mixed feelings, or perhaps even a little guilt, about watching the carnage and, by implication, endorsing it? 'I understand the objections to boxing and I've always been in favour of greater protection for the fighters, but I think you can call it a sport. I'm just against the way it's run.'

Voices collided as questions were fired at Sonny from every conceivable angle. Did it turn out to be as easy a conquest as he had envisaged? 'No, I thought it would be easier. The only time he hurt me was when he got up to one knee at nine. I thought he'd make it up. That hurt me.' This was no time for false modesty. 'It was only three left hooks. I hit him with a left hook to the body, and he tied me up. He had me tied up earlier in the fight but, when the referee said "break" this time, Patterson wouldn't break and I had to push him away. Another hook and a right, it was then I knew he was hurt. Then I hit him with another hook, a right and then one more hook to the head. The right? Nah, I don't think that hurt him. But earlier I got him with a right upper-cut. It was very nice. I think it lifted his left foot off the canvas.' The Patterson camp, too, were convinced that that right had been the punch that did most to sentence their man to his fate. 'Didn't seem to take that long,' mumbled Sonny when he was shown a tape of the fight during an interview for the closed-circuit audience. 'Sure didn't seem to take so long.' The outbreak of laughter, cackling and cruel, rent theatres from Broadway to Birmingham. After obliging a cluster of autograph-hunters, Sonny turned his attention back to the loser. 'Floyd is a heck of a man. [He] told me that, if the public lets bygones be bygones, he was sure I would prove to be a good champion. I say the same. I want to prove to the public that I can be a good and decent champion.' Pregnant with hope rather than expectation, the words ghosted through the night air, lingering like the final, desperate pleas of a man whose guilt has long been decided.

The brevity of the contest inconvenienced the Internal Revenue Service almost as much as it had Patterson. Six weeks beforehand, officials had begun planning an unprecedented swoop on box offices at Comiskey Park and the 260 theatres that would be screening the fight on closed-circuit television, the aim being to seize the promoters' share of the receipts for tax purposes. The reasons for this were twofold: first, Graff, Reiner & Smith Enterprises Inc., the company responsible for the closed-circuit transmissions, had effected a deferred-payment plan with the promoters, CSI, without first seeking IRS permission; and second, neither Graff, Reiner & Smith nor CSI had filed tax returns for 1961. The meticulous timetable, however, was thrown out of kilter by the speed with which Sonny completed his night's work: IRS officers had been instructed to wait until 10:30 p.m. before notifying the theatre operators that they were legally bound to hand over all receipts due to Graff, Reiner & Smith and CSI; Patterson was counted out at 9:43 and, although there was no problem in collecting the Comiskey proceeds, various ingenious delays had to be engineered in an effort to keep the 260 theatre managers in their offices for forty-seven minutes and so serve the order on schedule. Around $4.5 million was eventually taken. Sonny co-operated in good humour, posing for a photograph by standing on the street, suitcase in hand, thumbing a lift out of town. As ever, though, in the long term, it would be his pockets that went hungry.

Wrapped in a bathrobe, hair in curlers, cold cream smeared into her facial pores like so much war-paint, Sonny's good lady had stayed behind in the couple's plush $100-a-day penthouse suite on the forty-second floor of the Sheraton-Chicago, accompanied by her mother, Eva Crawford. As soon as the fight ended, Sonny had sent a couple of bodyguards to pick Geraldine up. 'I didn't even have time to get nervous,' she assured reporters. Geraldine had no taste for the battle herself. 'If it were up to me, I'd never have let Sonny do it,' she had said a couple of months previously. 'I'd take poverty over prize-fighting. If we have kids [of our own], I won't let them fight either . . . I'd much rather live simply without this anxiety and torment . . . I know he's done wrong but, if he weren't in the public eye, it would be forgotten. The sportswriters always keep bringing it up. It's like they don't ever want him to be good. How's a man going to be good if folks don't let him? Many nights we talk it over. Sonny knows himself, and he knows if he becomes champ he only wants to live to make everybody realise he's a better person.' Repeating his earlier statement, Sonny endorsed this. 'If the public allows me the chance to let bygones be bygones, I'll be a worthy champ. If they'll accept me, I'll prove it to them.'

But would he ever be given that chance? The immediate omens were far from encouraging. 'So pugilism has a new champion, for better or for worse. Liston will hardly be a model for American youth,' opined Arthur Daley, a boxing correspondent content, like so many others of his ilk, to justify his job by investing it with some dubious moral significance. 'About all he demonstrated is that boxing is a safer short cut toward becoming a millionaire than some of the illegal methods Sonny had previously tried . . . Whether this seedy business can endure with an ex-convict as its ruling monarch is uncertain at the moment. Its future lies in his massive hands for what may be a long time to come.' One prominent New York legislator – who preferred to remain anonymous since he did not want to 'prejudge' the report of a joint legislative committee investigating boxing which had only just completed a two-day hearing – stated that Sonny's accession 'could spell the death-knell for professional boxing in New York State.'

Watching the transmission of the fight at Loew's Victoria Theatre in Harlem, Ted Poston of the *New York Post* detected further discouraging signs. 'The stocky, conservatively dressed man half-rose from his seat . . . and his soft words carried far beyond his elevated box seat. He said, simply: "God help us." And, in the stunned silence of at least twenty seconds, he seemed to speak for over 2500 Negroes in their $6.75 seats, for the hundreds of standees ranged behind, for scores of others crouched in the crowded aisles, and for dozens of teenagers who had slipped through the back door, dashed from behind the TV screen and lost themselves in an earlier, joyful crowd, only half-heartedly chased by the cops. For Loew's Victoria belonged to Floyd Patterson for two minutes and fifty-five seconds last night. And no bad man in the worst melodrama had been hissed and hooted as wildly for the same length of time as was a villain named Sonny Liston.' Ahem. Go easy on the sauce, Ted. At Hotel Theresa on 7th Avenue and 125th Street, an establishment once owned by Joe Louis, the celebrations were noticeable only by their absence. 'No other Negro in all history has so united his people in a common hope,' said one guest; 'the vain hope that he'd get his block knocked off.'

Quite the most clear-headed response emanated from an editorial in the *Louisville Courier-Journal*, entitled 'We'll Take The "Old" Sonny Liston'. 'Now that Liston is the new heavyweight champion, the cry has already gone up for him to rise above his unsavoury past and bring "honour" to the crown. The Wheaties School of sportswriters is pleading with him to mend his ways and be the kind of man "children can look up to", the very model of a proper hero. This strikes us as arrant nonsense. First, it assumes that prize-fighters, regardless of their dispositions or past, are suitable objects for impressionable youngsters to idolise. Furthermore, if Liston suddenly is converted into a "good guy" for public relations reasons, it would be a dishonest trick to play on the youngsters. The biggest favour Liston could do for them is to act like the same heel all the pre-fight publicity said he was. Why hoodwink the young hero-worshippers into believing that only nice guys get to the top, or that a pleasant personality, a nice smile, and a strict adherence to the Boy Scout oath are the way to get ahead in professional fighting? Liston was in the ring for money. So was Patterson. Liston won because he is bigger, stronger, meaner and tougher. As for his chequered past, including his associations with the underworld, he's not the first prize-fighter with this kind of background to make the big time and he won't be the last. That's the kind of business professional boxing is. Liston is living proof of this (so, for that matter, was Jack Dempsey) and, as such, he is a typical representative of his trade.'

Sonny was also the perfect exponent of his trade, a trade peddling flesh-and-bone betting chips. Now that the two-armed bandit had coughed up, Frankie Carbo could be forgiven a grin as he bedded down in his cell. The Mob had recovered their status symbol.

The Sonny who emerged the following morning was a man at one with himself and his muse, a king flexing his orb and sceptre as if by divine appointment, warming to the spoils of victory with the glow of self-assurance they generated. Now came the real test: a round with Norman Mailer, the self-proclaimed heavy-weight champion of modern literature. Forever pounding out macho rhythms on his Corona keyboard and pummelling the reader with a cascade of sounds and images while stabbing away at his country's conscience, here was a man who defied all efforts to ignore him. An expert feather-ruffler, Mailer still unsettles peer and public alike, being described by one fellow-writer, Martin Amis, as a boozed-out blowhard. When Alan Lelchuk created a fictionalised Mailer in his book, *American Mischief*, he had him killed by a bullet to the anus.

Sickened by the victory of 'the man who knew most about Evil', Mailer convened a press conference two floors below the room in the Sheraton Hotel where Sonny was scheduled to hold his. The champion, as was now his right, was tardy, and the two con-ferences coincided. Slightly the worse for drink, Mailer used his for opportunistic purposes, proposing himself as the man to handle press relations for the return. The tragi-comic outcome in Comiskey Park appeared to have been a personal affront on a number of counts: to his judgement, to his sense of social justice, and to his concept of the function of boxing. 'I am the only man in this country who can build the second Patterson-Liston fight into a $2 million gate instead of a $200,000 dog in Miami,' he announced to the smattering of journalists present. Still seated, and refusing to leave, he was carried out in his chair by house detectives. Upstairs, Sonny sat at the centre of a long table, on the dais, flanked by a phalanx of bodyguards. Just as Mailer entered the room, the new champ ventured a disparaging comment about the press in general.

Mailer (shouting from the back): 'Well, I'm not a reporter, but I'd like to say . . .'

Sonny: 'You're worse than a reporter.'

Chorus of pressmen: 'Shut the bum up.'

Sonny: 'No, let the bum speak.'

Mailer (still shouting): 'I picked Floyd Patterson to win by a one-punch knock-out in the sixth, and I still think I was right.'

Sonny: 'You're still drunk.'

Chorus: 'Shut the bum up.'

Mailer shut himself up, though only momentarily. Approaching the dais, he walked behind Sonny with the intention of continuing their debate on a more personal level, only to be blocked by two sizeable black bodyguards, one of whom suggested that if he wanted to talk to Sonny he should approach him from the front. Obeying their instructions, he waited until Sonny had finished another conversation, then confronted him.

Sonny: 'What did you do, go out and get another drink?'

Mailer: 'Liston, I still say Floyd Patterson can beat you.'

Sonny (smiling): 'Aw, why don't you stop being a sore loser?'

Mailer: 'You called me a bum.'

At this, a gaggle of reporters gathered round. The adversaries now had an audience, and they knew it.

Sonny: 'Well, you are a bum. Everybody is a bum. I'm a bum too. It's just that I'm a bigger bum than you are.' Standing up, Sonny extended an elephantine right paw: 'Shake, bum.' And so they shook, Mailer pulling Sonny's hand, and thus his body, toward him, leaning his own head closer and speaking from the corner of his mouth as if whispering in a clinch. 'I'm pulling this caper for a reason,' he explained. 'I know a way to build the next fight from a $200,000 dog in Miami to a $2 million gate in New York.' Sonny stared back respectfully, with what Mailer later referred to as the 'profound intelligence of a profound animal'. 'Say, that last drink really set you up,' he mocked. 'Why don't you go and get me a drink, you bum.' 'I'm not your flunky,' Mailer corrected. 'He loved me for it,' Mailer would duly boast to the readers of *Esquire*. 'The hint of a chuckle of corry old darky laughter, cotton-field giggles, peeped out a moment from his throat. "Oh sheet, man," said the wit in his eyes.' Turning to the gallery, Sonny had the last, admiring word: 'I like this guy.' Thus it was that Mailer, his innate sense of intellectual superiority faltering, left the room 'a modest man'. He knew now that, in a bout of verbal fisticuffs between two men at the height of their contrasting crafts, 'I had met our Zen master'.

Nine

King of the World

He thought he was the King of America
Where they pour Coca-Cola just like vintage wine
Now I try hard not to become hysterical
But I'm not sure if I am laughing or crying
I wish that I could push a button
And talk in the past and not the present tense
And watch this hurtin' feeling disappear
Like it was common sense
It was a fine idea at the time
Now it's a brilliant mistake.

(Elvis Costello, *Brilliant Mistake)*

'Camera, lights, action – and cue Ed . . .' It is the first sabbath of Sonny's reign. The opening titles of *The Ed Sullivan Show* scoot past. Armchair America sits up. 'Now, out in our audience,' intones the eponymous host in that snooty nasal twang of his, 'the new heavyweight champion of the world, Sonny Liston.' Applause ensues, most of it merely polite. Like some would-be Moses commanding the Red Sea to part, Sullivan thrusts out his right arm toward the seats. The cameraman is so besotted with the odd-looking fellow on stage that he takes a while to scan the scene beyond. Eventually, the lens picks out a man whose dark, neatly-pressed suit blends disconcertingly with his shaven head and wispy moustache. Slowly, sedately, Sonny stands up, turns around and waves to the sea of white faces. The smile is broad, theirs too. Warmth is absent. 'Grand to have you here, Sonny,' whinnies Mr Ed. Welcome, my son, welcome to the machine.

The telegram from James H.J. Tate, the Mayor of Philadelphia, had certainly augured well. 'Your feat demonstrates that a man's past does not have to dictate his future,' it began. 'I know all Philadelphians join with me in extending best wishes for a successful reign and that you will wear the crown in the fine tradition of Philadelphian champions before you.' Sonny, though, hardly seemed the type to get carried away. Experience had repeatedly thrust home the absurdity of that. The night he beat Patterson, he rang his mother, who asked him how he was; he said he felt fine, but tired. After a reciprocal inquiry, he paused, then signed off, saying only, 'Well, I'll be seeing you.' However, on the flight home from Chicago on the afternoon of 27 September, the dam broke. Sonny simply bubbled. It was as if Tate's missive was the final seal of approval. Friends, moreover, had told him of plans for a home-coming parade. Forget those press punks. He had arrived. The tribulations of the past were surely behind him now. As the newly-crowned king of the world, he was looking forward to a regal welcome and duly spent the journey practising a speech. Never, it seemed, had life smiled on him with such unadulterated beneficence.

'He used me as sort of a test auditor, dry-running his ideas by me,' Jack McKinney, who sat next to Sonny throughout the flight, told William Nack of *Sports Illustrated* three decades later. 'There's a lot of things I'm gonna do,' Sonny informed McKinney who, unbeknownst to his companion, had been frantically ringing City Hall, trying to persuade a representative to meet Sonny at the airport. 'But one thing's very important: I want to reach my people. I want to reach them and tell them, "You don't have to worry about me disgracin' you. You won't have to worry about me stoppin' your progress." I want to go to coloured churches and coloured neighbourhoods. I know it was in the papers that the better class of coloured people were hopin' I'd lose, even prayin' I'd lose, because they was afraid I wouldn't know how to act ... I remember one thing so clear about listening to Joe Louis fight on the radio when I was a kid. I never remember a fight the announcer didn't say about Louis, "A great fighter and a credit to his race".

Remember? That used to make me feel real proud inside.' The manifesto continued apace. 'I don't mean to be sayin' I'm just gonna be champion of my own people. It says now I'm the world's champion, and that's just the way it's gonna be. I want to go to a lot of places – like orphan homes and reform schools. I'll be able to say, "Kid, I know it's tough for you and it might even get tougher. But don't give up on the world. Good things can happen if you let them." '

Only one thing jarred. Friends had phoned Sonny in Chicago to warn him of an editorial composed by the sports editor of the *Philadelphia Daily News*, Larry Merchant. 'A celebration for Philadelphia's first heavyweight champ is now in order,' wrote Merchant, tongue bruising the inside of his cheek. 'Emily Post [who, in the late 19th century, established a code of etiquette for America] probably would recommend a ticker-tape parade. For confetti we can use shredded warrants of arrest.'

When the plane touched down, Sonny headed toward the exit, McKinney beside him. As the staircase was wheeled into place, he adjusted his tie and repositioned his fedora, preparing to face his public. However, to his palpable consternation, the thin gathering below comprised no more than a cluster of airport staff, reporters, PR bods and the omnipresent paparazzi. 'His eyes swept the whole scene,' recalled McKinney. 'He understood immediately what it meant. His Adam's apple moved slightly. You could feel the deflation, see the look of hurt in his eyes. It was almost like a silent shudder went through him. He'd been deliberately snubbed. I knew from that point on that the world would never get to know the Sonny that I knew.'

But wait. Maybe the welcoming committee was inside the airport? Officials tried to steer him to the interview room via a private passageway, but Jack Nilon objected: 'The people want to see you, Sonny.' Unfortunately, most of those who did were being paid to do so. At the press conference, Sonny obliged the cameras and cuddled Geraldine. 'I'm going to be the same guy and do the same things,' he vowed, but offered the microphones little else. When he was asked about his financial situation, Nilon butted in:

'We'll make out. We won't starve.' At that moment, though, Sonny needed spiritual, not material, nourishment. That elusive sense of self was more distant than ever. He wasn't special. If he imagined that a reputation could be erased by a string of punches, as McKinney suggested he did, those hopes could scarcely have been dashed with greater irrevocability. Deposing that nice Mr Patterson merely affirmed his standing as the premier punch-bag of the era. In this context, victory achieved nothing, becoming a celebrity even less. Sonny had kissed Dame Fortune full on the lips, only to get a boot to the groin in return. Rarely had the futility of boxing, of redemption through violence, been embodied more ruthlessly. He had entered the confession box and emerged empty-handed, empty-spirited. Salvation? Not through this pulpit. He had been branded for life, just another steer in the unwanted herd. Two weeks later, he was stopped by police for driving 'suspiciously slow' through Fairmount Park. Meet the new boss, same as the old boss.

Thus it was that Mr and Mrs Liston packed their bags and left Philadelphia for Denver in early 1963. Sonny's snarling adieu, as we have seen, gained instant immortality: 'I'd rather be a lamppost in Denver than Mayor of Philadelphia.' Another year, another fresh nest in another distant tree. As it transpired, Sonny got his wish. The saltier dogs among the Denver police were soon cocking up their legs and aiming at him. According to Ray Schoeninger, a former sparring partner, he was pulled over on a daily basis at one point. 'They must have stopped him 100 times outside City Park. He'd run on to the golf course and, as he left in his car, they'd stop him. Twenty-five days in a row. Same two cops. They thought it was a big joke. It made me ashamed of being a Denver native. Sad they never left him in peace.'

There were other attempts to keep Sonny in line. One day he strode into the Beverly Rodeo Hotel in Hollywood, marched into the dining-room and proceeded towards the table seating Moe Dalitz, erstwhile rum runner and boss of the Cleveland Mob, now in charge of the Desert Inn in Las Vegas. As the pair spoke, Sonny clenched his fist and cocked it. Dalitz indicated the unwise nature of this method of negotiation with a chilling emphasis: 'If you hit me, nigger, you'd better kill me. Because if you don't, I'll make one telephone call, and you'll be dead in twenty-four hours.' Fully aware of the persuasive connections at Dalitz's disposal and the seriousness of his threat, Sonny turned tail and left. Nobody could ever explain the encounter.

That appearance on *The Ed Sullivan Show* may have trumpeted Sonny's arrival as another cog in the showbiz wheel, but money, despite Nilon's bluff assertions, was still a headache. Within a couple of weeks, he was refereeing a bout in Portland; another adjudicative engagement followed in Houston. Exhibition tours or, as a reluctant Sonny called them, 'eating money' tours, were planned for Europe and the Orient. The only gains he had gotten out of Chicago thus far had been that cursory twenty-five grand for training expenses. On 22 October, four weeks after he had won the title, the big cheque was still in the post. Jack Nilon charged that CSI were in breach of contract for failing to give Sonny the agreed down payment of $50,000 within forty-eight hours of the fight. Meanwhile, the remainder of the $282,000 now due was still being held by the IRS, because of the promoter's tax indiscretions. Indeed, Nilon alleged that the monies would not be released until after Sonny had given Patterson his rematch. So, that same day, it was announced that Sonny was breaking away from CSI and would make the defence under the auspices of a new promoter. Naturally enough, Tommy Bolan, CSI's president, denied any breach: 'If Nilon thinks we did, we'll have to let the courts decide whether or not we did.' Bolan added that an IRS representative from New York had advised him that 'a release of funds is imminent'.

What, then, of the authorities? Would New York now deign to recognise him? For once, the lights got as far as amber. However, just as the NYSAC seemed to be mulling over a change of heart, another skeleton appeared to sneak out of the closet. Claiming it had 'important evidence linking Liston with the underworld', the New York State joint legislative committee on boxing proffered another case, that of Cortez Stewart. A fairly negligible heavyweight, Stewart testified that, on 7 April 1962, Blinky Palermo had promised to 'move me along fast' if he agreed to be Sonny's sparring partner during the build-up to the Patterson fight; Stewart said that, while he did not know who Palermo was then, he later identified him from a photo. Stewart also claimed that 'the man' refused to guarantee the $50-a-day payment he had requested, explaining that Sonny was in debt and therefore could not afford it. The committee invited Sonny and his 'managers of record' to New York to 'comment on, affirm or deny' Stewart's testimony. Jack Nilon denied knowing either Stewart or Palermo and branded the former a publicity-seeker. Through his lawyer, Sonny turned down the invitation on the same grounds. The NYSAC promptly headed for the fence, recognising Sonny as champion while simultaneously stating that it was not yet ready to grant him a licence to box within the state. 'He must,' it stipulated, 'earn that right.'

Mexico City, the site of another projected 'eating money' venture, was just as unwelcoming. 'Mexico has categorically shut its doors and removed the *bienvenido* sign for Sonny Liston,' reported *Jet* magazine. No reason was given for this by officials of the State Department's migratory division, but the 'unofficial view' was that Sonny would set a bad example for Mexico's apparently innocent youth. Promoter Miguel de la Colina appealed to the Federal District Boxing Commission, requesting permission for Sonny to appear in exhibitions in the capital, but Luis Sporta, the head of the commission, was collaborating with Estes Kefauver.

Perversely, however, if Sonny ranked high on the 'not wanted' lists of New York and Mexico, he was welcome, if not quite for altruistic reasons, in Pennsylvania. For all the humiliation he had endured in Quaker territory, Sonny was first and foremost a sugar daddy, tolerated because of his potency as a money-spinner. But, even then, Sonny was no longer the prime attraction. In the spring of 1963, the Pennsylvania State Athletic Commission informally expressed a desire to host, not Sonny's return with Patterson, but a meeting between the champ and a pretty, lippy young Kentuckian, Cassius Marcellus Clay. Since striking Olympic gold in 1960, Clay's mastery of self-promotion had been plying boxing with increasingly heavy intakes of pizzazz, providing a regular fix for a business that could never overdose on overkill. As nimble with rhyming couplets as he was on his feet, he had not so much stolen Sonny's thunder as filched it from under his pillow and left a calling card. 'Say it loud: I'm black and I'm proud.'

Not being averse to the odd bankable windfall, Inter-Continental Promotions were keen to promote a match between Sonny and this witty whipper-snapper, even though the latter's standing was founded on less than solid fistic grounds. Having educated the ageing Archie Moore on the inadvisability of prolonging a career too deep into overtime, March 1963 saw Clay edge a disputed decision in a pedestrian affair against Doug Jones, convincing Pete Hamill that he was 'in danger of becoming a dreadful bore'. Predicting the duration of his contests was a splendid party trick – until it went wrong, which it did, and by some distance, against Jones, whom Clay had previously denounced as 'nothing but a bum'. In June, he flew to London, where 55,000 people filed down Empire Way and transformed Wembley Stadium into a forest of patriots rooting for one man instead of the customary eleven. Clay forecast a jive in five but, just as round four was drawing to a close with the Louisville Lip in artful control, Henry Cooper – 'Our 'Enery' – drilled him with his famed ' 'Ammer' of a left hook. Down went Clay, seemingly for good, only for a combination of the bell and a nifty manoeuvre with a pair of gloves to turn almost certain defeat into a stoppage caused by 'Enery's leaky left eyebrow – in round five. 'I'm not the greatest,' announced the victor. 'I'm the double greatest. Not only do I knock them out, I pick the round. I'm the boldest, the prettiest, the most superior, most scientific, most skill-fullest fighter in the ring today.' And more. 'I've received more publicity than any fighter in history. I talk to reporters till their fingers are sore.' The hype hailed down in torrents, but one thing was indisputable: if other boxers had comprehended boxing's *raison d'être* as fully as this, none had employed that knowledge with such an unerring eye and brazen desire for the main chance. This was showbiz, and Cassius Marcellus wanted to be master of ceremonies *and* top the bill. Here was the original MC Hammer.

He certainly upstaged the principals when preparations for

Sonny's reunion with Patterson began to gather pace in that most fitting of venues, Las Vegas, that humungous desert casino commonly referred to as 'Lost Wages'. According to his historian friend, Hank Kaplan, the fight was originally set for Miami on 4 April 'until Sonny smashed his knee up trying to teach a youngster how to drive a golf ball'. If this was so, the hush was deafening.

Few gave Floyd an earthly; attentions were diverted instead to the aftermath. One night, though, Sonny cut Clay down with the chortling ease of an Australian hacking down poppies. Entering Sonny's base camp at the Thunderbird Hotel, Clay pitched up against a wall and barked out insults as his target shot craps at an adjacent table. 'Liston was a mean-tempered son of a bitch, and he was losing, so naturally he's mad,' recalled Harold Conrad. 'Look at that big ugly bear. He can't even shoot craps,' quipped Clay, splintering the silence. Sonny glared back, grabbed the dice and rolled again. No go. 'Look at that big ugly bear,' digged Clay again. He can't do nothing right. Come on, for big ugly bear. Let's get it on. Come on. I'll whip you right now. Floyd Patterson was a nobody. You'll knock out Floyd Patterson, but I'm the real champ. I'm too fast for you, and you know it. Put up all your money, Sonny, if you think you can whip me.' Then Clay walked over to Sonny to address him more directly. 'I want you out of town by sun-up tomorrow. Las Vegas ain't big enough for both of us.'

By now, all other activity in the immediate vicinity had suddenly ground to a halt. The confrontation had become a spectacle. At this point, two different punchlines emerge, as is the way with boxing lore. In the one according to Conrad, Sonny hurls down the dice, gets up and offers Clay a succinct salvo of short shrift, saying, 'Listen, you nigger faggot. If you don't get out of here in ten seconds, I'm gonna pull that big tongue out of your mouth and stick it up your ass.' Others, doubtless in the quest for heightened drama, averred that Sonny also slapped Clay in the mouth. Conrad refutes this. 'I asked him later, "Were you scared?" and he said, "Yeah, man, that big ugly bear scared me bad." I was there. He [Sonny] didn't slap him, but he scared the shit out of him; you better believe it.' The Ali version, unsurprisingly, was more dramatic. 'Suddenly, he reached in his pocket and pulled out a long black pistol, pointed it straight at my head, pulled the trigger: BANG! BANG! I ducked. A chill went through my spine. BANG! BANG! He was still aiming at me. I leaped over the blackjack table, then the dice table, scattering chips and cards all over the floor, and ducking and dodging all the way out in the streets, and behind me the pistol: BANG! BANG!' Upon returning to his hotel room, Clay threw himself on to the bed, breathless. 'My heart was beating fast, my hands were shaking. I was thinking maybe I should leave Liston alone. I knew I was only acting crazy, but he might be crazy for real.' He was still in a state when a reporter came up an hour later and told him that Willie Reddish was having a laughing fit. Suspecting that Clay would pull a stunt, the trainer had given Sonny a gun – loaded with blanks. Fifteen–love.

The contract for Liston-Patterson II was more even-handed than that for the first bout, entitling both players to 30 per cent of the gate and TV revenues alike, although Floyd was due 35 per cent of the ancillary rights to Sonny's 30 per cent. In spite of the kerfuffle the previous autumn, the schism, remarkably, had been healed; the event would be promoted once more by Championship Sports Inc. Such harmony was somewhat out of step with the world outside on the eve of the fight. A similar concord was reached when the US, USSR and Britain agreed to draw up a treaty banning A-bomb tests in the atmosphere, but the Sino-Russian talks in Moscow had broken off. 'Castro Building Drab Red State,' warned the *New York Times*. A track and field meeting in Moscow was deemed front-page material when the Americans defeated their Soviet counter-parts in seven of the weekend's eleven events. 'US Guns Kill GI in Vietnam – Mistaken in Darkness as a Red,' thundered another headline. A septet of whites picketed the Gwynn Oak Amusement Park in Baltimore, protesting against the city's agreement to open the park to blacks and against the decision to drop charges against a civil rights demonstrator. Billy Bello, a 19-year-old welterweight from the Bronx who had made his national TV debut at Madison Square Garden two weeks earlier, was found in the hallway of his Washington Avenue tenement, needle-holes perforating one arm.

Marlon Brando was starring as *The Ugly American* in the cinemas; on 22 July 1963, Sonny Liston was billed to play the same role at the Las Vegas Convention Centre.

The brain-child of Bugsy Siegel, the gambling oasis had hosted one previous heavyweight title clash, in 1912, some nineteen years before the installation of the first legitimate slot machine coincided with the passing of a six-week 'quickie' divorce law. The evening ended in chaos when police broke into the ring in the ninth round and brought a halt to the Jack Johnson-Fireman Jim Flynn affair. Fifteen years earlier, in nearby Carson City, Jim Corbett had reduced Bob Fitzsimmons to a state of near-paralysis in the fourteenth. 'Jim,' the Cornishman remarked after rescrambling his senses, 'you gave me a bloody good licking. I will never fight you again.' Arthur Daley hoped this would provide a precedent: 'Perhaps Patterson will say the same to Liston next Monday. That would make the entire business worthwhile.'

The most popular bet was even money that the pair would cease hostilities by round six. The 110–degree temperatures had something to do with this, both fighters being forced to train indoors almost exclusively because of the dry, withering heat. Sonny sparred and did sit-ups in the Thunderbird pleasure palace's minute theatre, while Floyd got in trim at either the secluded Hidden Well Ranch a few miles out of town or, for public work-outs, the exhibit hall of the Dunes Hotel, admission $1 a head. But it was the billboard outside the Dunes that encapsulated the overriding reason for the odds. 'Training Headquarters, Floyd Patterson,' it trumpeted, below a plug for 'Sasha Semenoff and His Romantic Strings', a less muscular act currently packing them in at the hotel restaurant. Once again, the punk from Bedford-Stuyvestant was held to be little more than an appetiser for Sonny to gobble down.

Patterson was in peak condition, of that there could be no doubt. Accompanied by a pair of German shepherd dogs he would take a five-mile run every morning, occasionally throwing a croquet ball for the hounds to chase. While Sonny had been setting up home in Denver, Patterson had tired of his $100,000 Scarsdale home and opted to live full-time at his training camp in order to concentrate on the task ahead. He had been offered twice as much to fight Clay, but the opportunity to reclaim his manhood was irresistible. Harking back to the Chicago fiasco, Cus D'Amato insisted that his man would be a different proposition, just as he had been for his return with Johansson. 'Floyd was so distracted by the pressures that were bothering him that he was unable to concentrate. That's why he violated one of the fundamentals of boxing. He should have known better. When anyone clinches with Liston, he should come in close to tie him up or push him away fast to get out of range. But Floyd gave him hitting room from up close. This is easily correctable. He won't do it again.' But no one was fooled. The sentimental vote, the puritan vote and the white vote all went to Patterson, but the pragmatic dosh was riding on the bad nigger. 'Liston will take out Patterson the first time he hits him,' predicted Joe Louis. 'It won't go five rounds,' promised Sonny. 'It wouldn't go fifteen if I broke both my hands. I'll do just like the Indians did. When the bell sounds, I'll charge.'

Sonny made a marked impression on Jack Murphy, who interviewed him for the *New York Times* magazine. In fact, Sonny could barely have stamped his presence more explicitly when the pair met in the coffee shop at the Thunderbird. He refused to shake Murphy's hand and, with a sharp rejoinder, demanded that he refrain from smoking: 'That cigar has to go.' A clearly distressed Ben Bentley, now ensconced as Sonny's press agent, interceded. 'I should have warned you,' he said to Murphy. 'Sonny can't stand cigar smoke.'

'Liston looks mean and menacing, and his manner is often cool and hostile,' Murphy observed. 'Most of the people who serve the champion, including his chief trainer, Willie Reddish, seem intimidated by him. He is Big Daddy. When Liston gives the command, everybody jumps . . . His face is a mask that rarely displays any form of animation, yet he is also a showman with a keen awareness of his role as a performer . . . he is moody and impulsive, and his training programme is dictated by his whims. His trainer rarely knows from one day to the next whether Liston will box or take a nap. "I feel good today," he'll inform Reddish. "Let's call off the work-outs." ' Murphy also noted that it was 'no accident that the most spectacular part of his work-out is the final item on the bill'. This particular turn involved Reddish picking up a 12½lb medicine ball, and repeatedly slamming it into Sonny's abdomen from a range of no more than two to three feet. The smack of leather on skin echoes through the room, spreading a buzz among another 1000-odd capacity gathering. Sonny groans in mock agony as another 12½lb broadside cannons into his stomach. The laughter builds. More guffaws as Reddish pauses to mop up the pools of sweat swamping his brow. When a spectator holds aloft a camera and asks Sonny for a snapshot, the pose is immediate, arm waved high in fake recognition.

The tide of public opinion had not so much turned towards Sonny as glanced reluctantly over its shoulder. In the media, discussions on his merits as a boxer were now as common as discursions on his connections. Tolerance, to an extent, had supplanted disgust. To his credit, Sonny retained a deep well of mistrust. Sardonic asides proliferated. Asked to name his favourite baseball team now that his cherished Brooklyn Dodgers had made their treacherous move to LA, the response was drier than a vermouth-less Martini. 'I guess I'll be like the public and go with the winner.' The point was prodded home with no little insistence. 'I don't care what the public says – so long as I get the money.' Murphy moved in with a wicked-looking hook. Why did Sonny distance himself from the civil rights activists? The blow was parried, just. 'The NAACP wanted to make a political thing out of me fighting for the championship,' he grunted. 'I didn't see the sense of that. Boxing is a sport, not politics. After all the trouble they caused me, the NAACP had the nerve to ask me for $500 when I won the championship. Actually, they didn't ask me – they asked my lawyer. But it was the same thing, and I said no.'

Sonny was dismissive in his prognostications, constantly demeaning the job at hand. Ensnared by one especially frivolous mood, he suggested that the fight be held in a telephone booth. He was fulfilling contractual obligations, no more, no less. He had a measure of respect for Patterson the man, if not Patterson the fighter, but disapproval lurked. 'I have a little dislike for Patterson,' he had informed readers of *Ebony* before the Chicago show. 'But it's not because he wouldn't agree to fight me for so long, but because he hasn't fought any coloured boys since becoming champion. Patterson draws the colour line against his own race. We have a hard enough time as it is in this white man's world.' Although he omitted to mention Tommy 'Hurricane' Jackson, Sonny had made a worthwhile point.

'What can I do to sell the fight?' he wondered rhetorically to Murphy. 'Nothing I could say would make any difference. After all, the people saw what happened the first time.' He nevertheless trained with the intent of a man whose career was on the line. 'I expect Patterson thinks I will hold him cheap this time, but I won't make that mistake. I figure he will try harder, and he knows something about me and maybe he can make a better fight. I know if I got beat I'd try a lot harder the next time.' What, though, were Sonny's aims? 'I wanted to be champion because of the money, but the big thing is the satisfaction of being the best of anything. Joe Louis, he was always my idol, and I want to be even better than Joe. Everybody likes to break a record; I'd like to beat Joe's record.' But this was an undistinguished era for heavyweight boxing, and Sonny acknowledged that recognition would take time. 'I'll just do the best I can, with what I have to work with. I guess I can go back to fighting the same trash I fought before, or maybe there's a few guys I missed on the way up.' What about the boy Clay? 'Naw, he doesn't bother me none. His chatter just makes me laugh. That boy has got a big mouth – the only way he knows how to fight is with his mouth.' Those trusty old punchlines then had an oiling. 'Cassius can't lick a popsicle. He should be arrested for impersonating a fighter. I expect he'll run for a couple of rounds and I'll chase him; then it will all be over.'

More at ease with the press than hitherto, Sonny entertained the hacks amiably enough, but always on his terms. To a large extent, pride offset any desire to confess a need for acceptance, but there were moments of candour. 'After people meet me they say I'm nice,' he remarked during one conference. 'They is surprised that

I'm not at all like I'm supposed to be.' In the main, he rationed his words to maximum effect, although one day Peter Wilson heard him go into overdrive. 'There was this guy, see, an' he happened to know he could get into an ice box that belonged to the local butcher. So he keeps on gettin' in there an' stealin' steaks an' roasts an' ever'thin'. So fin'ly the butcher he gets wise an' he hides hisself in the ice box. An' when this guy comes reachin' in again . . .' Wilson watched as 'a hand like a black ham made the table shake'. The yarn spun on: '. . . the butcher he bring the cleaver down on this thief's wrist an' instead of the guy gettin' away with a steak or what-all, he only got time to grab his own hand and stuff it up his sleeve an' run for his cotton-pickin' life. An' outside he meets someone who knows how he's bin thievin' an' this other guy asks: "You got yours?" An' the first guy says: "Yeah, I got mine okay. Now you go in an' get yours." ' The story-teller was mightily amused by the time he delivered the punchline. Wilson, who saw Sonny as the butcher, waiting in the dark for his next victim, was not.

The tale of the tape embellished the portents for another mismatch. Sonny held a distinct edge in all the vital statistics: weight (215lb to 195), height, reach, fist, biceps, wrist, calf, ankle, thigh, chest and neck, not to mention self-belief. The level of public interest reflected the cynicism prompted by the swiftness with which the first fight had been concluded, and the consequent fear of *déjà vu*. Even Anthony Quinn, the actor, had thrown in his ha'p'orth, attesting that he could have tackled Sonny better at Comiskey than Floyd had. Demand for tickets ranging from $5 to $100 at the 8000-capacity arena was brisk, if scarcely overwhelming (6689 were sold *in toto*) and, while Tommy Bolan was bragging to anyone who cared to listen that receipts would exceed $300,000, in the event they fell appreciably short, at $247,690. SportsVision Inc., meanwhile, prepared to beam the bout to 143 closed-circuit screens in 109 American cities, a drop of close to 50 per cent on the number of external venues for Liston-Patterson I. Another difference was that Patterson could at least bank on a sharp get-away this time. For many years, Cus D'Amato's fear of heights had impinged itself on Floyd, but he had resolved to conquer this, working enthusiastically to obtain his pilot's licence. A two-seater, single-engine Cessna 172 would be close at hand.

The weigh-in replicated the one in Chicago: Sonny the choir-master glowering down, trying to drag Floyd's eyes into the firing-line, Floyd the errant soprano staring a hole in his boots. The difference in height was exactly an inch, 6ft 1in to 6ft-dead, but it looked like a foot. Patterson later insisted that while he was quite prepared to be called a coward, and indeed was happy to describe himself as such, this apparent meekness was not a mark of fear. 'I can never look *any* fighter in the eye because . . . well, because we're going to fight, which isn't a nice thing, and because . . . well, once I actually did look a fighter in the eye. It was a long, long time ago. I must have been in the amateurs then. And when I looked at this fighter, I saw he had such a nice face . . . and then he looked at *me* . . . and *smiled* at me . . . and *I* smiled back! It was strange, very strange. When a guy can look at another guy and smile like that, I don't think they have any business fighting. I don't remember what happened in that fight, and I don't remember what the guy's name was. I only remember that, ever since, I have never looked another fighter in the eye.'

As Floyd lay on the table in his dressing-room, self-doubt gnawed away. How could the body keep a promise that the mind was unable to make? As James Fox's Chas observed of Mick Jagger's Turner in *Performance*, he'd lost his demon. 'I remember thinking, "You're in excellent physical condition, you're in good mental condition – but are you vicious?"' he later informed Gay Talese. Viciousness was not important, he convinced himself. Not at that moment, anyway. 'Who knows?' he pondered. 'Maybe you'll get vicious when the bell rings.' Willie Reddish came by to wish him good luck, pushing viciousness even further from reach.

Patterson was first to enter the field of play. Picked out by a spotlight, Sonny was roundly booed as he followed. Floyd remained the defender of the faith. When the combatants were officially introduced, Clay, cutting a razzy figure in his white shirt, tie and polka-dot jacket, was ushered into the ring to add a little zing. Cheered good-naturedly by some and jeered less than zealously by others, he spotted a large sign held aloft by Sonny's corner-men. 'Clay has a big lip that Sonny will zip,' warned the pretend newspaper headline. At this, Clay sauntered over, grabbed the sign and ripped it to pieces, once for the TV cameraman, then again for those at ringside. Upon shaking Patterson's hand, he glanced at Sonny, threw his hands up and fled in mock terror. A group of spectators on the balcony had pasted a sign on the wall: 'Clay – The Desert Canary'. Back on his fifth-row perch, the canary cheeped merrily away. 'I'm the champ – the uncrowned champ . . . Come on, bring the bums out.' *The Star-Spangled Banner* found Patterson standing rigidly to attention, still boring that hole in his toes. Sonny shuffled his feet. Set against his white shorts, his maroon gloves positively dazzled.

Cus D'Amato's forecast that Floyd would adopt a more sensible tactical approach this time round was rubbished with indecent haste. Standing toe-to-toe once more, he managed to throw a few more blows, but Sonny treated them with disdain. Prowling the canvas with ominous deliberation and certainty, Sonny achieved the first knock-down after eighty-eight seconds with a left-right combination. Though not caught flush on the jaw, Floyd teetered slightly, then fell. 'Come on, Sonny . . . Sonny, ease up,' implored one spectator watching the action on the eighteen-by-twenty-foot screen at Loew's State Theatre in New York. 'I paid $7.50 for this.'

While enduring the compulsory eight count Floyd did not seem to be in any particular distress but, almost as soon as he arose, a left hook and a long right decked him again. Up at three, he waited until the count had reached the obligatory eight before resurfacing. The breathing space was of meagre value. One right to the chops was enough, bowling him on to his back. Body shuddering, he rolled over and raised himself on one knee, eyes aglaze. That was as far as he got before the toll scaled ten. Floyd had set an endurance record; clocking in at 130 seconds, this farce had lasted four seconds longer than the previous one. Back at Loew's State, one punter jumped out of an aisle seat near the back of the auditorium as the count neared completion and bolted for the exit. 'That's it.

That's it,' he announced. 'Never again.' Floyd was doubtless thinking something similar.

Sonny could have been forgiven a suppressed snigger or two. So this was prize-fighting? After thirty-six fights, thirty-five wins, 178 rounds and well under nine hours' labour, he had defended the greatest bauble in the entertainment world. In two fights requiring four minutes and sixteen seconds of half-throttle effort against one overmatched opponent, he had protected his quarry, a feat beyond the scope of Jim Braddock, Maxie Baer and Bob Fitzsimmons. Nigh-on ten years had passed since the night he dunked Don Smith in St Louis, but the wait had been worthwhile. 'What messed me up there was the eight counts,' he wisecracked to an uproarious accompaniment when the post-fight interviews were relayed to the closed-circuit throng. Yet where Chicago had offered royal blue skies, Las Vegas permitted only the fog of anticlimax. There was no glory to wallow in, no plaudits to drink in. He had merely done what was expected, perhaps more quickly than anticipated, but the surprise quotient was minimal to the point of invisibility. There had been no prolonged drama, no plot twists, no controversy – and not a drop of blood.

From Forrest City, Helen Liston, who had declined to watch either this or the Chicago bout and relied on neighbours for the result, approved her son's triumph with reservations. 'I guess you might say I was proud,' she told reporters, while describing boxing as 'just brutal'. When she was asked what she thought of the additional four seconds Sonny had consumed in dismantling Patterson, the family funny-bone emerged with a flourish: 'Well, Floyd's a good fighter. I guess he wanted to win pretty bad.'

'How could the same thing happen twice? How?' Floyd later asked Gay Talese, strictly rhetorically. 'That's all I kept thinking after the knock-out . . . Was I fooling these people all these years? . . . Was I ever the champion?' He was led from the ring, but the escort turned down the wrong aisle. 'They must have been thinking, "Patterson's not only knocked out, he can't even find his dressing-room." ' When the procession eventually ended, Floyd went into the bathroom, shut the door behind him and stared at the mirror. Two words issued forth from his pursed lips: 'What happened?' Fists began to pound the outer door. 'C'mon out, Floyd, c'mon out,' cried their owners. 'The press is here, Cus is here; c'mon out, Floyd.' He duly obliged. 'But what can you say? What you're thinking about is all those months of training, all the conditioning, all the depriving; and you think, "I didn't have to run that extra mile, didn't have to spar that day, I could have stayed up that night in camp and watched the late show . . . I could have fought this fight tonight in no condition." ' Apparently, Floyd had sustained nothing more debilitating than a headache. 'Liston didn't hurt me physically – a few days later I only felt a twitching nerve in my teeth – it was nothing like some fights I've had.' In terms of physical damage, his encounter with Dick Wagner in 1953 was considerably more painful: he had spent the next few days urinating blood. All the same, this had been a shattering blow to the spirit.

To cap it all, the Cessna was overburdened with luggage when Patterson took off, and the engine overheated ninety miles outside Las Vegas. He and his co-pilot radioed the airfield, booked a larger plane and turned back. But the terminal was choc-a-bloc with folk leaving town, compelling Patterson to hide in the shadows to the rear of the hangar (shades of those subway hideaways) – although the beard remained tucked away inside his suitcase. Nobody spotted him. If nothing else, he was still capable of a passable Houdini impression.

As soon as Sonny left the ring, the Louisville Lip sprang between the ropes and puckered up. Overcoming the three heavies from the Nevada sheriff's guard who briefly pinned him in a corner, Clay hollered another sermon. 'The fight was a disgrace. Liston is a tramp; I'm the champ. I want that big ugly bear. I want that big bum as soon as I can get him. I'm tired of talking. I want action. If I can't whip that bum I'll leave the country.'

For Sonny, an era had ended. His take amounted to $1.3 million (before distributions), but now the real moolah was within grasp. All he had to do was play straight to a crazy brat from Kentucky. Acclaim? For a black ex-con backed by dirty money? Forget it. Who needed it anyway? Just so long as he could put his money where this kid's mouth was, there would be compensations aplenty.

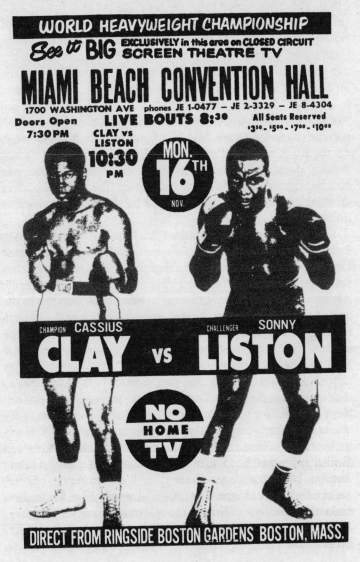

Ten

Miami Blues

Everyone has a will to win, but very few have a will to prepare to win.

(Vince Lombardi, former gridiron coach)

Demure and austere by nature, the dining-room of the Mayfair Hotel was suddenly transmogrified into a Dodge City saloon. The beefy, lantern-jawed cowboy with the determined glint in his eye abandoned his table and strode across the room. Coming face to face with his bounty at another table was Brian London, a useful Blackpool heavyweight with ideas well above his station who had been swatted away when challenging for Patterson's title some years previously. Instead of a Colt 45, he extended a hand, one that evidently preferred a shake to a shoot-out. Sonny, whose self-consciousness was particularly acute when eating, an activity he detested being observed in mid-delicto, merely carried on mauling a chicken bone. London, though, was not about to be dismissed so derisively. After a few seconds, Sonny reached over for a glass of water, still preoccupied, still, apparently, oblivious. The unwelcome guest thumped his fists on the table. 'You say there's no British heavyweight to fight you or spar with you,' exploded London, Lancastrian larynx to the fore. 'Well, I'm here to offer my services – free of charge. I've come all the way from Blackpool to make this offer to you. Now I'm going straight back.' Sonny glared back and kept chomping. London stomped off into the sunset, a broken man.

After a short break, Sonny had embarked on a barnstorming tour of Europe, accompanied by Geraldine, Nilon, Reddish and a sparring partner, Fonedo Cox, whose Christian name gave no end of trouble to anyone trying to announce it. Before reaching London in early September, the entourage had traipsed to Norway under the auspices of the Red Cross. Boxing was still legal there, and a crowd of 15,000 in Mysen lapped it up as Sonny strutted his stuff. This luncheon at the Mayfair Hotel was the curtain-raiser to a Harry Levene-promoted appearance the following day at the Empire Pool in Wembley, where Sonny trained and sparred in front of another admiring gaggle prior to the Billy Walker-Johnny Prescott bout. His farewell English performance was at Birmingham's Embassy Sportsdome on 18 September 1963.

Boxing News laid it on thick. 'What did he say in reply to London's outburst? Nothing. Now lazily sipping his water he stared at London as though trying to knock him down with those great big hypnotic eyes that are said to have twice demoralised Floyd Patterson on the scale.' Sonny was in fine fettle for the publication's question-and-answer session.

Reporter: 'Why didn't you shake hands with Brian London?'

Sonny: 'I was busy eating.'

'Why did you stare at him?'

'I didn't stare at him. I was looking straight through him at the guy behind him.'

'Will you accept his offer to fight or spar?'

'I accept, but not free. He'll need the money.'

And so it went on. 'Don't you think London deserves a fight more than Johansson?'

'Y-E-A-H,' endorsed Sonny, really hamming it up now. Cue howling chorus. Reporter throws in a cheeky jab:

'Maybe you're afraid to spar with him lest he finds out your secrets and beats you in a title fight?'

'Yeah. I'm afraid he'll find out my secrets and then not fight me.'

'What's your secret, Sonny?'

'Like the atom bomb. When it hits the target it explodes.'

London was not alone in trying to pit his macho wares against

Sonny's. When Sonny set up camp at the Savoy Hotel, one visitor to his suite was Reg Gutteridge, a renowned boxing reporter and ex-Royal Marine commando who had had a leg shot away during the Second World War and, unbeknownst to the champion, now sported an artificial limb. At one point during the interview, Gutteridge grabbed a knife and thrust it into the substitute leg. 'Can you do this?' he asked facetiously. Duly taken aback, Sonny was momentarily lost for words. 'No,' he answered after a lengthy pause, pregnant with astonishment, 'I can't do that. But . . .' At this he rose, loped over to the door and, with the merest twitch of those massive shoulders, proceeded to divorce the exit from its hinges. '. . . Can you do that?' he enquired, gently. Game, set and, incontrovertibly, match.

The cockney underworld was equally swift to sniff Sonny out. Those sultans of skullduggery, the Kray twins, had a penchant for basking in the reflected glow that flowed from the coat-tails of Ted 'Kid' Lewis, Freddie Mills and Terry Spinks, three members of that highly exclusive club of British world champions. The connection could never be regarded as healthy, and it almost did for Sonny. Paid £500 by Ronnie and Reggie for a spot of PR at one of their night-clubs, the Cambridge Rooms on the Kingston bypass, Reggie's nervy passenger barely survived the hair-rising ride back to the Dorchester. Not that rubbing shoulders with the British bovver boys held any other fears for Sonny. After all, compared with the Carbos and Palermos, the Krays were merely pick-pockets. Indeed, in his 1969 autobiography, *Me And My Brothers*, Charles Kray referred to Sonny as one of the 'guests of me and my brothers who still speak well of us'.

Before Patterson finally succumbed to all those taunts – or, depending on which version you believe, took pity on Sonny – there had been talk (make that hot air spouted) about 'Our 'Enery' fighting Sonny. Cooper, however, was dressed only for formality when he ultimately met Sonny on the London leg of the tour. 'I remember Harry Levene telling us about Sonny when he first entered the world rankings. My manager, Jim Wicks, said he had been warned that he was an animal and that I should avoid him. "Too

ugly," Jim would say to the press. "We only like to fight pretty boys."
He was very wary of him, because Sonny was a big guy and I was only
light. A fantasy grew around him. We thought he had two heads and
four pairs of hands. He was certainly a dangerous fighter, and he was
fine against guys who wanted to have a punch-up, but he couldn't
handle Ali. Having said that, Patterson had even faster hands than Ali,
but he could never believe that any fighter could knock him out.

'The stories that came out of Sonny's trip to London were
legend. According to one, he had it written into his contract that he
had to have three white women a day. I know he had a tough time of
it, but I couldn't feel sorry for him. Everybody involved on that tour
said he treated people like dirt. Levene arranged for a Roller to pick
him up off the tarmac when he flew in to London, the sort of
treatment reserved for royalty. Mickey Duff, Jarvis Astaire and
Levene got in beside Sonny, who took one look at Duff and said,
"Who are you? I don't like the look of you," then told him to get
out. So Mickey got out and took a taxi.'

While Duff and Astaire were responsible for the English leg of
the tour, Peter Keenan co-ordinated the Scottish and Irish legs,
setting up exhibitions in Glasgow and Belfast. A feisty Glaswegian
idolised by the Krays – who had set up, or so it was rumoured, the
whole British end of the Liston Roadshow – Keenan had been one
of the finest fisticuffers in Europe during the early to mid 1950s.
The only British bantamweight to achieve two outright Lonsdale
belts – Cooper's three make him alone in winning more – he twice
won the European title and claimed the Commonwealth crown in
1955, successfully defending it on five occasions. He also took the
then world champion Vic Toweel to a points verdict in
Johannesburg in 1952. On retirement, he turned to promoting.
'Sonny was just a big, daft boy surrounded by bodyguards, five of
them, all bantamweights, little guys. There was nobody fit to fight
him. He loved the piped band we brought to welcome him at
Renfrew airport but he couldn't understand the bigotry in Belfast.
He thought only blacks were treated badly. He kept on talking
about the march Martin Luther King was organising and how he
really wanted to be back home for it.

'Everyone loved him, but he had a drink problem. He loved Scotch. He also loved children, and although he had adopted a few daughters he didn't have a son and so he fell in love with my son, Peter junior. He was my only son, so I didn't want to let him go. In any case, Sonny was not fit for my son because of his drink problem. Peter took to him, though, and later went to stay with him for six weeks in Vegas, where he met Joe Louis and lots of other boxing celebrities. He had the time of his life. You should see his bedroom now. Full of pictures and memorabilia. Even after Sonny's death he would go over to see Geraldine for a holiday.'

One afternoon in his suite at Glasgow's Central Hotel, Sonny's hatred of smoke prompted a face-off between father and would-be father. 'He told me to put my cigar out,' recalls Keenan senior, 'but *no one* tells me to do anything, especially not in Glasgow. Then someone gave him a cane, and he knocked the thing out of my mouth. I told him that the only thing going out now was going to be him, out of the window – we were ten storeys up at the time – and promptly whacked him with a left hook. If they'd been Glasgow boys they'd have been smashing bottles, but his boys just froze. Sonny simply ignored it. He was a better-mannered person afterwards. Now he knew where he was. I felt sorry for him because he treated me like Mighty Mouse after that.' The Keenans still live together in the rough-and-tumble Knightswood area of Glasgow, Peter junior's vibrant, chirpy demeanour masking the brain damage he sustained in a recent car accident.

When Sonny returned to Denver, another escapade involving a vehicle drew a similarly gruff reaction to his run-in with Duff. Having set out from LA *en route* to New York, Clay was in Chicago one day when he decided on a gambit to drum up publicity for his mooted tilt at the title. Afraid of flying, he had bought a red bus, explaining that the good thing about buses was their tendency not to fall 30,000 feet when they broke down. Emblazoned across the top of the bus in a gaudy rash of colours was the rallying cry, 'World's Most Colorful [*sic*] Fighter'; below that, 'Liston must go in 8', both the handiwork of Cassius Snr, a frustrated artist-turned-sign-writer. This was Clay as Toro Molino, the character in Budd

Schulberg's *The Harder They Fall* who campaigned for his fights by trekking from town to town in a bus. On this occasion, he was bent on the 1000-odd mile diversion to Colorado. Accompanied by photographer-cum-aide Howard Bingham, brother Rudy, Ronnie King and Clay Tyson, a black comedian, he arrived on Sonny's lawn at around 2 a.m., having first given an anonymous tip-off, upon the advice of his backers, to a batch of newspapers and radio stations that he was going to break into the Liston residence. Sure enough, police sirens were wailing as the bus entered the pristine, white neighbourhood. 'We started yelling, "Oink, oink",' Ali remembered. 'Everybody heard. You know how them white people felt about that black man who had just moved in. We didn't help it much. Liston came out after the taunting but, before he could make up his mind what to do, the police told us to leave or we'd be arrested for disturbing the peace.'

Bingham had been dispatched to knock on the door as the snappers prepared to snap. Stirred from his slumber, Sonny draped a bathrobe over his slinky (and decidedly unbecoming) polka-dot pyjamas, went downstairs, picked up a poker from the fireplace and peered through the peep-hole in the front door. After a while, as the taunts and the oinks peppered the nocturnal air, he opened up. Bingham picks up the thread. 'He said, "What do you want, you black motherfucker?" You know that stare Sonny used to give opponents right before a fight when the referee was giving instructions? Well, that's the look I got from Sonny that night. So I got back to the bus pretty fast. One of the boys was in the bus, honking the horn, and Ali was on the lawn screaming and hollering about how he was gonna whup Liston bad. We all hollered for a while, and then Sonny came out on the lawn, so we took off. I had a good time that night.' Clay, who later claimed that Sonny smashed one of the bus windows with the poker and whacked a couple more, had the last word, as ever. 'You big ugly bear,' he screamed at Sonny as the latter stood in the doorway. 'The policemen and those dogs saved you. You no champ! You a chump! You gonna fall in eight, 'cause I'm the greatest!'

The publicity drive was not in vain. On 5 November 1963, names were assigned to dotted lines when Sonny and Clay convened in a room at Denver's Brown Palace Hotel. The challenger had his fun in front of the paparazzi, daring Sonny to 'get it on now'. For his part, Sonny sat and grinned, albeit a shade nervily. When he finally got a word in edgeways, there was a hint of panic, if only in the way he strove to make himself heard. 'I'll have to start training five days before the fight,' he asserted, barely holding a smirk at bay.

The haggling, needless to say, had been protracted. During a local Louisville TV broadcast back in August, Clay had announced the fight was off, which was a little odd since nothing, at that point, had been arranged for him to call off. He had talked too much and worked too hard to take the scant share offered him by Inter-Continental Promotions, he said, 'so, since I built it up, I'll tear it down. There will be no fight between Liston and I until the money is right. I'm the talk of the world. I am known as the predictor. The "Big Bear" needs me. So if I have to take low, I had just rather not fight. He either meets my price or he can dance elsewhere for peanuts. I don't need Sonny Liston. He needs *me*. I'm the hottest attraction to come along since talking pictures. Pick up any magazine, there's Cassius Clay on the cover. I'm not talking about boxing magazines. Anybody can get in those. I'm talking about the magazines that reach the non-fight fan. When you interest that type of person you've got it made. That's where the real money is.'

Even when the documents were finally sealed, giving the challenger 10 per cent more of the pie than Sonny had been offered for his first confrontation with Patterson, Gordon Davidson, a lawyer attached to Clay's backers, the Louisville Sponsoring Group, conceded that the syndicate was against their boy taking on Sonny. 'We argued that he needed more experience, that Liston was too strong for him right now. No use. He wasn't listening. We finally concluded Cassius doesn't try to learn anything from one fight to the next and really doesn't care about becoming one of the finest heavyweights who ever lived. All he wants is to be the richest. Wise or unwise, it's his decision and his career.'

Other voices could be heard in protestation, and not just because Sonny was now regarded as invincible. 'Such mismatches not only endanger the overmatched boxer, but degrade boxing from a great sport to a sordid racket,' railed Sol Silverman. An attorney who had taken up cudgels as a boxing investigator, Silverman had been enraged by the recent death of the former featherweight champion, Davey Moore, who had expired through injuries sustained in a fight with Sugar Ramos, inspiring an up-and-coming young folk hero by the name of Bob Dylan to pen a ballad. 'Let it be remembered,' continued Silverman, 'that professional boxing at this time can't stand another disaster. The proposed Cassius Clay-Sonny Liston heavyweight title fight is a dangerous mismatch which could result in grave injury to the young challenger. Besides, not one former heavyweight champion among the eleven now living regards Clay as being ready for Liston.'

Two days after the contracts were signed, Washington recognised the Ngo Dinh Diem regime in South Vietnam. Clay, fortunately, had found a way to stall his impending call-up papers. 'We don't want Clay to have something he is not entitled to,' argued William Faversham, the former investment counsellor who had united a disparate band of ten white Kentuckians, each one a millionaire or heir, to form the Louisville Sponsoring Group. 'But we feel this is an extenuating circumstance. If his entry into the service were delayed a few months it would give him his big chance.' A few months later, intentionally or otherwise, Clay flunked the army aptitude test, sparking a 'Draft That Nigger Clay' campaign headed by a lawyer from Georgia, who had already instigated a national 'Fire Your Nigger Week' campaign aimed at white firms with black employees.

In the meantime, in Florida, Chris Dundee had been deploying his persuasive tongue on brother Angelo's behalf in an effort to convince Miami to stage the fight. The Dundees, it seems pertinent to point out, were both part of the Carbo connection. While on a special assignment in Washington DC in March 1958, District Attorney Frank Hogan's spies spotted the Czar sharing a meal at Goldie Ahearn's with, among others, Sam Margolis and Angelo Dundee. An innocent gathering? Perhaps. Far more guilty was Chris Dundee. According to Truman Gibson's testimony to a

New York grand jury in April 1958, Chris had rung him earlier in the year to discuss closed-circuit TV rights for the forthcoming Sugar Ray Robinson-Carmen Basilio shindig, hoping to obtain a franchise for the telecasts in Florida and Georgia. Gibson resisted his entreaties, so Dundee handed the phone to . . . Carbo, a dab hand at friendly, and generally irresistible, persuasion. For once, however, Frankie flunked. No dice. Even Czars have to play by the book on occasions.

Bids to stage the Liston-Clay contest had already been received from Minneapolis, Los Angeles, Las Vegas, Atlantic City and Chicago – though not New York, naturally, nor, for much the same reasons, California. That mean mug staring out from under a Santa Claus hat on the cover of December's *Esquire*, left eye partly obscured by the rim to enhance the sinister image, was still an eyesore to many. Sitting on the knee of this Father Christmas carried a government health warning. If this was the magazine's idea of a good wheeze at the expense of its white, upwardly mobile readership, it certainly had all the right ingredients. The very thought of Sonny as Santa was enough to turn the WASPs of America into profound disbelievers.

Hidden so carefully from the outside world as a rule, the child in Sonny emerged during that *Esquire* shoot. George Lois, the magazine's art director, approached his subject via Joe Louis, a mutual friend; reluctant though he was, Sonny agreed to a session in Las Vegas. If anyone bar his boyhood idol had done the asking, the project would never have reached first base. However, after Carl Fischer had snapped his first snap, Louis was again called in to intercede. 'That's it,' snapped Sonny as he got up and rid himself of the asinine red-and-white bobble-hat. As he approached the door to leave, Lois grabbed his arm. No words were necessary to free his hold. Sonny just stopped and glared down at him, then proceeded to his pew at the casino craps table downstairs. The 'Brown Bomber' well understood his sound-alike's plight and, at Lois's request, went to track down Sonny. Upon finding him, Louis walked up from the rear and executed a manoeuvre beloved by teachers and parents alike, taking Sonny by the ear and marching him towards the lifts as if he had caught him sneaking a crafty drag behind the bicycle sheds. 'Come on, git,' muttered Louis as he guided Sonny across the room. *Esquire* got their man back.

Back, though, to the fine print. In Pennsylvania, a new administration had ruled that the PSAC should not grant a licence enabling Inter-Continental Promotions to stage a Liston-Clay get-together. In the view of the State's District Attorney, Sonny owned stock in the company and would thus violate the local boxing code by having a fiscal interest in his opponent. A member of the PSAC informally suggested a get-out to the Nilons' lawyer, Garland Cherry, who owned a 5 per cent stake in ICP, not much less than Sonny's share. The informant recommended that either the rights be sold to, or else a contract entered into with, another promoter in the vicinity. This unnamed insider expanded on his advice when testifying at the Senate's boxing hearings of 1964: 'In other words, deliver the bundle of rights to some local promoter who is acceptable to us, make your money as you will, and whatever provisions or commitments you want, as long as the man who applies to the boxing commission is one who is acceptable to us, and there are not commitments between himself and one or the other fighter.'

ICP declined to bow and scrape any further. There was no reapplication. New York and California were targeted next, with an unsurprising dearth of success. The fancied runners were now down to three, New Jersey, Florida and Nevada, each a major gambling emporium; the Orange State edged home when Chris Dundee and William B. MacDonald Jnr agreed to purchase the promotional rights to the live gate for $625,000, a huge sum. The pockets that were mainly responsible for this belonged to MacDonald, 'a guy,' according to Harold Conrad, 'who'd made a big score in real estate or oil or something, and wanted everybody to love him.'

For Dundee read Barnum, for MacDonald, Bailey. A contract drawn up on 29 October 1963 stipulated that Clay would receive 22½ per cent of the profits plus a victory bonus of $50,000, if applicable – the aim, maintained the lawyer, Gordon Davidson, being to secure a 25 per cent share for his boxer. In return, ICP would promote Clay's next fight, name his opponent and nominate the venue. In order to guarantee a return, furthermore, half of Clay's purse would be held in escrow. Sonny frowned on the challenger's purported 25 per cent take, even though Robert Nilon insisted that the return clause constituted insurance against defeat. Upon ferreting out this information during his subsequent investigations, the Florida State Attorney, Richard E. Gerstein, did his sums and calculated that this cosy arrangement might have made losing a teensy bit worthwhile. However, the Miami Beach Boxing Commission claimed never to have received this contract which, in any case, did not have Sonny's signature on it. What he did put his imprimatur on was another document signed the same day, one that did not include the rematch clause and gave him 40 per cent of the gate receipts plus ancillary rights. One can hardly sign a tacit understanding, can one?

Neither can you legislate against the fickle nature of public approval. Leaving his Miami training base on 21 January 1964, Clay travelled with Malcolm X to New York and addressed a Nation of Islam (aka Black Muslim) rally, having previously been sighted at a similar gathering in Philadelphia. He was pictured on page 1 of the *New York Herald-Tribune* the next morning. The pong evolved into an almighty stench when, eighteen days before the protagonists were due to protagonise, Cassius Snr was quoted in the *Miami Herald*, saying his son was now a member of the Nation of Islam. This was an admission Clay himself did not make until the day after the fight, when he stunned the assembled news media – and hence the majority of the western world – by proclaiming his belief in Allah.

For a measure of how this news was likely to go down in less-than-liberal Florida, one had only to go back to 1961. Harold Conrad was in Miami awaiting Joe Louis's arrival for a hotel lunch meeting amid negotiations for the latest chapter in the Patterson-Johansson saga. All of a sudden, the owner of the establishment (or was that the man fronting for the owners?) sidles over and requests that the publicist eat in his own room instead of the dining-room. 'He said,

"This is a white man's hotel",' recollected Conrad. 'They'd let a Nazi in, and not Joe Louis.' Clay, for his pains, was now identified with a religious sect that supposedly regarded white folk as the very devil and violence as a credible means of exorcism – and that, of course, could do irreparable damage to the gate. Rather than Good against Evil, the bill now pitted Evil against Evil. 'We wound up with two bad guys,' concurred Chris Dundee, 'which is OK for wrestling, but not boxing.'

For all his apparent desire to please, the tubby, bubbly, ruddy-faced MacDonald was not about to consign either his investment, or his Rolls Royce convertible, or his yacht, to the dumper, so he summoned Clay into his office. 'Is it true that Malcolm X out there in the gym is here by your invitation?' 'It is.' 'I also understand you have a Captain Samuels in your camp and a security guard on your sponsors' payroll, and Black Muslim cooks in your camp. Is this true?' Another nod. 'Already this fight is jeopardised,' MacDonald continued. 'I've got to have a chance to make my profit back. And there's only one way, and you've got to do it now, today. You've got to clean house. Then you got to get on radio, television, tonight. You got to deny you're a member of the Black Muslims.' 'And if I don't do that?' 'If you don't,' answered MacDonald, in a soft though unequivocal tone, 'the fight's off. I'm calling it off. You're through. You're finished.'

For once, Sonny's criminal connections were trivialised. Black power was even more repugnant than Mob power. Conrad promptly donned his mediator's cloak and persuaded Malcolm X to leave town for the remainder of the build-up. That appeared to satisfy MacDonald, and the rendezvous remained. Not, mind, that Sonny's camp was free of unpopular elements. Enter Ash Resnick, director of sporting events at the Thunderbird Hotel. Resnick was a bookie, too, and had been blacklisted from just about every track in Southern Florida. Now he was hitching a ride on the gravy train. Pep Barone and Sam Margolis were also in attendance when Sonny trained at the Surfside Civic Centre in Miami Beach.

As expected, the combination of two such compelling yet unpopular rivals hit the gate hard, although this also had something to do with the price of admission, with ringside seats going at $250 a behind. The capacity of the Convention Hall in Miami was 16,448 but, as the day drew nearer, the chances of MacDonald and Chris Dundee pulling in the 10,000-odd they needed to break even grew ever more forlorn. In the event, 8927 tickets were sold, MacDonald losing $363,000 all told. The fight was nevertheless previewed as the world's most-watched sporting event yet, and others were going to make a mint. More than 1.1 million vantage points were available at the nation's 271 closed-circuit venues, including 16,000 at the Memorial Sports Arena in Los Angeles and 13,000 at Detroit's Cobo Hall. In addition, millions of Europeans would see a delayed transmission of the fight (which was due to take place in the middle of their night) via satellite and kinescope. Theatre Network Television Inc., the company that had purchased the screening rights from Inter-Continental Promotions, predicted record takings of $3.2 million. Once the outlets had extracted their 50 per cent share, ICP would be entitled to 85 per cent of the remnants. WABC Radio, meanwhile, had paid ICP $115,000 to transmit coverage. The pie was certainly deep enough for Sam Margolis and the rest of Frankie Carbo's extended family to gorge on.

The publicity treadmill was demanding but useful. Not many acts succeeded in elbowing the Beatles from the spotlight in 1964, but Sonny managed it. Kennedy was dead, the Warren Commission had succeeded in kidding most of America that Lee Harvey Oswald had acted alone, and the self-loathing that now gripped the nation had partially manifested itself in a crazed hunger for British pop groups, for innocence and optimism. Holding down each of the top five slots on the *Billboard* singles chart during one historic week, the Mersey beat boys were embraced with even greater ardour across the Atlantic than they were at home. Now, though, nine days before the fight, Sonny was on the same bill. As he sat in the audience watching them strum and yeah-yeah their way through *I Want to Hold Your Hand* – introduced as a ditty that 'would suit Cassius' – for *The Ed Sullivan Show*, Harold Conrad claims that Sonny elbowed him in the ribs, saying, 'Are these motherfuckers what all the people are screaming about? My dog plays drums better than that kid with the big nose.' Having arranged for Sonny to be there in the first place, Conrad had also fixed up a meeting at Clay's gym between the challenger and John, Paul, George and Ringo. When this quintet of 1960s icons met up, the subject was money, specifically how much they had all made. 'You guys ain't as dumb as you look,' cracked Clay. 'No, but you are,' replied Lennon, acerbic as always.

When the final ringing cadence of *All My Loving* became submerged in sensurround shrieks, the gaze of the cameras left the stage. Sullivan extended his besuited left arm toward the outer fringes of the crowd jamming the ballroom at Miami's Deauville Hotel. 'Ladies an' gennelmen, out in the audience tonight . . . [pregnant pause] . . . heavee-weight champy-onn of the world . . . Sonny Liston.' The switch from sex symbols to dread symbol was seamless. The shock of the new succeeded by the monster of the ages. The cheers faded into a polite ripple as Sonny rose, looking positively sober in a pale grey suit and white shirt with a diminutive, Beatles-y collar. A wave of the regal left hand acknowledged the twinset-and-pearl brigade around him, reluctant courtiers all. He complemented this with an immense, toothy, vaguely sheepish smile. Sitting down, Joe Louis to his left, the king of the ring waggled the other arm. Sullivan then re-engaged his microphone and interjected from his pulpit. 'Sonny, how are you?' Silence. Sonny, who hasn't heard a thing, carries on displaying his teeth. 'Sitting with him, another great champion and one of the real class guys of sports,' Sullivan announces, 'Joe Louis. Stand up there, Joe, and take a bow.' A grim-faced Louis stands up for the briefest of seconds as the applause mounts.

At this, on prance Allen and Rossi, comedians, apparently. The camera spins stagewards. Allen, one assumes, is the dapper good-looker, Rossi the short, curly-haired bum wielding a pair of grossly oversized gloves. 'HELLO DERE' runs the lettering on the back of the obligatory robe. In continuity terms, the transition from Sonny to this peculiar duo is fiendishly planned. 'You're a fighter?' wonders Allen, demonstrably the fall guy in a pastiche that tries hard to bounce like Groucho and Chico but barely bobbles. 'No, I'm the mother of the Beatles,' cracks Rossi, an Italian-sounding accomplice. 'How many fights did you have?' 'A hundred.' 'How many you lose?' 'A hundred – you can't win 'em all.' 'What's your trickiest punch?' 'My left hook.' 'Why your left hook?' 'I use my right hand.' The sparring pauses as the guffaws ring out. 'Rocky is my nickname.' 'What's your real name?' 'I can't remember . . . wait a minute . . . Hap-py Birth-day to you . . . Marty.' 'What do you do after each fight?' 'I bleed.' 'What did you do when you fought Cassius Clay?' 'I stuck my tongue out at him.' 'Why?' 'He was choking me.' 'When did you know you were in trouble?' 'Right after the national anthem.' 'Are you gonna fight Sonny Liston?' Rossi glances at Allen in mock terror. 'He's the biggest guy in the world.' 'If you did meet him what would you predict for the night of the fight?' 'I predict rain, snow flurries.' 'I'm talking about the outcome of the fight.' 'Early knock-out. I'll hit him in the dressing-room with a pipe. Let the Urban League send *me* a letter.' There you had it. The party line. Despite Clay's poetry, boxers were still oafs, still gorillas, still meat.

The challenger certainly knew the score. 'Where do you think I'd be next week if I didn't know how to shout and holler and make the public take notice? I'd be poor and I'd probably be in my home town, washing windows or running an elevator and saying "yes suh" and "no suh" and knowing my place. Instead of that, I'm one of the highest paid athletes in the world. Think about that. A southern coloured boy has made $1 million.' A week later, moreover, the biggest southern gorilla of them all would earn nearly $1.3 million for forty-five minutes' toil tops. Now ain't *that* America?

To see Sonny in training for the fight was to witness a lavish production number. Busby Berkeley might have designed it had his notions of sport extended further than Esther Williams's breast-stroke. The focus of attention was a ring set on a stage on the second floor of the Civic Centre, a grand piano to one side, flanked by the Star-Spangled Banner and the Florida State flag. Every afternoon, punters streamed in, plonked down their fifty-cent admissions and filled the 200-odd blue leather chairs facing the stage. Attention was rapt as the show began, a portable screen in front of the stage affording a reminder of Sonny's destruction of Patterson in Las Vegas mingled with various plugs for the gambling Gomorrah. The fight footage comprised one account at normal speed and one in slow motion, a recording that amplified with unnerving precision the shattering power now awaiting Clay. To George Plimpton, 'the concussive force of Liston's attack became shockingly apparent, the anatomy of destruction, every blow, alternate hooks, one after another, absolutely predictable because in slow motion each was telegraphed: Patterson's body quivered like a struck custard as he sailed to the canvas.'

While the onlookers were still gulping down their awe, a young lad clad in a University of Miami sweatshirt removed the screen, revealing the champion's instantly recognisable frame in the middle of the ring. Dressed in a pair of snugly-fitting black trunks and a shirt extolling the virtues of the Thunderbird Hotel, Sonny cut an impassive, impossibly huge figure. Applause rang out. Each member of his entourage took a turn to step forward upon being introduced by the announcer, carrying a towel and bowing awkwardly as they did so, like a collection of proud waiters visibly uncomfortable with the Hollywooden glitz they had been requested to embellish.

The announcer proceeded to present a series of manoeuvres, beginning with a three-round shadow-boxing session in which Sonny and a partner donned lightweight gloves and never once landed so much as a blow in anger. Photographers, professional and otherwise, were instructed not to use flash bulbs since these might blind Sonny and prompt him to hit his accomplice-in-sham. After each of the exercises, Willie Reddish dabbed theatrically at his charge's brow and cheeks with his towel, mopping and wiping the sweat. 'Liston looked fast and tireless,' observed Plimpton. 'His opponent skipped and wheeled, his ring shoes squeaking on the canvas, moving very fast, as presumably Clay would do; but Liston always seemed to loom above him, an attendant thunderhead. We were seeing the part of the show that emphasised Liston's speed.

Heavy applause when it was done, and up front a row of small girls whacked their hands together like applauding seals.'

Stage-hands now dismantled the ring. 'The champion at the light bag,' proclaimed the announcer as Sonny prowled forward to beat a percussive tattoo with a rhythmic insistence and stamina that had the throng inhaling their breath in hushed reverence. More applause. Reddish then joined him in the spotlight, huffing and puffing and generally making a great play of picking up a 15lb medicine ball which he then heaved repeatedly into Sonny's stomach. The trainer staggered off after about ten or so of these thrusts, Sonny's expressionless eyes following him intently. 'What they are trying to tell us,' quipped one sceptic, 'is that a medicine ball ain't going to make it to be champion of the world.' Cue a series of limbering-up exercises followed by the grand finale, Sonny skipping rope on a plank of wood accompanied by the moody swing of *Night Train*. 'Note,' recommended the omnipresent announcer, 'that the champion's heels never touch the board. He does this all off his toes.'

To Plimpton, the effect was mesmeric. 'We watched, hypnotised, the swing of the skipping-rope, the churning motion of his legs, until the human quality seemed to leave him. When it was over, a good stage-manager would have drawn the curtain, and let us go to remember that suspended rage. But at this point an attempt was made to humanise Liston. He was towelled off, fetched up in a gold-trimmed robe, and those in the audience who wanted to have their picture taken with him were invited to a table at the foot of the stage to pay ten dollars for the privilege.' Sonny's face, Plimpton continued, resembled that of a contented cat. 'If a girl stood beside him, he would drape a hand across her shoulder. Once he bent slightly and picked up a black woman, wearing a flowered hat, who weighed 200lb. The camera shutter clicked. A piece of costume jewellery fell off her and crashed to the floor. Her body shook as she giggled. Liston continued to hold her aloft. One of his *cuadrilla* produced a high, keening wheeze of appreciative chuckling, leaning forward to pound his knee. Liston set her down and looked for the next. The woman, her hat now gone askew, retrieved her jewellery. She seemed relieved to get off the stage.'

The promoters, too, were doing their bit for the newshounds who gathered daily in the bar of the Rooney Plaza for a succession of early-evening parties, shipping in Marty Marshall, the tall, elegant source of Sonny's solitary professional loss, who was introduced by a man inviting all and sundry to 'shake the hand that broke Sonny Liston's jaw!' The press lapped it up, plying the amiable black man with questions about his fifteen minutes of fame. 'I heard a story about the champion this morning,' one hack piped up, directing the yarn at Marshall in the hope of eliciting a reaction that would convert myth into fact. 'He does his road-work, you know, out at the Normandy golf course, wearing that hooded sweatshirt, and there was this greenskeeper working out there, very early, pruning the grass at the edge of a water hazard, very quiet, spooky, you know, and he hears this noise behind him and he looks over his shoulder and Liston's there, about ten feet away, looking out of his hood at him, and this greenskeeper is so scared he gives a big scream and pitches forward into the water.' Marshall smiled. 'Yeah, I can see that.'

To the educated eye, however, Sonny appeared to be taking his training chores rather lightly. Dr Ferdie Pacheco, Clay's physician, recalled a 'leisurely, almost cavalier' approach. 'He always finished training the same way, saying, "I don't know what I'm training this hard for. I'm going to knock this kid out in one round." ' If Sonny harboured any doubts about his ability to see off the young upstart whose unique routine had been packing 'em in at the shabby Fifth Street Gym, he gave little outward indication. Had he not won the battle of wits at the Thunderbird casino? Did not forty-three of the forty-seven leading boxing writers polled by UPI favour him? Defeat was not on the agenda. His handlers and advisers seemed more concerned with integrating Sonny into white upper-class America. He had rented a large house in a wealthy white neighbourhood, next door, no less, to Dan Topping, the owner of the New York Yankees, the traditional aristocracy of baseball. Clay, meanwhile, would take evening promenades with Malcolm X through the black areas of Miami, causing mouths to gape. Black champions, after all, tended to latch on to the white powerbrokers.

'Again and again,' recalled Malcolm X, 'Cassius startled those Negroes, telling them, "You're my own kind. I get my strength from being around my own black people." '

'I feel he's gonna be a cinch, but I'm not lettin' it go to my head,' Sonny assured the press at one juncture, cracking an ice-pick of a smile that implied it probably already had. 'Even if they carry him in on a stretcher, I'll be cautious. All I want is for them to carry him out on one.' One foolhardy hack enquired whether he had contemplated going the distance. Transfixing his inquisitor with what one particularly unimaginative report described as 'the hypnotic beam of a cobra mesmerising a victim', Sonny summoned as much disdain as he could muster. 'Cassius kin bring his lunch with him if he wants. I'll be ready to fight all day and all night.'

'Sonny hurts a man whenever and wherever he hits him,' averred Joe Louis, whose wife, Martha Malone, was handling Sonny's legal affairs. If Sam Cooke and Norman Mailer were regular pilgrims to Clay's work-outs, Sonny had the 'Brown Bomber' in his corner as full-time cheer-leader and blackjack partner. This was to be expected, of course. Aligning oneself with the champion was all but *de rigueur* for a celeb like Joe. After all, Joe still reeked of Heroism and Respectability, an extremely rare combination for a black boy in these times of interracial upheaval. Having Joe in your camp was like brandishing a Good Housekeeping Seal of Approval. Sonny must be all right; Joe likes him. It is also tempting to wonder whether Joe himself was motivated in part by sympathy for a persecuted brother-in-arms.

'Rocky was the same way,' Joe elaborated, likening Sonny to Marciano. 'When I fought him, he pounded my arms so much that I couldn't raise my hands to my face for a week afterward.' Louis compared Clay's speed to that of one of his own trickier adversaries, Billy Conn. 'But Conn knew how to fight. Everyone knew how to fight in my day, even the bums. That Clay has the speed, all right, but he don't know what to do with it.' 'He's got the edge in everything but talent,' concluded Sonny, spitting the words out like poison-tipped blow-darts.

Rumours, as ever, abounded. One had it that Sonny's sexual

antics were more strenuous than his official fitness regime, that he was carrying on with two other women besides Geraldine, whom he was said to sleep with on the eve of every fight. So much for abstinence. Quite why boxers should be required to undertake a sexual fast whenever they are about to go into the ring has always eluded me. One can only think that this is because they have voracious sensual appetites (probably something to do with that innate need to conquer). The image of Cathy Moriarty running her painted fingernails over Robert De Niro's torso in *Raging Bull*, teasing his flesh beyond craving point, remains an enduring one.

Harold Conrad endeavoured to persuade Sonny to get his priorities right, to little avail: 'He [Sonny] told me, "Don't worry, Hal, I'll put the evil eye on this faggot at the weigh-in and psych him right out of the fight."' Lax or not, Sonny still looked in menacing condition, if a tad overweight. For his part, Willie Reddish sent a shudder through the Clay camp by asserting that his fighter had yet to hit anyone as hard as he was able to. 'That's right,' reasoned Sonny. 'I don't think it's possible for any fighter to hit a man as hard as he can. There's a moving target, and you just can't hit it perfectly.' Was Sonny intending to hit Clay as hard as he could? 'No,' was the almost indifferent retort. 'Just hard enough to put him to sleep.'

When the subject switched to his charge's fiscal habits, Jack Nilon contended, more than a little enigmatically, that Sonny 'throws money around like a man without any arms'. On the one hand, a man with no arms cannot hold on to money but, on the other, he cannot throw away what he cannot hold. An odd statement. A generous streak was noted by Paul Abdoo, a 44-year-old Denver photographer on Sonny's payroll who was supposedly permitted to keep all the profits emanating from his snapshots of the champion (autographed items sold for $1 apiece, pose-with-Sonny pics for $5). 'Sonny's been real good to me,' insisted Abdoo, who was veering toward the down-at-heel when first asked to take Sonny's official championship picture. When Sonny went to Abdoo's studio and introduced himself as 'Sonny Liston, the heavyweight champion of the world', or so the story goes, the photographer retorted, 'I'm the Marquis of Queens-berry,' and swiftly adjourned to his dark-room. Sonny then knocked on the dark-room door and submitted a plaintive correc-tion: 'But I really am the heavyweight champion.' From that moment, apparently, a firm friendship began to evolve. 'I don't care what a man is, see,' explained Abdoo, 'either I like him or I don't. Champion or not, Sonny's a good guy.' The subsequent footnote, however, isolated Abdoo's chief reason for liking Sonny: 'I'll stay with him because I don't know how good it might get.'

There was a chance, however, that it might not get much better. Unbeknownst to anyone outside his immediate circle, Sonny had been undergoing a course of cortisone injections, as State Attorney Gerstein's investigations later revealed. The reason for this was an injury to his left shoulder, one that had apparently compelled him to miss a spat of sparring sessions with Amos Lincoln. That said, when he did get to grips with Lincoln, who was reputedly brought in to make Sonny look good, the results could be spectacular. 'Amos Lincoln was the best sparring partner Sonny had,' claimed corner-man Milt Bailey, 'but one time he hit him so hard his helmet flew off. We thought his head had gone with it. Sonny was in great shape.'

At the penultimate work-out before the fight, Eddie Machen rocked the boat by revealing how his decision to take on Sonny with his mouth rather than his fists had proved so unsettling to his baffled foe, but that commotion soon subsided. Another quickly usurped it when Sonny took what was arguably his first public stand on racism. Or perhaps that should be *dared* to take his first public stand on racism. Asked why he hadn't marched in Alabama, Sonny had once dead-panned, 'I ain't got no dog-proof ass.' Yet, on the Saturday preceding the Convention Hall bash, Jack Nilon stated that, unless the New Orleans venues dispensed with racially segregated seating, they would be prohibited from screening the fight. 'There is a provision in every contract between Theater Network Television and the individual theatres that segregation will not be permitted. There is a report that this is not being observed in New Orleans, and it is now being investigated. If it is not straightened out, remedial action will be taken.' Explaining the meaning of 'remedial action', Nilon made a motion with his hand simulating a plug being snatched from a wall socket. 'Pull the plug,' he said, emphatically. 'We simply won't show it.'

In response to this, the Loew's State and Saenger theatres on Canal Street chose to adhere to their policy of never opening to a racially mixed audience. Three cities – Montgomery, Alabama, Jackson, Missouri, and Waco in Texas – had previously been refused permission to show the telecast after grousing about the segregation clause, yet other southern venues, such as Atlanta, Jacksonville and Knoxville, had signed the contract and accepted the provision. A joint statement from the New Orleans twosome read as follows: 'In view of Sonny Liston's feelings, as set forth in his weekend statement, and the laws of Louisiana, which we are advised are incompatible, we regret that the closed-circuit telecast has been cancelled. Refunds will be made at the box office.' If one episode encapsulated the depth of Sonny's well-being, this did. Only supreme confidence could have enabled him to risk such a political gesture and stick firmly to the principle involved. The clause had been inserted at his insistence. 'I feel that the colour of my people's money is the same as anyone else's,' he said. 'They should get the same seats. If not, I don't want these places to have the fight.'

If Sonny's fortress had an impregnable aura to it, Clay's was felt to be wholly vulnerable. 'At the moment,' wrote Arthur Daley in the *New York Times* of 22 February, 'Cassius Marcellus Clay may very well be – to borrow his own florid description of himself – the "prettiest and greatest" of all heavyweight fighters. Before Tuesday midnight, however, the situation could very well undergo a rather violent metamorphosis. On that evening, the loud-mouth from Louisville is likely to have a lot of vainglorious boasts jammed down his throat by a ham-like fist belonging to Sonny Liston, the malefic destroyer who is the champion of the world. The irritatingly confident Cassius enters this bout with one trifling handicap. He can't fight as well as he can talk.'

Daley then drew a parallel between Clay and Captain Queeg, the crazed figure at the centre of the *Caine Mutiny*, immortalised on screen by Humphrey Bogart, who would click steel balls in his hand as he sat in the dock, sensing the trial seeping through his fingers. 'After his final sparring session in the seedy old Fifth Street Gymnasium the other day – he was to shift a day later to the more antiseptic auditorium – Cassius sat on a chair inside the ring ropes and talked and talked. He kept jiggling two circular metal weights in his hands while he yackety-yacked in somewhat self-conscious amusement. The weights clicked as he flicked them from hand to hand, and up from nowhere popped a rather haunting memory. It was the image of Captain Queeg.' Clay, moreover, looked 'dreadful' to Daley in his penultimate sparring session. 'He didn't show a good jab, a good hook, a good cross, a good combination, a good anything. One sparring partner, Cody Jones, hooked in at will to jaw and body. If Cassius was studying defensive encounters by permitting this, he sure waited until the last moment to do it. There was one thing, though, that Cassius did with consummate skill. It was when he was shadow-boxing in front of a mirror. The mirror gave him an exquisite opportunity to admire himself. He took full advantage of it.'

There was much to admire. Beyond all the posturing and those finely sculpted, pulchritudinous features (when, pray, was the last time anyone could sell a heavyweight champion on sex appeal?) stood a gifted athlete. Uncommonly fleet of hand and foot, he was that rare bird, a defensive artist. He also had sound minds in his corner. 'Liston was awesome,' acknowledged Angelo Dundee in Dave Anderson's instructive tome, *Ringmasters*. 'But he always had trouble with tall guys. He always had trouble with awkwardness. That was the whole key. His only loss had been to a tall guy, Marty Marshall. That's what I was basing my thinking on. What bothered Liston was height, awkwardness and speed, things that prevented him from leaning in with that great left jab he had. He used to really lean in with that jab. But I figured I knew what Liston was thinking. That this kid can't really fight, that he runs too much. But he didn't know this kid's strength. To me, there was no way this kid could lose to Liston as long as he didn't let Liston jab him. The whole key was for my kid to surround that jab by going to his left, away from Liston's jab. I figured once he surrounded the jab, Liston would lose his mobility. My guy's height was another factor. Liston usually fought guys he dwarfed.'

But could Clay take a punch? His having fallen foul of "Enery's 'Ammer' took on more ominous overtones in discussion of his chances against the most powerful puncher of this or any other era. Hence the masochistic afternoons with 'Shotgun' Sheldon, in which Clay would prepare himself for the barrage that Sonny would surely unleash by encouraging his sparring partner to direct his swings exclusively toward his stomach. The only way to conquer pain is to confront it.

Clay had also been practising self-projection. What followed at the weigh-in divided observers but, whatever one's interpretation, it was almost certainly the challenger's master-stroke. Aside from the homosexual jibes that Benny Paret had so mistakenly flung at Emile Griffith two years earlier, the scales had never been known for producing anything remotely above the mundane, but the 1000 or so members of the media who congregated in the Cypress Room in Convention Hall now witnessed something utterly without precedent. At 10:30 a.m. on 25 February, the morning of the fight, Clay swept through the door. Alternately swishing a heavy, wooden African walking stick and thumping it on the floor, he was clad in a blue denim jacket, 'Bear Huntin' ' inscribed in red on the back. Flanking him were Angelo Dundee, Sugar Ray Robinson, and his talisman of an assistant-trainer, Drew 'Bundini' Brown. Robinson, resplendent in a maroon sports jacket, and Brown, sporting a similar number in exclamatory yellow, guided Clay through the milling throng as their man shouted hoarsely, *ad nauseam*, 'I'm ready to rumble, I'm the champ, I'm ready to rumble . . .' Brown then joined Clay in a full-lunged, less-than-impromptu rendition of their war-cry, 'Float like a butterfly, sting like a bee. AAAH! Rumble, young man, rumble. AAAH!' Pausing at the steps leading up to the platform, the Queen Bee turned toward the cameras and sniped at Joe Louis's presence in Sonny's camp, a preference Clay evidently resented. 'You can tell Sonny I'm here with Sugar Ray,' he goaded. 'Liston is flat-footed and Joe Louis is flat-footed, but me and Sugar Ray are two pretty dancers.'

At 10:37, the entourage repaired to a dressing-room, where Clay undressed and put on a white terry-cloth robe. Clearly perturbed by the hubbub, a posse of Miami Boxing Commission representatives followed him in and warned that he would be fined if he continued to misbehave. Dundee and Robinson in turn lectured him on the sacrosanct nature of the occasion, but the plan – to mess with Sonny's mind, to attack first – was too far advanced to go back now. What was it Clay had told brother Rudy beforehand? 'I'll jump him and, when I do, you hold me back.' Only the embarrassed Robinson was unaware of what had plainly been rehearsed, albeit mostly in Clay's brain. At 11:09, Clay bounded back. At first, he refused to climb the steps to the platform. 'Let 'em up, this is my show, this is my show,' he then demanded when the uniformed guards prevented Brown and Robinson from coming up with him. Robinson smiled and shook his head. 'I'll keep him quiet,' Brown muttered. 'I'll have to be up there to keep him quiet.' Eventually, the trio were all waved on.

Two minutes later, Sonny and his band entered to sparse applause. At this, Clay began to gesticulate feverishly, jumping up and down like a baby kangaroo that had just discovered its ability to defy gravity. Robinson and Brown patted his shoulders as if trying to calm him down. Peeling off his gold-and-white silk robe, Sonny stepped on to the scales, tipping them at 218lb, 3lb more than expected. As he stepped down, a caterwauling sound burst from the other end of the platform, courtesy of a familiar heckler: 'Hey, sucker, you a chump, you a chump. Are you scared?' As Clay kept up his tirade, Dundee, Robinson and William Faversham restrained him, fearful he might attack Sonny. A quizzical, confused expression consumed Sonny's ageing features. That buxom bottom lip drooped, ready to pout. The eyes were sombre, completely mirth-free. He cupped his hands around his mouth. 'Don't let anybody know. Don't tell the world,' he said, calmly, for Clay's ears only.

The meaning of this has never been satisfactorily explained and has admitted a variety of interpretations. Was Sonny taking the mickey? Or was he genuinely concerned, in some strange, paternalistic way, that Clay might be making a fool of himself? The latter would seem to have been an uncharacteristic response. He sounded placid enough to those present, but who knew how much turmoil was bubbling away behind that inscrutable mask? 'Sonny said, "You ain't afraid of me, you're afraid of my left hook," ' Jack Nilon later avowed. Angelo Dundee, however, was adamant that not a word had crossed Sonny's lips. 'Liston was so shook up he couldn't talk. He just didn't know what to make of the kid.' Clay himself heard the message loud and clear. 'I'm delighted,' he thought. 'He actually believes I'm a fool.'

In the midst of this tumult, Morris Klein, the chairman of the Miami Boxing Commission, grabbed the microphone and attempted to defeat the din: 'Cassius Clay is fined $2500.' The official also threatened to withhold the trouble-maker's purse were he to pursue such tactics during the fight. Dr Alexander Robbins, the commission's physician, somehow managed to hold the bouncing Clay down long enough to take his blood pressure. With Sonny looking on, more bemused than amused, Dr Robbins discovered that Clay's pulse was ticking over at an extraordinary 110 beats per minute, more than double the normal rate of fifty-four (Sonny's, interestingly, was also well over, at eighty compared with his usual rate of seventy-two). 'Sure it's high,' reasoned Angelo Dundee, 'but he was only acting, he was only putting on a show.' One reporter, Jimmy Cannon, wondered aloud whether this signified fear. Nodding, Robbins declared that Clay was 'emotionally unbalanced, scared to death, and liable to crack up before he enters the ring. We'll have to call the fight off if his pressure doesn't come down before he goes into that ring.'

When Clay took his turn on the scales, coming in at a relatively light 210½lb despite having weighed around 214lb after ceasing training the previous Friday, no one seemed particularly bothered. Pounds and ounces had merely provided the backcloth to a riveting little two-act extravaganza. The star had improvised a shade and come close to losing his voice, but the script, in essence, was followed. With the ugly sister so utterly overshadowed, this was pure pantomime. Whether it had had the desired effect was another matter. 'Clay could get under Liston's skin more than anyone knew,' Milt Bailey subsequently admitted. That said, Bailey did not believe Sonny was unnerved. 'Clay was a loud-mouthed kid trying to build his ego up. We figured he was scared to death, and it would only be a matter of time before Sonny stopped him talking.' Ferdie Pacheco checked Clay's blood pressure again shortly after the weigh-in and, much to his astonishment, found a normal reading. 'Liston has been boasting he's afraid of no man alive, but Liston means no sane man,' Clay informed the medic. 'Liston's got to be afraid of a crazy man.' With that, he drifted off for a nap. If Sonny slept, it is doubtful he did so with any soundness.

As Clay made his way back to the dressing-room, he was pursued by King Levinsky, once one of Joe Louis's bums-of-the-month and now a tie salesman touting his wares from a cardboard suitcase. 'He's gonna take you, kid,' yelled Levinsky. 'Liston's gonna take you, make you a guy selling ties . . . Partners with me, kid, you can be *partners* with me.'

The comparative number-crunching showed that Clay had the upper hand in height (6ft 3in to 6ft 1in) but lagged in terms of both reach (82in to 84in) and ammunition (Sonny's fists measured 14in to his opponent's 12in). His record, mind, was marginally cleaner than Sonny's: Clay was unbeaten in nineteen professional contests, stopping all but four of his victims, while Marty Marshall blotted the champion's CV. As the deadline beckoned, however, Clay grew increasingly distracted. He had been receiving threatening phone calls throughout the past week. The usual contents of these one-sided conversations ran along the lines of, 'Nigger, you'll not win that Sonny Liston fight,' or words to that effect. The pace had hotted up that morning. 'I'd gotten calls saying, "You'll be lucky if you make it in the ring, you loud-mouthed bastard." Then the caller would hang up and another caller would say, "If Liston don't get you, we're gonna get you. You'll never be the world heavyweight champion." At first I didn't pay any attention, but Captain Samuels said, "The white power structure wants you whipped."'

Some months earlier, a story had been published claiming that Harold Johnson, a former world light-heavyweight champion, had taken the ring groggy after eating a doctored orange. The memory of this merely hardened the paranoia. The only people in attendance whom Clay now trusted were his brother and Captain Samuels. 'He was particularly suspicious of Angelo,' reflected Pacheco, 'because Angelo was Italian, and in his mind he'd begun to associate Angelo with the gangsters around Liston. Remember, the Muslims – and it was clear by then that Cassius was a Muslim – had never been in boxing before. All they had to go by were Hollywood movies where the Mob fixed everything, and Liston was with the Mob.'

Gossip was still flowing as the witching hour approached. First it got round that Clay was intending to duck out. Then a radio news bulletin revealed that he had been seen at the airport, preparing to fly to Mexico. Instead, at 9:59 p.m., Clay came jogging down the aisle at Convention Hall, 'The Lip' writ large across the back of his white, skimpy, mini-skirt of a robe. The cheers that accompanied him were part-sympathy for what he was surely about to receive, part-gratitude for the showmanship that had raised the occasion high above the norm. Stealing through the ropes in a single bound, he shadow-boxed in a corner for six full minutes until Sonny appeared on the distant horizon. The challenger's composure, borne out by a pulse rate of sixty-four, was astonishing. This was not a man with fear in his heart.

Malcolm X, who had re-emerged that day, substantiated this impression. 'Along with Cassius, I really was more worried about how his brother, Rudolph, was going to do, fighting his first pro fight in the preliminaries. While Rudolph was winning a four-round decision over a Florida Negro named Chip Johnson, Cassius stood at the rear of the auditorium watching calmly, dressed in a black tuxedo. After all of his months of antics, after the weighing-in act that Cassius had put on, this calmness should have tipped off some of the sportswriters who were predicting Clay's slaughter. Then Cassius disappeared, dressing to meet Liston. As we had agreed, I joined him in a silent prayer for Allah's blessings. Finally, he and Liston were in their corners in the ring. I folded my arms and tried to appear the coolest man in the place, because a television camera can make you look a fool yelling at a prize-fight.'

Installed as a prohibitive 7–1 favourite, Sonny was encased in his trade-mark white terry-cloth robe as he set off on the long trek from dressing-room to ring, hood pulled tightly over his forehead. Beside him, Willie Reddish, Milt Bailey and Joe Pollino wore T-shirts provided by the Thunderbird Hotel. Ash Resnick was also close by, having been reserved a berth in Sonny's corner. In many of the cinemas not screening the fight, Rock Hudson and Paula Prentiss were doing brisk business with *Man's Favourite Sport*, but mankind's preferred pastime on this particular night was a trifle less lovey-dovey. There were other conflicts in the news, most notably Quebec's threat to secede from Canada. Earlier in the day, the leader of the National Association for Puerto Rican Civil Rights had accused a cop of running his beat as if it were 'a plantation'. The *New York Times* was presiding over a long-running literary wrestling match provoked by Arthur Miller's latest play, *After The Fall*. 'It should be renamed *The Loves of Arthur Miller*, or "How I influenced a pretty girl (with a horrible Brooklynese accent) to have an operation on her nose",' suggested Margaret O'Grady in a letter to the editor. Nobody, meanwhile, was quite sure whether the new Kirk Douglas–Burt Lancaster blockbuster, *Seven Days In May*, a melodrama about an attempted military coup in Washington, was trying to add to the ever-thickening pile of Kennedy conspiracy theories. This Miami showdown was thick with those but, for now, all that mattered was that the participants had both got to the altar on time.

The hood was eventually removed just before the ring announcements, unveiling Sonny's sparsely-populated head and bringing that mephistophelean moustache sharply into focus. The muted reaction to Clay's name died quickly. A similarly disinterested response, leavened with the obligatory jeers, greeted the words 'Charles "Sonny" Liston'. As Barney Felix, the nominated referee, issued his instructions, Sonny looked up and fixed Clay in his sights, a furrowed brow embellishing the mask of malevolence. Eyes shifting downward to meet those of his shorter assailant, Clay stared back unflinchingly. 'I got you, sucker,' he whispered. The words hit Sonny like a bucketload of spittle. 'Stand tall,' Dundee had ordered his charge a few moments earlier. 'You're bigger than this sucker. Make sure you look down on this sucker.' The trainer wanted him to 'instil his height in Liston's mind. Liston liked people to think he was even bigger than he was. He would wear big boots to make him taller. He would stuff big towels under his robe. He always had little short guys around him. I've used the same trick. I don't like tall guys around my heavyweights because I want the fighter to project a huge look.'

As they awaited the opening bell, Sonny flexed his shoulders, Clay his dancing shoes. Sonny then began the action with a succession of off-target lunges before finally catching the waltzing Clay on the chin. Channelling every last ounce into the blow, he then missed extravagantly with a booming left hook, stumbling in the process. He pounded Clay's rib-cage in a clinch but, as the round wore on, it was the younger man who asserted himself, keeping Sonny at bay with his long left lead, sometimes shoving it, palm open, into the champion's splayed nose. Weaving his head out of harm's way with consummate ease, he was also countering with growing confidence. First came a right-left flurry to that close-cropped head, rat-a-tat-tat. Then another. Then, as the bell was about to clang, he snaked in a cheeky left to the temple, flicking his wrist just before contact. The timekeeper clanged four times before the duellists desisted.

During the break, Clay affected a yawn. Luckily, he was wide awake when Sonny started round two with a cruel left. This staggered Clay, but Sonny now adopted a more cautious approach. Contempt had given way to sense, if not quite respect. The projected walk-over obviously contained a few pot-holes. At one point he bundled Clay into the ropes, but the dancer pirouetted away. Reddish, according to Bailey, had urged Sonny 'to bide his time, figuring that, sooner or later, he would catch this guy. But he couldn't.' Commentating on TV, Joe Louis advised Sonny to 'forget Clay's head, 'cause he moves it too fast'.

If its predecessor had been indecisive, round three was Clay's by a street. Opening up with a cluster of quicksilver combinations, he forced Sonny to wobble. When he drew back, a cut was visible high on Sonny's left cheek-bone. The armour, incredibly, had been pierced. When Clay took a breather, Sonny ploughed forward, ungainly in movement, desperate of punch. Apeing Patterson, he leapt and threw a massive left hook that missed by some distance, but the draught flung Clay into the ropes. Bobbing along like an oversized robin on speed, Clay continued to dodge everything while purloining points at will with his insistent, eloquent left jab, a weapon that had a disconcerting tendency to be fired from all manner of angles. Sonny's stiff-necked movements rendered him a sitting duck. 'You're 40 if you're a day,' Clay had asserted during a televised interchange between the fighters some weeks earlier. For the first time in Sonny's career, the case of the missing birth certificate seemed worthy of Poirot. By the end of the third, he was bordering on 50.

Joe Pollino worked on Sonny's wound between rounds, but it was his legs he should have been attending to. Trained to go three rounds tops, Sonny's were simply not up to chasing. He caught and shook Clay momentarily half-way through the fourth, but otherwise flailed away fruitlessly. Clay's eyes appeared to be smarting for some reason, but that didn't stop him from whacking Sonny on the chin in the final second, a telling strike. It was not a hard shot, but the sheer effrontery of it shattered a thousand illusions.

Blinking furiously, however, Clay reclaimed his stool in some distress. He wanted out. 'I can't see,' he shrieked. 'My eyes are burning. I can't see.' As Dundee attempted to rinse his eyes with a sponge, Clay cried foul. 'Cut the gloves off. Show the world there's wrongdoing going on.' The trainer quickly deduced that something had rubbed off on Clay's gloves – either the coagulant Pollino had been using on Sonny's gash, or else some liniment from Sonny's shoulder. Whatever it was, it had found its way into his boy's eyes when Clay brushed his forehead with his own gloves – a peculiar, reflexive ritual common to most fighters, partly designed to wipe away sweat, mostly to ensure the brain is still alert. At this juncture, however, the tale forks in a more suspicious direction. It was held in some quarters that Pollino had for some years been carrying around a potion to be used in case of emergency. This, most assuredly, was just that and, as Pollino would subsequently confess to Jack McKinney, he had duly applied it to Sonny's gloves between the third and fourth rounds, as instructed by the bewildered, despairing champion. The evidence was cast far beneath the ring.

Concentrating on effect rather than cause, Dundee set to work on Clay's psyche. 'Forget the bullshit. This is the world championship. Sit down.' Pushing Clay down, he began to clean out his eyes with a towel, discarded that in favour of the sponge and rinsed them instead. 'I put my pinky in the corner of his eye, and then I put it in my own eye, and it stung, it burned like hell. There was something caustic in both eyes.' By now, Barney Felix had realised something was afoot and approached the challenger's corner. Clay was still hollering. The bell was about to bellow. Aware that the referee might well stop the fight, Dundee rammed in Clay's mouthpiece, stood him up and shoved him back toward the killing field. 'This is the big one, daddy. Stay away from him. Run,' he exhorted. 'Don't let him knock us out,' boomed 'Bundini'. 'Use the yardstick on him. Yardstick 'em, champ.'

Clay duly re-engaged Sonny, his right eye on the verge of closing. 'Beat that nigger's ass, Sonny,' barked a voice from the ringside. 'Beat that nigger's ass.' Hammers poured into Clay's ribs as he clung on to Sonny's head, but the expected crucifixion never materialised. What ensued, in fact, was reminiscent of a mime show: Sonny lunged, Clay feinted and parried, but the aggressor's boots were leaden, our animalistic Astaire's too spry. Even when Sonny did locate the target, landing a stiff left to the temple, he was strangely hesitant in following up. Guilt or fatigue? Probably the latter.

Not that Dundee saw much of this. As soon as battle had recommenced, brother Chris had run up to him, breathlessly. 'Ange, show these guys you didn't do nothing. They're all looking to do a number on you.' The warning was heeded. Behind Angelo towered 'two Muslims . . . looking at me in a definitely hostile way, figuring I'd done something wrong. So I said, "Are you guys nuts? I want to win this thing as much as you do." ' By way of attempting to prove his integrity, the trainer took some water from his bucket and threw it into his own eyes. This seemingly convinced his two companions that he had not been doctoring the water. Malcolm X observed all this from seat No. 7, feeling faintly smug. 'Seven has always been my lucky number,' he would reflect. 'I took this to be Allah's message confirming to me that Cassius Clay was going to win.'

As his eyes regained clarity towards the end of the fifth, Clay halted his clockwise perambulations and reverted to attack, twice peppering Sonny's nose with a quiverful of featherweight left jabs that evoked Woody Woodpecker's metronomic persistence with tree-trunks. If there were any lingering doubts that Sonny had missed the boat, those blows erased them. Clay resumed the offensive in the sixth, stringing together fifteen unanswered punches while Sonny flailed away, battering the smoke-filled air. There was no leverage in Sonny's missiles and, although he did connect with a left to the chin, the ratio of hits to misses was a sorry one when set against Clay's unwavering sense of direction.

At the conclusion of the sixth, Sonny plodded back to his corner, a ponderous, worn, shadow of the boxer who had extinguished Patterson. His face was wan, puffed, beaten, his body limp, sagging, beaten. At first, instead of taking his seat, he remained standing. Eventually persuaded to sit, the eyes spoke before the tongue could move. 'I can't lift my arm,' he grunted, finally. 'That's it.' The best-kept secret in town was about to wriggle out. It was that left shoulder. Initially, there was a degree of confusion as Reddish reinserted the mouthguard. Sonny, allegedly, spat it out and reiterated his intention not to go on with due emphasis – 'That's it, I said.' 'Well, y'know,' said Reddish, resignedly, 'another day, another time.'

It was all over. Those who pooh-poohed the injury when it became public knowledge would hark back to Jess Willard, the only other heavyweight champion of the glove era to quit on his stool. 'It broke Willie's heart, I tell you,' Bailey sympathised. 'Willie was hurt more than anyone else.' As Joe Louis was informing the closed-circuit audience that 'Clay got all the confidence he need', the flapping in Sonny's corner became clearer. Peering over Dundee's shoulder, Clay tried to work out the signs. Felix was deep in conversation with Reddish and his cohorts. Faces were falling. The next thing anyone knew, the challenger was in the centre of the ring, jigging a jig, arms aloft. Dundee and 'Bundini' joined him there, Angelo standing back as the rumblers rumbled. The prettiest had overcome the ugliest. An exceptional if over-confident bruiser had been outwitted by the most exceptional boxer of all. Allah had outmanoeuvred the Mob.

For what it was worth, the three adjudicators somehow contrived to have the pair on level terms at the end of the sixth. On a 10-points-per-round basis, Felix had awarded Sonny and Clay 57 apiece; Judge William 'Bunny' Lovett favoured Sonny, 58 to 56, and Judge Gus Jacobson went for Clay, 59 to 56. The chasm between Lovett's card and Jacobson's was remarkable: the former had Sonny winning four rounds while the latter awarded Clay five. The tendency of American judges to reward aggression, no matter how ill-focused or off-beam, may explain this warped interpretation, but it did little to ward off the shower of egg-yolk now raining down on the world's boxing scribes. The motor-mouth who had earned a cheap volley of laughter before the first bell with the line, 'It's even money Clay won't last the national anthem', deserved more than most.

Clay had his say as soon as Felix raised his hand. 'Eat your words,' he shouted, glancing down to spray vituperation over the press corps fringing the ring. 'I told you I was gonna do it. Allah ordained it,' he proclaimed to the jumble of journos that gathered in his dressing-room twenty minutes later. 'Whatcha gonna say now? It won't last one round? He'll be out in two? How many heart attacks were there? Oh, am I pretty.' On he careered, rubbing it in like a masseur armed with a bottomless pot of oil. 'You can't call it a fix because I didn't stop the fight – the doctor stopped it. Oh, I'm so pretty. Whatcha gonna say now, huh? I watched Sugar Ray Robinson and Jake La Motta for eight months – the same fight, over and over. That's what I've been doing. I'm too quick for him, too fast, too fast for any heavyweight alive. You newspapermen [*sic*] made it tough on Liston. Don't ever make a 7–1 favourite. Just let me go in even money.' By now, bedlam reigned as friends, handlers, trainers and just about everyone in the place crowded around Clay, pawing at him as he fidgeted, nervous tension manifested in perpetual motion. Did he want a rematch? 'If he wants a rematch he can have it, but I don't think he'll want it. Sonny was not even a match for me, but he must apologise. The man was dirty and he couldn't even hurt me.'

While the new monarch held court, Sonny let Jack Nilon do his talking. 'I was the one who made the decision,' insisted the manager, far too often for credibility. 'Sonny wasn't tired, believe me. He said he simply lost all the sensation in his shoulder. His left hand was numb. You couldn't send a man out to fight with one hand. Sonny said, "I'll go on," but I didn't pay any attention to him. He wasn't tired. He just lost the use of one hand, that's all.' Nilon was enjoying himself in Cloud-cuckoo-land. 'This boy [Clay] throws a better punch than we figured. But I'm sure if Sonny hadn't had this misfortune, that as the fight went on into the third, fourth and fifth rounds, Sonny would have put him away.' After this, Sonny was spirited to the nearby St Francis Hospital, crying as he left the dressing-room. 'He was disgusted,' said Joe Pollino, who remained behind. 'He was broken up.' As Sonny headed to the car park, left arm in a sling, a bandage under his left eye, he told reporters that the loss of his title made him 'feel like when the President got shot'. At the same time, it was 'one of those little things that happened to you'. Six stitches were inserted beneath the offending eye, and Sonny spent three and a half hours in X-ray before Dr Robbins delivered the verdict: 'We came to the conclusion that Sonny Liston suffered an injury to the biceps tendon of the left shoulder, with the result that there is separation and tear of muscle fibres with some haemorrhage into the muscle belly. This condition would be sufficient to incapacitate him and prevent him from defending himself.' Dr Robbins added that no further examination was necessary and that he would recommend to the Miami Boxing Commission that Sonny's purse be released.

It was now that Jack Nilon revealed that Sonny had indeed first hurt the shoulder in training, and that, as a consequence, he had missed four sparring sessions, on 3–5 February inclusive and 14 February. As to why they had proceeded with the fight, the manager explained matter-of-factly, 'We thought we could get away with it.' What Nilon did not say was that Sonny, according to various sources, had wanted to call the whole thing off, only to be swiftly disabused of this fanciful notion. Hank Kaplan was aware of this story, and believes it. 'I heard from a friend I trusted implicitly that, when Sonny discovered that shoulder injury, he went to the Miami commissioner's office, where he was given short shrift. The way I heard it, the commissioner told him, "You're not going to do *this* again," which was a reference to that golf course incident that stopped Sonny's second fight against Patterson from taking place in Miami. Anyway, Sonny said, "If that's the way you want it," and stormed out.'

It had been too late to stop the party. The invitations had all gone out. Then, as State Attorney Gerstein would discover, Dr Robbins, upon examining Sonny prior to the fight, had somehow either failed to detect, or at least to report, the ailment. This in itself did not point to a fix – if it is difficult to picture Sonny's pride allowing him to be party to such a notion, it seems equally significant that Gerstein's rummaging should ultimately fail to provide any indictable evidence – but the fact remained that betting odds had fluctuated alarmingly at ringside. The day after the fight, CBS-TV stated that the line had shifted from 7–1 to 10–1 to 4–1, with a sizeable wad available for Clay. Inside knowledge of the injury among the gamblers is not beyond the realms of possibility, particularly given the presence of Ash Resnick. Resnick, after all, had been conspicuous by his presence backstage throughout Sonny's rehearsals. Anyway, the Miami City Council announced its intention to conduct an investigation, although Arthur Daley didn't seem to give a fig either way. 'Poetry and youth and joy had triumphed over the 8–1 odds,' he gushed to the upper brass of New York the following morning.

Back in Jefferson City, Sonny's old temporary residence, howls of derision had erupted in the prison halls where, UPI reported, 'officials said some inmates felt Liston "threw" the fight. Other prisoners thought it was pretty cheap when he did not come [out] for the seventh round.' That the smell of something afoot was so pungent was in many ways a back-handed compliment to Sonny. Ignorant of the injury, the crowd in Convention Hall had mingled cheers with boos when he failed to emerge for the seventh, mirroring the depth of public disbelief. 'It can't be,' exclaimed one onlooker. 'I don't believe it. Shoot him, shoot him.' This was Mister Monster, the King Kong of Christendom. Now Mister Monster had chickened out. Even when word did get out about the shoulder, the cynics comprehensively outnumbered the believers. There was even talk of Sonny having hurled a chair against the wall when he got back to the dressing-room. How could a man with a gammy shoulder do that? Fix.

'I don't think he quit,' proffered Chris Dundee. 'Sonny just got old during the fight.' Father Alois Stevens vouches for the veracity of the shoulder alibi. 'I was staying in the annexe of the St Francis Hospital and, when they brought Sonny up to the emergency room, we were there. His arm was still numb. I watched his eyes when the doctor took a scalpel to his shoulder. No reaction. Sonny said it didn't hurt, that he didn't feel anything. But he lost because Clay was a great fighter.' Having viewed the bout on countless occasions while editing it for domestic consumption, Bill Cayton deserves his say. Formerly Mike Tyson's co-manager and owner of the world's most expansive array of fight footage, he is convinced that the injury was sustained, or at least exacerbated, at the very start. 'People have scoffed at the shoulder story but, if you watch the tapes as I have, you can see Liston never once threw a leveraged left hand. He couldn't throw his left at all. He was pushing it. The first real punch he threw he missed and, when you miss with a punch that you've thrown with real bad intentions, you can hurt yourself. He wrenched the muscles. From that moment, his left was tentative. You can see it.' At the time, Joe Pollino traced the mishap to a later stage. 'Liston threw a hook in the fifth round. Clay stopped it in mid-air, and Liston felt something crack in his left shoulder.' That someone close to Sonny should refer to him by his surname summed up this enigmatic character with a sad succinctness.

The most plausible explanation seems to be that the shoulder injury certainly hampered Sonny, and made him even more intent on a quick kill. Indeed, had one of those early haymakers connected, he would probably have fulfilled his objective. That he didn't testified to a problem he himself had referred to a few weeks earlier, namely that of hitting a moving target. Clay, moreover, did not so much move as hover, conjuring up a ghostly apparition as he darted in and out of view. But even if that dreadnought left had been up to full velocity, it is unlikely that Clay would have gone under. Frightened he may have been, but the challenger had done his homework. The blarney had worked, making his opponent wonder and thus unsettling him. For Sonny, confusion outside the ring begat uncertainty and frustration inside. Compounded by an exaggerated faith in his own omnipotence and a consequent failure to prepare properly (admittedly, he had not gone three rounds with anyone for three and a half years), this in turn begat a crippling loss of confidence.

Like many others, Bill Cayton witnessed a butterfly emerging from the chrysalis that night. 'Ali went into that fight a good fighter but he came out a great one. He matured, he grew in confidence. That night he became the fighter who was on the road to becoming the greatest fighter of all time. He was terrified, sure, but Sonny couldn't punch him. Then, when he agreed not to quit and came out for the fifth, he realised that not only was Sonny not fighting the fight he thought he would, but that he couldn't hurt him.' Not for another ten years would Clay/Ali match this level of strategic perfection. In Kinshasa, however, George Foreman would not have a half-blind opponent at his mercy; Sonny did, and still Clay survived. Never was his genius more vividly expressed.

Just before the fight was due to be screened, a fire broke out on the balcony of the Loew's Kings Theatre in Brooklyn, forcing the 1000–strong gallery to evacuate. When they returned, according to the *New York Times*, 'some streetside opportunists' snuck in for a free show. What they beheld was possibly the most palatable excuse for the existence of professional boxing. Skill, stealth and psychology had slain the dragon.

When all was said and done, mind, Sonny came out the richer (before distributions, of course), and Bill MacDonald lost his deposit. In all, courtesy of his purse ($326,187), a half-share of ICP's $234,375 (of which Sam Margolis snaffled 55 per cent and doled it out accordingly) and a slice of the record closed-circuit takings, Sonny, as far as the world knew, was due some $1.3 million, double Clay's swag. Gate receipts, meanwhile, were $402,000, which was $223,000 less than the promoters had guaranteed. Nilon was more concerned with the future. 'We're simply out of business,' he lamented. 'There is no contract for a return bout. We don't even know if there's going to be one now. We understand the kid is going into the Army now for two years. What can we do? We're out of business.' Of all the economically truthful statements uttered between the conception and death of one of the most feverishly dissected events in modern boxing history, this ranked high.

Back at the Municipal Auditorium, the first mixed audience ever to watch a fight in New Orleans had behaved impeccably. The scene was eerie. On one side of the wall dividing the auditorium, the New Orleans Philharmonic Symphony orchestra pizzicatoed and plucked and peeped, appreciated with some difficulty by a collection of predominantly white ears. On the other, voices, mostly black ones, hissed and hooted as Sonny held fast to his stool: 'Fix!'

In the wee small hours of that February night, Harold Conrad claimed he found Sonny drinking in bed, feeling morose, small, alone. Things stink even more when you are unused to the smell, and Sonny hadn't had a whiff since the Viet Minh entered Hanoi. When Conrad told him that Miami was thick with talk of tank-jobs, self-admonishment surrendered to outright fury. 'Me? Sell my title? Those dirty bastards!' A glass shattered against the wall.

Eleven

Exile from Maine Street

Somebody started saying it was an inside job
Whatever happened to him
Last time they saw him on the Bow'ry
With his lip hanging off an old rusty bottle of gin

(Van Morrison, *The Great Deception*)

It was 25 December 1964. Sonny was sitting in a police patrol wagon, hands clasped together, two cigar-like thumbs preventing his chin from embracing the grimy floor. A pork-pie hat perched precariously on his head, brim barely wide enough to cover that shiny pate. The snappers snapped the void in his gaze. Christmas? Bah, humbug.

The bleak midwinter found Sonny on the less amiable side of the law once again. The ever-vigilant (especially in his case) Denver cops had arrested him for driving under the influence of alcohol, an activity that those close to him fervently denied he ever indulged in. 'Sonny went under a lot of harassment here, but that's the lot of the celebrity,' reasons Charles Cousins, a Denver native and now deputy commissioner of the Colorado State Athletic Commission. 'Father Murphy introduced us and brought him over to my house. We were friends. He wasn't as bad as his image, I had no problems with him. Not a real outgoing type.' Since this was the first time Sonny had been stopped for such an offence, it seems reasonable to assume a decent alibi. None was offered; but that, given the circumstances, was understandable. Six weeks earlier, he had been on the verge of attempting to regain his title. He had trained with unprecedented rigour and vigour, defying the years as he did so. He was ready. The engine had been ignited. Then, three days before lift-off, the mission was abandoned. Muhammad Ali (as now was) had a hernia. An incarcerated inguinal one, to be exact. Sonny might just as well have set out to conquer Everest and tumbled down a manhole a couple of feet from the summit.

As a backcloth to this, the civil rights movement had been making progress toward its own distant peak, culminating in a Senate seat for Bobby Kennedy, a staunch supporter, and a crushing election victory for the Democrats. There was still some clambering to be done, however. 'Let us close the springs of racial poison,' Lyndon Johnson had pleaded after signing the Civil Rights Act of 1964 but, for all the President's apparent sincerity, he was soon empathising with King Canute. Thirteen days later, on 15 July, a right-wing extremist named Barry Goldwater mowed down all-comers at the Cow Palace in San Francisco to land the Republican presidential nomination (fortunately, Johnson would beat him hands-down in November). Before the month was out, law and order had broken down in upstate New York as race riots ravaged Rochester. The city's unemployment figures were the lowest in the state, so poverty could certainly not be blamed. When Governor Nelson Rockefeller sent in the National Guard on 27 July, 500 looters and Molotov cocktail-shakers were arrested and a curfew imposed. The following day, Malcolm X launched the Organisation for Afro-American Unity, 'a non-religious, non-sectarian group organised to unite Afro-Americans for a constructive programme toward attainment of human rights . . . Whether you use bullets or ballots, you've got to aim well; don't strike at the puppet, strike at the puppeteer.'

The World Boxing Association, meanwhile, had gone for the puppet, temporarily stripping Ali (*né* Cassius X) of his title for 'conduct detrimental to the spirit of boxing', a flimsy euphemism that failed to convince anyone – least of all the NAACP – that the association's motives bore no relation to the new champion's stance on race and religion. With Malcolm X having broken away, Ali was now the public face of the more religious, less vindictive

Nation of Islam. Yet the public still perceived the Nation, Black Muslims, Malcolm X and hatred as one explosive package, an image first captured in 1959 by Mike Wallace's documentary, *The Hate That Hate Produced*. To reporter Jimmy Cannon, Ali was now a 'more pernicious hate symbol than Schmeling and Nazism'. To Budd Schulberg, he was 'part of a global family of non-whites among whom Caucasians were in turn a minority doomed to eventual defeat'. Even Senator Richard Russell, a hardline segregationist but one intent on preserving order in his Georgia constituency, accused the WBA of being 'intolerant, bigoted and narrow-minded'. Senator Jacob Javits, a liberal New York Republican, sided with Russell despite the fact that the differences in the pair's views on civil rights were about 'as profound as any in the chamber'. That the Senate should host such a debate underlined once and for all that the ownership of the heavyweight title carried rather more symbolic significance than that of a means of assessing strength.

In the event, the athletic commissions of New York, Pennsylvania and California refused to endorse the WBA action, but the flak carried on regardless. On 20 March, Ali went to Madison Square Garden to watch a fight involving his skilful Cuban stable-mate, Luis Rodriguez, only for Harry Markson, the Garden's boxing president, to bar him from being introduced under his adopted moniker. In the November issue of *Playboy*, he bared his soul. 'I don't want to go where I'm not wanted . . . Integration is wrong. The black man that's trying to integrate, he's getting beat up and bombed and shot. But the black man that says he don't want to integrate, he gets called a "hate teacher". I've heard over and over, how come I couldn't be like Joe Louis and Sugar Ray? Well, they're gone now, and the black man's condition is just the same, ain't it? We're still catching hell.' Sonny, for one, would endorse that last sentiment heartily.

Nothing, though, was going to stop a rematch. Although there had been no return clause in the original contract, there had been an 'understanding' that the two fighters would reconvene on an unspecified date in the not too distant future. As soon as this became clear, however, the WBA turned its temporary snub into a permanent one, duly crowning Ernie Terrell after Sonny's exsparring partner had beaten Eddie Machen in an eliminator. Contrary to Jack Nilon's fears, the Army did not need, let alone want, Ali. Although the Nation of Islam's Herbert Muhammad was beginning to muscle Ali's backers, the Louisville Sponsoring Group, out of the picture, the group's leader, William Faversham, continued to do his best to keep the draft board at bay. On 26 March 1964, Ali gave him a helping hand, resitting the military qualifying exam under the gaze of three Army psychologists, and flopping once again. Reclassified 1-Y ('not qualified under current standards for service in the armed forces'), he was free to carry on boxing.

However, Sonny's waning status, the Miami investigation and Ali's religious persuasion, not forgetting his suspect mental aptitude and apparent lack of patriotic zeal, meant that the venue pickings were even slimmer than they had been for the first fight. Ironically, not to say remarkably, those perennial enemies, New York and California, approved, as did Europe, and Massachusetts. But despite considerable resistance among New England's more jingoistic citizens and Veteran committees, a promoter named Sam Silverman secured the contest for Boston by stumping up the readies (a reported $50,000, less than a twelfth of that proffered by MacDonald and Dundee for the first engagement, underlining the attraction's receding magnetism). Silverman's track record was less than unblemished, but then he had been in the game too long for it to be otherwise. In 1953, he had promoted a controversial televised fight in which the lightweight champion, Jimmy Carter, knocked down the jejune Tom Collins more than ten times in what was considered a gross mismatch, one that heightened concern over whether the networks now controlled boxing. Silverman, apparently, was also one of Frankie Carbo's pawns.

The slated date was 16 November 1964. While Ali took himself a wife and trotted off to Africa to shake hands with President Nasser, creaking the scales at 245lb on his return, Sonny set to work with the earnestness and single-mindedness he had dispensed with in Miami. This time, the strut would be bedded in the firm soil of dedication rather than the quicksand of arrogance. He was certainly in the best shape Milt Bailey had ever seen him in. 'The Bear' looked good. Word got around. The bookies were backing him to the hilt.

On 5 November, at a Plymouth golf club on a corner of the White Cliffs resort that overlooked Massachusetts Bay, a gathering of 300 spectators paid $1 apiece to watch a ninety-minute work-out. 'A faster and trimmer Liston drove three sparring partners around the ring,' reported Robert Lipsyte in the *New York Times*. A more voluble play-by-play account was given by Al Braverman, a portly New York gallery owner and ex-pug hauled in as camp co-ordinator with a special brief 'to see Sonny didn't get out of order'. An exuberant chatterbox with a keen sense of theatre, Braverman would boom his narration into a microphone: 'These exercises are to loosen up the circulation,' and so forth. Sonny snorted angrily when one left hook missed Amos Lincoln, but otherwise displayed little emotion. Against the swift Fonedo Cox he circled and jabbed; against Lincoln and Curtis 'Honey Boy' Bruce he unleashed the left. Lincoln and Bruce both looked more winded after their stints than Sonny did after all three of his. There was no skipping to *Night Train*, however; according to Stan Zimmering, a 41-year-old physical instructor from Denver with a second-degree black belt in judo, the beat was 'too slow'. A revealing incident occurred while Reddish was kneeling in a corner of the ring being interviewed for a TV report. 'Hey Willa,' barked Sonny. 'Willa!' At that he walked across the ring and kicked Reddish's shoulder through the ropes. Duly chastened, the trainer dropped the microphone immediately and went back to work. There was only one star in this show.

Braverman discovered this early on. 'A friend of Liston's came to me and said, "I want you to handle Liston. Only you can do it." I said I would have to sit down with him and talk to him first. When we sat down, I said to Sonny, "You know who sent me to you?" "Yeah," he said. "Well," I went on, "if you should call me motherfucker or embarrass me in any way, I'll break a bottle over your fuckin' head. I'm tellin' you right now." So he said: "Al, we ain't gonna have no trouble. If I hear you announce me on the mikey-phone I'll come to the press conferences. Just make sure you announce me." So when he came to training or whatever and the press were there, I would announce him on the mikey-phone. One time I introduced him as "the ever-smilin' Sonny Liston".'

Sonny claimed he was training harder than he had for Miami and said he had 'a surprise' for Ali, who was in his estimation only 'a fair fighter', not nearly so brave as Patterson. 'I fought a stupid fight [in Miami]. I shouldn't of run after him. I had something he wanted and I should of waited for him to come to me. I'm not making any conditions . . . predictions, I mean. I'm keeping that a secret for Clay [*sic*]. I think I'll come out ahead.' Was he bitter? 'I'm bitter, but not bitter enough to lose my head. When I catch him, you'll know I'm bitter.' At that, Sonny pulled a huge pocket-watch from his dungarees. 'Time to go,' he informed the assembled press, and did, chuckling as he went.

The mood in both camps, superficially at least, seemed light-hearted. Following a playful suggestion from Ali, Angelo Dundee announced his intention to wire Floyd Patterson and ask him to serve as his man's sparring partner. 'I'll even pay my own expenses to Boston as soon as he phones me to come,' said Floyd from his home in Marlboro, New York, 'but I promise not to hurt him or floor him. I'm in very good shape right now.' Sonny joined in the fun: 'I need sparring partners who can go more than one round. Maybe Patterson is good enough to work with Clay [*sic*], but I need somebody who will give me a better work-out.'

Wearing his customary red cap, the sad-eyed Reddish appeared bemused by the PT instructor's presence. 'I don't know what Zimmering is doing. Exercise, walks – I guess it don't do Sonny any harm or any good.' Zimmering was clearer about his function. 'I try to keep his mind free from what's happening. When Sonny and I take walks after meals, I talk about my new shirt, about my wife coming up for the weekend, that kind of thing.'

Sonny breakfasted at 10, striding into the sunny dining-hall with Geraldine a few steps behind. Casually dressed, a dungaree suit, tweed cap and white sweatshirt were familiar accoutrements. Husband and wife always sat at the picture window overlooking the rocky shoreline, Geraldine ordering Sonny's eggs and checking his mail. 'Isn't this cute,' she trilled one morning, 'another little poem.' A self-conscious eater and ever wary of the stares and leers, Sonny rarely lifted his head. Zimmering was the only other regular at the table, Reddish usually occupying a nearby one with his fellow-Philadelphian, Archie 'The Penal Man' Pirolli, the gruff, greying, 68-year-old camp secretary. The what? 'Some nights I stay up until 2,' explained Pirolli, 'just signing Sonny's autograph for all the people who want pictures, and the payroll, and the mail. Some guy wants two tickets to the fight so he can hypnotise Clay at ringside.'

Cognisant of Sonny's child-like sense of humour, Braverman became the Minister for Fun. 'I'm running out of gimmicks,' he wailed one day. 'The rubber scorpions were great. Sonny really went for that. And the hot peppermint gum, a lot of laughs.' He then pulled out an enormous syringe and plunged it into Pirolli's arm. The needle promptly collapsed, and with it Braverman as he pulled back the plunger to allow a crimson liquid to fill the syringe. Pirolli, hamming it up, looked appropriately shocked. 'Like blood, it looks like blood,' roared Braverman. 'Sonny'll love it.' Sonny, in actual fact, had a morbid fear of syringes, and Braverman knew it. Fighters, he reasoned, were 'like babies, got to give them toys. Keep their minds off the fight.' Teddy King, one of Sonny's trusty seconds, had had a turtle dropped in his soup the previous day but kept up the habit of a lifetime by declining to smile. Teddy's idea of fun was to wear his cap – embroidered, naturally, with the letter L – askew.

'As long as I was with him, for those coupla months, Sonny was absolutely fantastic,' Braverman asserts. 'I never had a problem with the son of a bitch. He had a great sense of humour. I built him a shock box which he wrapped in Christmas paper and had a hell of a time shocking people with it. Then I got him that big syringe to keep him happy. That got him crazy. At other times you wouldn't know what to think because he would always be glowering at you. Like a child, like a baby. He was a forgiving guy. I remember Mort Sharnik coming up to me and saying that *Sports Illustrated* wanted him to talk to Sonny, but that Sonny didn't want to know because he didn't like reporters. So I took Mort on a training run with Sonny the next day. Leaving Mort a little way behind, I ran alongside Sonny and said, "Do me a favour, Sonny, talk to him. He's a good friend of mine and he won't write a bad story." And Sonny said OK. He was a very suspicious man, very self-conscious. He didn't get on a platform for the blacks because the only things he cared about were Sonny Liston and his wife. And children. He loved children, do anything for 'em. He trusted 'em. Didn't trust adults. He could give you a glare so baleful you'd just wanna fold up.' To Sonny, the great thing with children was that 'they got their own little way of thinking, they're not jealous.' Unfortunately, for reasons he and Geraldine kept to themselves, the Listons were unable to have any of their own.

More often than not, Sonny would head off after training to watch TV and take a walk with Zimmering before retiring to a cottage on the edge of the golf course until dinner, which usually comprised steak. There were camp followers aplenty. In exchange for 'walking-around money', Joe Louis was there to lend moral support and help with PR. Fred Brooks, the president of SportsVision, the closed-circuit TV company, was a regular visitor. So, too, Sam Silverman, Sam Margolis and the fast-talking Robert Nilon. Louis apart, Sonny never acknowledged their presence. As ever, confidants were few. 'I watch him but I don't hang around with him. I don't pal with him,' revealed Reddish, who liked it that way. 'I don't want to lose that edge of respect he has for his trainer, so I can tell him what to do.' Zimmering got closer: 'He's a lovable guy, he'd give you the shirt off his back. Smart, witty, very intelligent. He does nice things. We were passing through Chicago, on our way back to Denver last month, and I was looking for some souvenirs for the family. I passed by a case of jewellery, and I looked at it, but I couldn't afford it. Sonny came up behind me and bought up half that case of jewellery and he gave it to me and said, "Give it to your wife, give this to your mama." I have a job back home. Sonny doesn't pay me. He knew I couldn't take money from him, we're that close friends. But he gave me something I could take.'

On 9 November, Dr Nathan Shapiro of the Massachusetts

Boxing Commission pronounced Sonny and Ali to be in peak condition, thus killing off fears about Sonny's shoulder. The shoulder, Dr Shapiro opined, that 'allegedly' caused those Miami blues. Memories, though, were quick to flood back. On their way to the medical, Ali and his buddies had threatened to pull Sonny and his handlers out of their car as it drew up outside the Department of Public Safety. Inscribed on the back of Ali's blue dungaree jacket, in a slight variation of the theme, were the immortal words 'Bear Hunter'. 'I'm bear huntin',' the hunter announced. 'I'm huntin' that ugly bear Liston. Pull 'em outta that car and put 'em in a cage.' The police restored order, but the silly season had begun. As Sonny was being weighed by Tommy Rawson, the associate boxing commissioner for Massachusetts, he laughed out loud. Ali was predicting a nine-round KO, but the gleam in Sonny's eye suggested a swifter execution – in his favour, naturally. Archie Moore, now the PR aide to the San Diego Chargers gridiron club, had tipped Ali to win the first debate, one of the few to do so. Now he fancied a KO for Sonny 'any time after the seventh round'.

The plot then took an irrevocable twist. On Friday (natch) the 13th, Ali was comfortably ensconced in his suite at the Sherry Biltmore Hotel in Boston having just wolfed down a dinner of steak, spinach, potatoes and a tossed salad. While watching Edward G. strut his stuff as Little Caesar, he began to vomit, prompting his brother, Rudy, to call a doctor. At that moment, Angelo Dundee was watching a closed-circuit telecast of a football game between Boston University and the University of Miami. When, at half-time, the commentator announced that Ali had been taken to Boston City Hospital, he dashed there himself and discovered an operation in progress. It was a congenital condition, ruled the surgeon, although Sonny maintained that it could have been prevented 'if he'd stop all that hollering'. A loop of Ali's intestines had seared through the muscles lining his abdomen, then descended, planting a growth the size of a lime in the lower right wall of the bowel. A decade later, he would benefit similarly when an eye injury to George Foreman delayed their Zaire confrontation. That Foreman should rank Sonny as his foremost source of inspiration (albeit from a negative perspective of the man) adds a certain touch of intrigue.

Sam Silverman called the match off just after Ali was shipped off to hospital at around 7 p.m. Dr Morris Prizer, the executive physician, said the hernia had become acute because of the rigorous training schedule. 'Bundini' Brown said it might have been the heavily-weighted shoes (an extra 3lb in each foot) which his man had been wearing to practise foot-work. Dr Shapiro, anxious to cover himself, said the vomiting might have done it. The suggestion that Ali might have been slipped a mickey was discounted by the authorities, yet there was never any chemical analysis of the contents of his stomach.

Sonny had done five miles of road-work that morning before cancelling his afternoon work-out and going out to buy a suit. After dinner, he, Geraldine and Father Stevens had taken a walk. 'Although he was unhappy at losing his title, Sonny seemed pretty upbeat while I was in Boston,' Father Stevens recalls. 'That night someone came up and told us about Ali's hernia. He [Sonny] was obviously upset but didn't show a lot of emotion. He took it stoically. He wasn't a cussing man. Others were more upset.' Sonny's first public reaction, typically, was to make like Henny Youngman: 'Well, let's all put our aprons on and go to work and pay the bill.' Later came a more serious admission: 'Shit, I worked hard for this fight.' He wished it had happened earlier, 'instead of waiting till all the hard work was over.' To Milt Bailey, there was no disguising the fact that the first heavyweight title fight to be cancelled at the last minute for reasons other than rain was a cruel set-back; he had never seen his man in such good shape. 'All that talk about retaliating for Malcolm X; none of that bothered Sonny. What hurt him most was when Ali had the hernia. To have to wait six months and go through the training all over again; that definitely hurt, physically and psychologically.'

Arthur Daley came to the same conclusion in the *New York Times*. 'He [Sonny] peeled off weight until he no longer seemed quite the malevolent and terrifying ogre who had twice destroyed Floyd Patterson in less than a round. But his Spartan regimen did something to him. He seemed to shrink in size and instead of looking his announced age of 30 he looked closer to 40 . . . now Liston will have to go through that arduous routine again. The postponement will hit him much more rudely than it will the buoyant Clay, still bubbling with vivacity and [the] swift recuperative powers of youth.' Not so much *coitus interruptus* as *spiritus interruptus*. What happened on Christmas Day six weeks later cannot have been unconnected.

There were other, more sinister theories behind the cancellation. Ali was not in the shape he had been in in Miami, while Sonny had never looked better. Ticket sales had been disappointing, so too closed-circuit sales. Ali was quarrelling with his bride. Massachusetts had supported the WBA's refusal to recognise the fight. Above all, Ali had apparently known about his condition for four months and had gone as far as to schedule an operation for after the fight. Could it, *The Ring* conjectured, have been a 'ploy to force Liston out of training and force him to achieve peak condition for a second time, some task for a man of Liston's age' (at the beginning of the year, Dan Daniel had composed a highly uninteresting, highly unsubstantiated column in the same magazine, asserting that Sonny 'has passed 40')? Conjecture, though, was all it was. Herman Greenberg, the chairman of the Massachusetts SAC, confirmed that both fighters had been in tip-top shape, and he knew this, apparently, because he had planted 'agents' in each camp. Massachusetts, to be fair, was divided in its enthusiasm, but closed-circuit sales were actually said to be good.

The pariahs took a pounding. SportsVision had been due to screen a telecast at more than 200 venues, claiming seat sales of 600,000 and an ancillary rights package worth $4.6 million. With no insurance protection and refunds promised, Fred Brooks estimated his company's potential losses at between $100,000 and $400,000. 'We took a bath,' conceded Sam Silverman, who said $235,000 had so far been taken at the box office. According to its spokesman, Harold Conrad, ICP expected to take a loss of $75,000. Each camp paid its own expenses. In the meantime, Garland Cherry, the Nilons' lawyer, caused a stir by asserting that, contrary to what Conrad had said, neither ICP nor Sonny had yet received their due from the Miami deal. On 16 November, Sam Margolis, speaking in his capacity as an ICP vice-president, offered a double-headed consolation prize to the closed-circuit exhibitors who had lost out: a middleweight title match betwixt Joey Giardello and Rubin Carter followed, perhaps, by a bout between Patterson and an improbably gutsy, if tactically limited, young Canadian, George Chuvalo. By comparison with the original bill, this was akin to substituting two Keatings for one Magritte.

It was not long before the Boston Rag was off for good. Those Veteran committees and America-the-Beautiful arch-patriots eventually won the day. Whither now? While Ali convalesced, Faversham and Co. kept casting the net, hoping to land a more compliant fish from the ever-shrinking shoal. What they hooked was a sprat in the shape of St Dominic's Arena, a small youth club-cum-minor league ice hockey arena in Lewiston, an unprepossessing little textile town in Maine, population 41,000. With a capacity of around 6000, here was proof, if any were needed, of the irrelevance of live gates to boxing. On this occasion, around one million people were expected to watch the contest on some sort of screen or another, Canadians and Mexicans included. Even the Brits were being lured, the BBC making strenuous efforts to obtain permission to use the Early Bird satellite and so screen the fight live, before dawn.

Back in Lewiston, the townsfolk seemed less than ecstatic at the prospect of receiving their fifteen minutes at the centre of the sporting universe. 'I'd throw both those bums out of the state,' barked a filling station attendant. 'You don't go to see fights on what they pay you here,' shrugged a female factory worker. Sam Michael, a 59-year-old public official doubling as promoter, over-compensated for this antipathy: 'In the months to come, people who never saw Maine before will think of the state for a vacation.' In the same type of 'borrowed licence' deal cited as the official reason for the fight being booted out of Boston, ICP guaranteed Michael $15,000 plus $5000 expenses.

Not since that swindling rogue, Doc Kearns, dragged Jack

Dempsey to the run-down Montana cow town of Shelby (population 500) had there been a more unlikely venue for a heavyweight title fight. Kearns's idea of generating publicity was to sell $70,000 worth of tickets to the impoverished Montanans, charter a locomotive and caboose for $500 and then make a swift get-away after his man's lack-lustre points win, more than $¼ million in his saddle bag. Three banks in Shelby folded as a consequence, but this disturbed Kearns's conscience not a jot. 'They're lucky that I didn't sue them for the rest of the dough,' he wisecracked later.

Sonny adjourned to the Poland Spring resort as D-Day was shunted back to 22 May 1965, sharing his living quarters in the nearby Mansion House with a retinue of 150 Catholic priests currently on retreat at the same residence. The return to the grindstone was far from easy. 'Old fighters react to training like beautiful women to washing floors,' opined Norman Mailer. 'But Liston did it twice . . . and the second time he trained, he aged as a fighter. They [Sonny and Amos Lincoln] had wars with one another every afternoon in the gym. By the day before the fight, Liston was as relaxed and sleepy and dopey as a man in a steam bath. He had fought his heart out.' Lincoln was allegedly paid an extra $100 to make Sonny look good in his last work-out, but fooling the punters was easier than deceiving reality.

The tenor of the Ali camp changed with the murder of Al Hajj Malik al-Shabazz (*né* Malcolm X) on 21 February. The erstwhile voice of the Nation of Islam had not seen eye-to-eye with the pacifistic approach of Martin Luther King; indeed, he had alienated many blacks, including Elijah Muhammad, who had dismissed him from the Black Muslims in 1963. His passing none the less coincided with an outbreak of renewed black unrest. On the first of the month, Dr King and some 300 supporters had been arrested in Selma, Alabama, for parading without a permit. They were protesting against the sluggish pace of electoral reforms intended to give blacks the vote in a state where whites were outnumbered by six to four. A month after that fatal bullet was fired in the Audubon Ballroom, Dr King led 25,000 marchers to the steps of the state Capitol in Montgomery, where he presented Governor

Wallace with a list of grievances. Back in Selma – where an attack on three liberal clergymen by a white gang had recently provoked half a dozen nuns to front a demonstration – bombs were discovered in a black church, in a funeral parlour and at the home of a leading black lawyer.

Small wonder, then, that Ali, whose own leanings were toward Elijah Muhammad, should begin to fear for his own safety. Word was that a collection of Shabazz's associates were bent on avenging the assassination by rubbing out the most popular Muslim in the Nation of Islam. Two carloads of armed men, reportedly, were heading to Maine from New York. 'Gunmen Stalking Clay' boomed one headline; 'Black Muslim War Endangers Muhammad Ali' squawked another, more liberal paper. The week Ali pitched camp in Chicopee, Massachusetts, five FBI agents turned up at his hotel and installed a twenty-four-hour guard. Every morning, a couple of police cars would accompany him to the track where he worked out; every morning, five policemen would scamper across the field and check for ambushers before he could begin running. Police snipers filed along the fringes, concealed behind bushes. Plain-clothes policemen circulated conspicuously among the crowds at the gym.

Following a visit to Poland Spring seventy-two hours before the gloves were due to be raised, Angelo Dundee questioned Sonny's training tactics. 'I went over there and walked in. Nobody stopped me. He looked terrible sparring with Amos Lincoln, then he tried to skip rope and got his feet tangled up. Maybe just to do something, anything, to impress the spectators, Liston let Reddish throw a big leather medicine ball into his stomach. Boom, boom, boom. Some of the people were ooohing and aaahing like this was really terrific, like what great shape he must be in. I turned to the guy next to me and said, "Why don't Willie throw the medicine ball in Sonny's head? That's where my guy is going to hit him." '

Robert Lipsyte espied a man whose mind did not appear to be properly focused. The night before the fight, he and Dick Gregory went to see Sonny. Gregory had volunteered to distribute Thanksgiving turkeys in Mississippi, and the pair went to Poland

Spring to get money. When they arrived, according to Lipsyte, Sonny was slumped in front of the TV, watching the movie *Zulu*. 'There was a scene where three or four white guys with repeating rifles were mowing down the cream of the Zulu nation, wiping them out. Liston just sat there, staring at the television, and I had the sense his mind wasn't anywhere.'

Another visitor to Sonny's room that night was Jose Torres, whose Cus D'Amato-taught peek-a-boo style had just helped him dethrone Willie Pastrano, the world light-heavyweight champion. Acting as teacher, the erudite Torres explained how he had beaten Pastrano by cutting the ring short. Sonny stated his intention to follow suit, but the dimensions of the St Dominic's ring were not about to oblige him. Only a week earlier, a young reporter, Dave Anderson, then with the *Journal-American*, had popped by the Ali camp in Chicopee, *en route* to Lewiston. Suspecting that the contractual clause stipulating a twenty-foot ring might not have been strictly adhered to, Angelo Dundee asked Anderson to measure the perimeter. 'My guy needs a twenty-foot ring,' he explained. 'He needs room to manoeuvre. In a small ring, Liston's got an edge.' In fact, Anderson found the ring to be sixteen feet square and, later, that it had been borrowed from the nearby Brunswick Naval Air Station gym. The Nilon boys denied any knowledge of this, let alone admitted malice aforethought. Interestingly, however, a larger ring winged its way in from Baltimore shortly after Anderson filed his story.

By now, Sonny's concentration on the matter in hand had been well and truly broken. As if all that talk of vengeance squads were not enough, corner-man Teddy King later recalled two Black Muslims warning Sonny he would be killed if he won. Joseph H. Farrand, the Lewiston police chief, got wind of the rumour and duly instructed his men to search spectators before they entered St Dominic's. Whether or not there was any substance to all this, the incessant speculation can scarcely have enhanced Sonny's peace of mind. The comedians had had their fun prior to the previous fight: 'I'm betting on Clay – to live,' nudged Joe E. Brown; 'Clay should last about eighteen seconds, and that includes the three seconds he brings in the ring with him,' winked Jackie Gleason. Now, though Sonny remained favourite (on the eve of the fight the odds were 13–10), the humour was missing.

There were whispers, moreover, of drugs. On his way to St Dominic's for the fight, Peter Wilson watched aghast as one of Sonny's corner-men (he couldn't, or wouldn't, identify which one) walked straight into the back of a row of parked cars, seemingly stoned off his box. This does not surprise Bill Cayton. 'Around that time, it was reported to me by my sources that Liston had gone on drugs. I don't know if it was cocaine or heroin, but it was probably heroin and, apparently, he stayed that way for the rest of his life.' Father Stevens saw 'no evidence one way or the other', while Geraldine always denied the charge. Three decades on, Al Braverman hedges his bets. 'I never saw him touch junk or play with dope when I was with him, but then that's only what I saw.' Yet if Sonny had sought refuge in drugs around this time, then one would not have to search too hard for reasons. If being the champ could not bring him fulfilment, being an ex-champ was hardly likely to drive away his demons. The postponement merely hastened the decaying process.

Not that this was evident when Dr Ralph F. Turgeon examined Sonny at Poland Spring, nominating him 'the fittest man I've ever examined'. The day before the fight, Sonny hid behind the white wooden doors of the Mansion House while the locals on Lisbon Street and at Bates textile mill shelled out $25 for the cheap seats. Not that many, mind. Michael claimed ticket sales were approaching 6000 but, with the 1510 freebies, the actual turnout was 2434. The pot, swelled by TV, radio and overseas sales in excess of $1.7 million, would yield nearly $½ million for each of the contestants. According to Chief Farrand, 240 cops would be in attendance. To protect SportsVision's investment, the once-bitten Fred Brooks had taken out a $1 million life insurance policy on Ali. This, naturally, was interpreted as lending credence to the assassination-mongering. At the weigh-in – a relatively peaceful affair by comparison with the Miami extravaganza – Sonny tipped the scales at 215¼lb, Ali 206lb. The only ruffle came when Sonny's original tonnage was announced as 219½lb. A horde of protests followed, and the scales were readjusted.

In a few days' time, the most newsworthy coloured face in the world would belong to Vivian Malone, the first black to graduate from Alabama University. For now, though, all eyes were on the smooth, lissom frames of Charles Liston, now a slender 6–5 favourite, and Cassius Marcellus Clay. Marciano, Louis, Patterson and Jimmy Braddock, a puggish parade if ever there was one, stood to attention as Robert Guilet, the latest New Sinatra, rendered the national anthem, 'in a smeared, syncopated version,' wrote Alistair Cooke, 'unmatched for musical gall since Bing Crosby put out his first recording of *Adeste, fideles.*' Jersey Joe Walcott, controversially brought in as referee to heighten interest, arrived late, huffing and puffing as he climbed through the ropes. Sonny entered in his wake, one observer describing his expression as 'sulky'. Then came Ali, 'who never,' Cooke noted, 'ceased from Morris dancing except when he bared his teeth three inches from Liston's corner.'

To many, what ensued was more dirty dancing than the Morris variation. Ali surprised Sonny from the bell, taking the offensive and landing a straight right. A few seconds later, another right appeared to shake Sonny, whose advances seemed hesitant. Less than a minute of otherwise tentative probing had elapsed when Sonny, trundling forward as his target shuffled and quickstepped, aimed a slow, low left. The timing was awry, however, and just as Ali looked to be in the process of skipping further away he moved his head slightly to the right, the jab grazing the left side of his face, then made a grab for his holster and snaked a lightning right into the side of Sonny's head as it hovered invitingly around hip level. Jose Torres's Spanish radio commentary testified to the quality of the punch: '. . . a perfect shot to the jaw, right on the button . . .' Others were less convinced. Seemingly no more than a flick, it was as if Ali, wrote Alistair Cooke, had 'backhanded a bothersome fly'. Either way, Sonny never saw a thing until it was too late. The blow lifted his left foot off the canvas. As it came to earth, the rest of his body crumpled in sympathy. Cooke was not alone in watching sceptically as he 'reeled and crashed with all the verisimilitude of a Friday-night television wrestler.'

Cue chaos. Instead of going to a neutral corner, Ali stood astride Sonny, right arm cocked. 'Get up and fight, sucker,' he demanded, forgetting the rules amid the furnace of the moment. He wanted to give the crowd value for money; he also wanted to 'whup him bad'. That Miami shoulder alibi niggled. 'I didn't want him making excuses or quitting. I wanted him to get up, so I could show everyone how great I was.' Walcott tried to intercede but he, too, had lost control. Instead of refusing to start the count until Ali had retreated in the prescribed manner, Walcott tried to pull him away, omitting to communicate with the inexperienced timekeeper, Frank McDonough, a former newspaper printer who began pounding out the count with a gavel from the instant Sonny returned to terra firma. After ten seconds, Angelo Dundee, who had been keeping a keen eye on McDonough, claims to have yelled over to Walcott: 'Joe, Joe, the fight's over. Check the timekeeper.' After seventeen seconds, Sonny was upright again but, by now, Ali was jigging his jig, arms aloft. Walcott, who had still not uttered as much as a 'one', wiped Sonny's gloves and allowed battle to recommence. All of a sudden, he detected a cry from above the mayhem: 'It's over. He's out.' The voice was that of Nat Fleischer, an esteemed, impassioned journalist and historian, but no official – although Dundee is adamant that the shouting came from the equally small, sandy-haired chap sitting next to him, McDonough. The Society for the Preservation of Boxing Myths suppressed that angle. The obedient, frazzled Walcott promptly turned his back on the brawlers, walked toward the side of the ring where Fleischer was seated, crouched, listened briefly, then prowled back into the centre of the ring to halt the contest once and for all. The duration of the fight was announced as a minute, even though 142 seconds had drifted by when Walcott finally pulled down the curtain.

Dundee jumped into the ring and went over to console the glassy-eyed Sonny, by now slumped on his stool. 'I said, "Tough night, Sonny." He didn't say anything. He looked right through me. He was out. He was definitely out. When the fight was stopped, he was on his feet, throwing shots. But the only reason he was on his feet throwing shots was his instincts as a fighter. All those people chanting "Fix, fix, fix" that night were not able to look in Liston's eyes like I did. But who knows how much all that [rumours of threats to kill Ali] had been playing on Liston's mind.' Ali was proud to inform the press that the deed had been done through his interpretation of Jack Johnson's previously unknown 'anchor punch', a manoeuvre involving a late twist of the wrist that many sceptics compared rather to the corkscrew punch patented by Kid McCoy. None the less, he later concurred with Dundee, stressing the cumulative effect of all those policemen, FBI agents and bullet-proof shields. 'I believe the pressure got to him. There has never been a fight less fixed.' When his turn came to confront the media, Sonny refused to employ the excuses at his disposal. Was that the response of a bent fighter? 'There was only one punch, a short right to the side of my face,' he said, pointing to his left cheek-bone. 'I couldn't hear the count, but it was a good punch. I have been hit harder, though, by Cleveland Williams.' Did he quit? 'No, I did not.' Was he thinking of retirement? 'I don't know.'

The consensus view was far less restrained. The crowd, such as it was, was steaming. This was partly because of Ali. Nobody in Lewiston liked that jumped-up Muslim much. Of course it was a fix. Look at those ticket prices. For what? On the surface, you couldn't blame them. Illinois Congressman Robert Michel dubbed the bout 'disgraceful'. Demanding a Congressional investigation and proposing a national commission (what a revolutionary step!), he pointed out that the receipts for the last three heavyweight championship bouts had been in excess of $12 million for roughly twenty-one minutes of action. 'Before the fight, I said I wouldn't spend twenty-nine cents to see it,' Michel said smugly, 'and I was right.' Not for the first time, Senator Zaretzki proposed an anti-boxing bill in New York. Aaron M.I. Shinberg, a Democrat from Haverhill, Mass., filed a resolution urging a moratorium on professional boxing and the closed-circuit televising of fights 'until such time as a thorough investigation of professional boxing has been conducted on a nationwide basis by a federal agency or a committee or sub-committee of the US Congress, and the findings of said investigation have been reported and recommendations of said agency, committee or sub-committee adopted.' A Brooklyn Democrat, Max M. Turshen, declared boxing to be no more than 'modified murder' and depicted the fight as 'a horrible example of this so-called sport'. He, too, proposed a bill, to 'end this evil once and for all'.

The *Corry Journal* in Pennsylvania bared its prejudices with a snooty front-page apology: 'Due to the nature of last night's fight, the *Journal* feels it does not warrant coverage. Don't look for it on the sports page.' In a report headlined 'Comedy Of Errors', Arthur Daley strove to cover his back after having asserted that there was no way in which Ali could win 'with one punch'. Tongues would wag, he assured the Big Apple, 'about the strange ending of this wretchedly mishandled, bush-league production for many years to come'. 'A PIFFLING FARCE' yelled the midday edition of the *London Evening Standard*; 'PARODY OF A FIGHT' snorted *La Suisse*. Down in Mexico, *La Afición* railed about 'a coarse and indignant farce'. The Soviet government organ, *Izvestia*, brought some dignity to the histrionics: 'What happened to Liston? To this question no one can give a sensible answer yet. It is not impossible that more efforts will be needed not only from boxing experts but from investigatory organs.' Even the peacenik *Manchester Guardian* was moved to carry a story on the front. Well, they did have the delicious Cooke on the spot. 'If the word fiasco were not in the language,' he spat, 'it would be necessary to get an Italian to invent it to describe the shortest and stupidest championship match in the history of boxing. It is conceivable that even Sonny Liston's patron, Mr Blinky Palermo, may never know the truth. Mr Palermo is at the moment serving time in the Federal Penitentiary, but he was well represented by "associates and business connections".'

'Was the match a horrid hoax as a prelude to Liston's saying goodbye to the ring?' pondered Nat Fleischer. 'Goodbye it doubtless is, because who would pay to see this man fight again and do so with a sense of confidence in the bona fides of intention and result? Liston is through. It must be said that he did boxing very little, if any, good in his entire career.' *The Ring* was flooded with letters of a similar hue. 'Never before in the history of sport have so many paid so much for so little,' claimed one. Gene Tunney was never a fan of Sonny's. 'I doubt he ever bothered to learn the fundamentals of boxing. Dempsey would KO him in two rounds,' he once said of him. 'In a bar-room, it would be even.' Now, on the Fighting Marine's 67th birthday, any grudging morsels of admiration evaporated for good. 'This is the worst, most offensive debasement of boxing that I've ever seen or even read about.' To Arthur Daley, there was one consolation: 'For small favours let us be thankful. At least the boxing racket is completely rid of the deflated ogre, the unsavoury Sonny Liston.'

Yet there was not one shred of evidence to flesh out the accusations that Sonny had decided, as Ted 'Kid' Lewis's manager, Charley Rose, put it, 'to go into the swimming-pool'. As Fleischer himself conceded, 'it might have been done in more convincing fashion'. Indeed. If you're going to make it look good, there can be little sense in going down at the first opportunity. Al Braverman echoes this view. 'I was standing right behind Fleischer. When Sonny went down, Walcott panicked. He didn't know what to do. He stood there, tugging Ali, trying to get him into a neutral corner. He then ran over to the side of the ring where Fleischer was, and Nat said, "It's over, he counted him out." Then Walcott ran back to where Liston was and pinned his arms. He stopped the fight without hearing a count of one. Not even one. He couldn't handle the situation. Nat Fleischer didn't have a fuckin' thing to do with the fight. He was just Nat Fleischer, the historian. Sonny got hit, sure. High on the cheek-bone. It dazed him. But if it was a tank-job, why did he get up? If he'd wanted to tank he could have stayed down. No one could have got near enough to the camp to bribe him anyway. And I know I never saw no Black Muslims. Afterwards, Sonny wanted to walk out the back door, so I said: "There ain't no fuckin' way, you're going out the front with me. You're gonna face those reporters. You walk out the back door, they say something happened to you. You gotta come out front with me." And he did, and he was fine. People say Geraldine was angry with him because she thought he'd thrown it. Bullshit. I saw him embracing her in the hotel later. A great woman, a smart woman.'

Teddy King, who believed that Sonny's heart was never in the fight, heard something rather different going on as he was standing outside his boss's room that night. 'I . . . overheard Geraldine laying him out for quitting. She was really letting him have it, and Sonny just stood there and took it like a little kid. When we came in the room, he said, "Tell her I got hit, Teddy." I didn't know what to say, so I just kept my mouth shut and nodded.' Ali's next opponent, Patterson, who had flown to Maine from Sweden, also dropped by. Earlier, he had told the press that 'it was a good punch . . . the best right hand I've seen since Joe Louis.' To him, there was no question of deceit. 'I knocked on the door. Sonny was all alone, so I asked if I could come in. He said to do so, and I began talking about the fight, telling him not to feel bad about it, giving him encouragement, telling him about my experiences. The funny thing was that he never once said anything, and I was there for a good half-hour. When I said I had to go and began heading for the door, he finally said something. "Floyd," he said, making me turn around, "thanks." I thought to myself, gee, I got some response. Maybe I reached him.'

Jose Torres went backstage as well. Before the fight, Sonny had told him about his time behind bars, how other prisoners would be subjected to rape and sodomy, whereas he was spared because everyone was scared of him. Sonny in turn had been fearful of the less balanced prisoners. The conversation came back to Torres that night. 'The room was empty. Liston was embarrassed and very depressed. My first question was, "Did you see the punch?" And he told me, "Yes, but I saw it too late." That was it. In boxing, the punch that knocks you out is not the hard punch. It's the punch you don't see coming.' Torres was not sure whether Sonny really wanted to get up. 'Sonny was afraid of crazy people, and he thought Ali was crazy.' Two years later, Sonny endorsed this. 'Ali knocked me down with a sharp punch. I was down but not hurt, but I looked up and saw Ali standing over me. Ali is waiting to hit me, the referee can't control him. I have to put one knee and one glove on the canvas to get up. You know Ali is a nut. You can tell what a normal man is going to do, but you can't tell what a nut is going to do, and Ali is a nut.'

What, though, of Walcott? More pertinently, how did he come to be in such an invidious position in the first place? Barney Felix, who refereed the Miami bout, was less than half an hour from taking off from Florida to run this one when he received a call from a Lewiston official. Given the racial climate, it had been decided to make the match 'all-Negro'. Or that, at least, was what they told Barney. 'My wife breathed a sigh of relief, and I think I did too.' He felt Walcott should have used force. 'If I am in the ring and I am absolutely unable to force Cassius into a neutral corner, and my picking up the count is delayed, I might take a shot at Clay's jaw myself.' To Felix's way of thinking, Sonny should have been permitted to carry on. 'There is no legal count as the referee has not picked up the count from the knock-down timekeeper. [What if] Liston, still not knocked out legally, picks himself up, knocks Cassius unconscious and walks into a neutral corner. The answer? Liston again is champ.'

For his part, Walcott pleaded not guilty. 'Nobody can point the finger of suspicion at Jersey Joe Walcott. The reason I stayed with Clay and kept pushing him away was because I was afraid he was going to kick Liston in the head. Clay was like a wild man. He was running around the ring and shouting for Sonny to get up. Can you imagine what they would be saying about me if Clay had kicked Liston in the head? And, you know, he might have hit Sonny as he was getting up. If he did that he might have injured Liston permanently. Like all referees, I was there to protect the fighter on the floor. Liston was a whipped man. I could see that by the glassy look in his eyes . . . Clay never gave me a chance to start counting. I couldn't hear the count from the knock-down timekeeper.' The former champion pronounced himself happy that the climax was on the level. 'The punch Clay dropped Liston with is one of the most devastating punches I've ever seen. Sonny was hurt, real bad. I was afraid after seeing Clay knock Sonny off his feet with one punch. I think I did right under the circumstances.'

Ah, the circumstances. In what must rank as one of the most Sennettesque episodes in boxing history, Ali had gone loopy, Walcott had forgotten his lines, and Sonny had been adjudged knocked out by an inaudible, not to say illegal, count. Yet in Torres's estimation, Sonny was beaten, not by Walcott, nor by drugs, nor by the postponement, nor even by the punch itself, but by his subconscious. 'Deep down, in the innermost part of his soul, Sonny Liston feared Muhammad Ali. And, even more, he feared the Black Muslims.' Ali, as time would prove, was indeed a man whose skills deserved fear, but Sonny's fear was not a physical one. Sure, Ali was crazy, and that unnerved Sonny, particularly while the man was looking down on him, fist at the ready.

Ali was certainly an enigmatic mass of contradictions. 'He was never what anyone wanted him to be,' wrote Robert Lipsyte. 'A black symbol who rejected Malcolm X, a champion who boasted, a selective pacifist, a separatist libertarian, a lovable religious zealot, and a campus speaker who denounced marijuana, unmarried sex, and integration.' But that perceived craziness masked another source of fear. Ali, the Nation of Islam and Martin Luther King were all in the vanguard of a world Sonny had distanced himself from, a world he could not comprehend. Sonny would always be the jailbird thug, the bad nigger, no matter what those civil rights folk achieved. Maybe it suddenly dawned on him that the courage required to enter the ring was nothing next to the bravado needed to take a militant political stance? Having realised that, perhaps he began to cower? He certainly began the fight hesitantly, shorn of his customary zest. He may well have been fearful of the snipers rumoured to be flanking the ring, even though the police search had produced nothing in the way of hardware. More significantly, the scar left by Clay's psychological superiority in Miami was deep. The bizarre circumstances of the Lewiston Laugh-In merely opened the stitches.

The more the memory recedes, the more groundless appear all the suspicions. Granted, the perspective time affords has a handy knack of diminishing one's sense of outrage. Now, furthermore, we tolerate Don King, where once we vilified Blinky Palermo. But having started out believing that chicanery was afoot, the fact that I no longer do so has nothing to do with emotional castration, nothing to do with the apathy instilled by a society whose response to a disaster such as AIDS is to build up its immunity to caring. It is attributable to one simple factor. Here was a man with an ego to match his ham-like fists.

Sonny Liston take a dive? Not the Sonny Liston a select few were lucky to know. 'He had too much pride,' avers Father Stevens. Even so, he shed a lot of the excess that night. Like Mariner 4, bound at that moment for Mars, Sonny had passed his destination and was losing speed on his orbit round the sun. Not so much the Great Deception, more the Great Dejection. He would not be forgiven, whatever the truth of the matter.

Twelve

The Last Ride

It is cold and the wind is blowing
We need something to keep us going
Mr President have pity on the working man
Maybe you've cheated
Maybe you've lied
Maybe you have finally lost your mind
Maybe you're only thinking 'bout yourself
Too late to run. Too late to cry now
The time has come for us to say goodbye now
Mr President have pity on the working man
Mr President have pity on the working man

(Randy Newman, *Mr President*)

'There is nothing going on around here,' Geraldine advised the prying reporter at the other end of the line. 'Charles has no match coming up, and there have been no negotiations. Charles got some money for the Lewiston fight but he has not been paid for the Miami Beach fight. If he fought now, the government would take all the money, so there is no use of making any matches. We aren't in need. We don't need money now. But it's lucky for us that we have been saving. If Charles had been one of those spendthrifts, we would be in a real bad way. In spite of talk about his being old, he is only 34 and has quite a few hard contests left. Maybe we will go to Europe.'

And so, harried by politicians, commissions and a disgusted boxing fraternity, not to mention the Denver cops, hemmed in by income tax problems and unpaid earnings, Sonny and Geraldine fled to Europe. With them went Geraldine's daughter, Arletha, now 19, and the couple's adopted daughter, Eleanor, now 13. It was back to the days of fighting for eating money. Sonny, as far as mainstream boxing was concerned, was now *persona non grata*. Even though there was no physical evidence of it, the agreement to hold a return bout with Ali after Miami was all the witch-hunters could pin on him, but it was enough to prevent Sonny from receiving the monies due to him. After Lewiston, there would be no more pre-arranged rematches.

On 29 June 1966, three weeks after James Meredith, the first black to defy the colour bar at the University of Mississippi, had been shot in the back and legs during a civil rights march, Sonny resumed his fistic career in Stockholm, just as Uncle Sam's bombers were preparing to drop in on Hanoi with a similar purpose in mind. His opponent in an Ingemar Johansson promotion was the German champion, Gerhard Zech, a southpaw who had recently gone the distance with his compatriot, Karl Mildenberger, in a forlorn bid for the European title. Sonny made rather shorter work of the job than the man who, six weeks later, would take Ali into the twelfth. After seventy-one seconds of the seventh, the blot on boxing's landscape uncorked a short left-right combination that left Zech a bloody mess from a squashed nose and a gash over the right eye.

Away from the vindictive glare of the North American media Medusa, Sonny seemed more relaxed, albeit apparently in the grip of a severe attack of self-delusion. 'I like Sweden. Its people appreciate boxing. I hope to remain here for at least two more bouts. I would like to face Karl Mildenberger and Floyd Patterson, who is popular here. Then I'm certain I'll be ready to face Clay [*sic*] in another championship match if he is still the title-holder.' And Sweden liked Sonny. After one fight, a young mother walked up to him and Geraldine and asked them to adopt her baby. 'Negroes know how to treat children,' she explained. The request was granted willingly. A son at last. Freed by amiable libel laws, however, some observed a darker figure. 'Liston,' J.A. Tree reported in *The Ring*, 'aged over 42 and a grandfather, presented a somewhat pathetic picture for a one-time world champion, and a once big earner. He says that he does not have the lavish financial resources he generally is supposed to possess after two fights with Patterson and a pair with Clay. Where did the money go? Did he ever get it? Sonny and his missus just smile the grim smile.'

Contrary to Sonny's fond imaginings, another tilt at the title was completely off the agenda. Only the previous December, *The Ring* had dropped him from its unofficial world ranking list, the first time a former heavyweight champion had been removed from the top ten so soon after attempting to regain his title. Over the ensuing months, the magazine's offices were festooned with letters of complaint as well as vindication. George Girsch sought to justify his publisher's rationale: 'In many quarters, it is felt that Liston is unfit to box any more. Surely no long lines of promoters are queueing up at his door.' While the last assertion was bang on the nose, the more salient point was that Sonny had become too hot a potato, even for Frankie and Blinky's henchmen. The Nilons had gone, so too Sam the Sham. Perhaps even the Mob could not compete with the waves of political change? By some quirk of coincidence, the authorities had turned on the heat just as Sonny's usefulness passed its sell-by date. There would no longer be any protection from the Chicago connection.

The following year, 1966, Sonny was reported to have met Nat Fleischer 'in Europe', whereupon he launched into a vehement protest at *The Ring*'s persistent refusal to rank him. 'Isn't it time to give me a break,' Sonny allegedly pleaded. 'What did I do wrong to begin with?' The ever-vigilant Fleischer explained that he could not be rated because he was ineligible to box in every state of the United States bar Nevada; also that he had been barred by the British Boxing Board of Control and the European Boxing Union, 'thus there is no basis for rating you'. The Man Who Thought He Was A Timekeeper was unable to resist a final dig. 'Frankly, you are the Forgotten Man.' Given the physical disparity between the two, it is difficult to picture Fleischer actually saying this to Sonny's face, but you never know.

Happily, the Forgotten Man could still remember how to deploy his fists. Less than two months after decking Zech, he was knocking Amos Johnson senseless in Gothenburg. In the same city the following March, he buried the erratic Dave Bailey within three minutes. Four weeks later, he was back in Stockholm to face Elmer Rush. While Ali was declining an invite to tour Vietnam on the grounds that he had no great quarrel with the locals, Sonny made his stand with a six-round KO.

Arriving home in the summer of 1967, Joe Pollino, who had acted as Sonny's 'manager' in Sweden, declined to discuss his client other than to rail against the system that had forced him into exile. 'Liston occupies a position without precedent in professional boxing history. He stands barred on reportedly powerful evidence connecting him with unsavoury characters, and yet, on no presentable evidence at all. He appears to be barred for losing.' Pollino went on to attack the original refusal of the New York SAC to grant Sonny a licence: 'Before . . . commissions adopted the broad and not too safe assumption that a fighter was to be judged entirely on results. Their broad policy was based on the smell of things . . . [they] displayed a penchant for tracing odours to their sources.'

Despite this, Eddie Dooley, Roy Long and Albert Berkowitz all asserted that they would repeat the NYSAC's 1962 stance if Sonny applied again. (Around this time, incidentally, it was revealed that Sonny's lawyer had advised him not to accept an invitation to face an NYSAC interrogation shortly after Melvin L. Krulewitch and his chums had rejected that ill-fated licence application five years previously.) 'Not a chance,' snapped Dooley. 'We would turn him down now. His situation has not changed. The brief encounter with Clay at Lewiston looked bad.'

Yet only after Lewiston had decimated Sonny's marquee value did Illinois and Nevada remind themselves of the New York findings. Only then did they strip Sonny of his licence, and even then Nevada returned it. Jim Deskin, the executive secretary of the Nevada Boxing Commission, outlined the thinking behind the change of heart. 'The Nevada Boxing Commission felt that the WBA had reinstated Cassius Clay, and that both Clay and Liston had been suspended for the same reason, that is, "the return bout clause", and they felt that if Clay had been reinstated it was incumbent on this commission to issue a licence to Liston.' Deskin said that Sonny had written to him during his time as WBA president the previous year, asking to be reinstated by the world body. 'I placed this on the agenda of the executive board meeting in Panama. However, I took ill the first day, and apparently it got lost in the shuffle or was inadvertently overlooked by the board, and it was the consensus of opinion of the executive board that Sonny Liston appear before the board at the Reno WBA convention on 20 August 1967. There the matter stands.' Lost in the shuffle? Inadvertently overlooked? Oliver North could have had no finer role model.

Dan Daniel got all high and mighty in *The Ring*. 'Boxing appears to want nothing more to do with Liston . . . Sonny had a penchant for hooking up with the wrong guys. If you have that flair you are bound to end up behind the eight ball. And that is precisely where Charles "Sonny" Liston now finds himself. He asked for it, he got it.' Sonny, however, was a trash-can for boxing to dump its guilt into, and therefore he had his uses. He was also a cyst that needed removing, but a prolonged crucifixion would be so much more fun. As Sonny arrived on the convention floor in Reno, Bob Evans, the WBA president, must only barely have suppressed the cackle bubbling below his dead-pan tone: 'We never suspended Liston. Suspensions are made by commissions. Sonny, if you can get a licence anywhere you are at liberty to fight where you are wanted.'

Sonny soon found out where he wasn't wanted when he replied to Evans. Since he could now be licensed, he would very much like to take part in the WBA-organised elimination tournament designed to find a successor to Ali, who had been stripped of his title after turning down the Army's generous offer of employment. Sonny's request was turned down with rather less justification. The field, apparently, had been closed. While the outer door had been left mockingly ajar, the entrance to the inner sanctum banged firmly shut.

Yet fragments of hope remained. California, once a firm

supporter of the New York ban, now welcomed Sonny as some kind of prodigal son. After flattening Bill McMurray in the fourth round of his American come-back in Reno on 16 March 1968, Sonny was paired with Cincinnati's Billy Joiner in LA two months later, knocking him out in the seventh. The Listons had by now returned to Vegas, settling into an eye-catching $50,000 split-level home on Ottawa Street. 'Liston is not in want,' sneered Dan Daniel. 'He has a luxurious home in Las Vegas, plus two of the richest models the Cadillac people turn out. He has a swimming-pool, and adjacent to his baronial acres is the Star Dust golf course. Charley lives in evident contentment. But Geraldine complains, "There is no money coming in." '

This was not strictly true. In 1967, Sonny had been hired to make the briefest of cameo appearances in Bob Rafelson's anarchic comedy, *Head*, a cinematic vehicle for those poptastic sensations, the Monkees (only one of whom was a bona-fide musician; in the year of *Puppet On A String*, this Anglo-American combo were the foremost Pinocchios). Also in the cast was another former macho icon, Victor Mature. Sonny, unsurprisingly, was seen knocking out one of the adorable quasi-primates. To a sceptical mind – i.e. one in tune with the director's undisguised contempt for Corporate America – the scene that led up to this could have been interpreted as a lament for Sonny. Promising his girlfriend that 'they pick the round, I pick the guy', a skinny white runt of a boxer proceeds to run the rule over an array of would-be opponents, arranged as if they were part of a police identification parade. After selecting the last candidate in line, an impassive, mute Sonny, he explains his decision: 'I like him. He looks like a nice guy and I like his smile.' In the ring, Sonny performs as if he were a statue with movable arms, a punching machine. Preening sadistically in the crowd is what we take to be a mobster, all black fedora and grinning spivviness. Everyone is urging the white boy to stay down when Sonny sends him reeling for the umpteenth time, everyone but the Black Fedora. The only difference in real life was that they picked the guy, Sonny the round.

Geraldine, meanwhile, had taken a job as a casino hostess. 'I used to see her occasionally on the Strip or working at the Circus Hotel,' recalls Joey Curtis, now the president of the American Veteran Boxers' Association. An acquaintance dating back to Sonny's formative years as a pro, Curtis first met him when 'Sonny started coming to Jimmy Toppi's Olympia Gym in Philadelphia. He'd just come out of the can, and I was training there myself. He had a body like a tank. He was very, very eager: he knew he had a lot of ability. On the outside he wanted to be the baddest cat in the world, the roughest son-of-a-bitch on two feet. If he had wanted to kill a man in the ring he could have. But he was a pussycat. We stayed in contact until the mid-1950s, then met up again in the late 1960s. I rarely saw him, so when I saw Geraldine I would always say, "How's the champ?" and she'd say, "Fine, great." But I heard he was into drugs.'

Then, in July 1968, there was a breakthrough of sorts. In a nationally televised bout at San Francisco's half-empty Cow Palace, Sonny was matched against Henry Clark, a swift puncher of 23 ranked No.9 in *The Ring* ratings. With upper-cut and hook to the fore, experience prevailed in the seventh despite the fact that Sonny's preparation for the fleet-footed Clark was said to have been light on road-work. No details of the purse were announced, but Sonny was back in favour: *The Ring* now deigned to rank him at No.7. 'Since Clark was a rated heavy and Charley beat him,' Nat Fleischer conceded, grudgingly, '*The Ring* and your correspondent were placed in a position which dictated returning Sonnyboy to the Top Ten.' Coming from Fleischer, this was tantamount to a grovelling apology.

Back at the Cow Palace, Sonny had been running around waving a piece of paper. It was, he claimed, his birth certificate, placing his age at 36. No one believed a word, of course. In truth, Sonny had a habit of shooting himself in the foot on that front. When completing his licence application form for the first Ali fight on 12 February 1964, he had entered his date of birth as '8 May 1934', more than two years after the approximate date his mother had insisted on. Yet if he was now 36 he would have had to have been born in 1932, as this new certificate indicated. To compound the confusion, and acknowledge his own uncertainty, Sonny had stated his age as 30 on the application form in Miami; according to the information he had submitted in the line above, he was 29.

For Sonny, the year that saw the civil rights movement lurch from James Earl Ray to Black Power to Mayor Daley ended with a new trainer in tow, 'Dandy Dick' Saddler, the rough-house featherweight champion whose reign had been so unhappily truncated by a car crash. There were also four brisk demolitions inside two months to celebrate. Sonny Moore made it as far as the third in Phoenix, Willis Earls as far as the second in Juarez. In Pittsburgh, a crowd of 4213 watched Sonny dispose of the overmatched Roger Rischer in the third in a benefit bill for Ben Anolik, an ailing ex-promoter. Hisses and catcalls besieged the fighters as Sonny, looking more than a little ponderous, floored Rischer in the first for a count of eight. Rischer got up and ran for cover but was caught against the ropes in the third. A couple of left hooks and a straight right, then a conclusive left, and *The Ring* had a new No.5 contender. In Baltimore, Sonny stepped into the ring with his old mucker, Amos 'Big Train' Lincoln. 'Liston picked up his coffee and donut money for the year,' jibed *The Ring*'s John Ort after a left hook had done for Lincoln in round two. The mismatch would have been over even earlier had referee Ruby Goldstein not elected to ignore the fact that Lincoln's corner had already thrown in the towel after a three-punch combination had sent their man sprawling. Lincoln ended up draped over the ropes for three full minutes while the doctors strove to revive him. For Sonny, the pickings appeared plentiful, with $35,000 emanating from closed-circuit revenues alone. By Christmas, he was *The Ring*'s No.4.

In March 1969, Billy Joiner was unhinged again, this time in St Louis, Sonny disappointing in his first fight there for nearly eleven years by winning on points – only the twelfth time he had been taken the distance in fifty contests. Next up was George 'Scrap-Iron' Johnson, who had recently gone ten rounds with the dangerous Joe Frazier but failed to survive the seventh against Sonny in Vegas. In September, Sonny Moore asked for more in Houston, and duly got it, left helpless in three. 'How Much Has

Ageing Liston Left?' asked the cover to November's issue of *The Ring*. Not a lot, declared Dan Daniel in response to the 500 or more letters that had poured through the magazine's letter-box over the previous six months, pleading Sonny's case as a valid contender. Daniel, as ever, cited age as the reason, but what about Archie Moore? Was he not said to have been between 45 and 48 when he was forced to relinquish his light-heavyweight crown in 1962? Moore himself believed that Sonny had 'looked better with each fight since "Dandy Dick" took over' and could better both Frazier and Jimmy Ellis, the other principal pretender to Ali's throne. 'But I also believe he'll never get the chance. What do either Frazier or Ellis need with Liston? He'd be too strong for either one of them.'

Moore maintained that 'condition is the key for Sonny' but, if that was the case, the portents for his crucial December meeting with Leotis Martin were far from good. This was an opportunity to shake up the pundits once and for all. Martin, after all, had kept Frazier at bay for almost nine rounds in the first section of the WBA eliminator series. But if Sonny recognised the import of the Vegas engagement, he certainly did not show it in training. 'The last thing Sonny would do was train,' attested George Foreman, who had sparred with Sonny at his home gym in Houston prior to the second Sonny Moore bout and was retained as a training partner for this fight. 'He'd want to party all the time, and sometimes he would do so much he didn't even know his name. He was on top for seven rounds against Martin, then began tiring in the eighth and got kayoed in the ninth. I thought, "Good gracious, I don't ever want to be put asleep like that." ' In his eleventh professional contest, Foreman expended two minutes in knocking out a journeyman by the name of Bob Hazelton on the undercard of that same Hilton bill, but he learned more about his chosen trade on the drive back to Ottawa Street with a silent, visibly depressed Sonny. 'I decided right then that if you were going to be a boxer, you'd have to be in training all the time.'

'Father Time & Martin Direct Liston To Exit' exclaimed *The Ring* in the wake of the right-left-right, machine-gun volley Martin let rip after barely one minute of the ninth round, leaving Sonny 'spread-eagled like a bear rug in front of a fire, and as lifeless'. Sonny, a 3–1 favourite, had won the first six rounds, sending Martin plummeting in the fourth with a left hook. The judges' scoring at the end was 37–34, 38–35 and 38–36 in his favour. 'If he had taken a beating, I would advise him to quit,' avowed Dick Saddler. 'But he was winning, moving along like a real star, when three lucky punches landed. There still is a lot of fight left in Sonny.' If this seemed a mite optimistic, then Martin was the first of the pair to quit. One of Sonny's blows instigated an eye injury that compelled his vanquisher to retire six months later.

Just as Martin was about to fade into obscurity, Sonny demonstrated how much fight he had left in him at the Jersey City Armory on 29 June 1970, when he took on an ex-Marine named Chuck Wepner, a.k.a. 'The Bayonne Bleeder' and Sylvester Stallone's inspiration for the *Rocky* films. The 4012 gathering included Ali, who pointedly ignored anyone calling him 'Clay', as well as Britain's latest young heavyweight hope, the Hungarian-born Joe Bugner. What they beheld was a free plug for the abolitionists. Barney Felix played his part by refusing to stop the contest in the third, when Wepner was bleeding from both eyebrows and a broken nose. Johnny Tocco, that wily old trainer from the St Louis era, was back in Sonny's corner, and in the sixth he implored Felix to show some humanity. It was then that Davey Pearl, now Sonny's 'unofficial' manager, witnessed a side of Sonny he'd never seen: 'He told me he was afraid to hit him any more.' Tocco's memories have a resonant, technicolour tinge: 'It was like blood coming out of a hydrant.' When Dr Reginald Farrar, the attendant physician, finally got around to prodding Felix into calling a halt at the end of the ninth, Wepner's manager, the multi-talented Al Braverman, tossed a handful of water across the ring and snarled at both medic and official. OK, so his man had an inch-long slice under a left eye that had swollen grotesquely. OK, so one eyebrow had been erased by a three-inch gash. And the other was severely cut. And a ragged wound decorated his forehead. And his nose was busted. All right, so he needed fifty-five stitches. But Wepner was one of those beings born solely to fight. Pain meant nothing. That's why he was able to go fifteen rounds with Ali in Cleveland five years later. 'I let up on him [Sonny] in the ninth,' the 6ft 5in Canadian revealed. 'I didn't want to knock him out.'

Braverman's recollections, typically, are laced with the sadistic humour needed to stay sane in the boxing game. 'Liston kicked the shit out of Wepner almost every round. He got tired of hitting him. Wepner's whole career was a fuckin' miracle because he couldn't even spell "fight". He had two left feet and two left hands. But we won the next thirteen fights after that and wound up getting a shot at Ali. Wepner couldn't outfight you, but he could outlast you, outgut you. What was great about him was that he believed all the lies that I told him. When he fought Ernie Terrell he came back to the corner at the end of the fifth and said he thought he'd broken his tongue during a clash of heads. "You got another one?" I asked him. "Yes," he answered. In the next round, Terrell stepped back as blood spurted from Wepner's head. You could've put three fingers in that cut. "It's a scratch," I shouted. "Are you a faggot?" ' As to whether there was any substance in the stories about Sonny having ignored instructions to throw the fight, Braverman, who once ridiculed the very idea, is now merely coy: 'I can't swear he wasn't asked to throw it.'

If he had been, there was scant evidence. While Wepner earned less than $4000 after contracting to pay Sonny's purse from 50 per cent of the net receipts, the victor received $13,000. It was quickly accounted for. Some weeks earlier, Sonny, still hanging around with the 'wrong' people and allegedly immersed in the drug-strewn Las Vegas underclass, had placed a $10,000 bet with his close friend, gambler Lem Banker. 'I knew he was in desperate need of cash,' said Banker, who put the money on an undefeated, up-and-coming heavyweight, Mac Foster, to defeat the ageing, cumbersome Jerry Quarry. Quarry retired Foster in the sixth. On the flight back to Vegas from Jersey City, Sonny opened a brown paper bag, counted out $10,000 in small denominations and passed the wad to Banker. The remaining $3000 was distributed among Tocco and the other corner-men.

Davey Pearl, a former referee and constant companion since Lewiston, observed Sonny at closer range than most during this period in his capacity as unpaid guru. 'I didn't want the money. I just wanted to be his friend. Shortly after the Wepner fight, Geraldine asked me and my wife over and proceeded to hand me $500. I said no, I can't take it. I felt sorry for him. The top people in Las Vegas were forever coming up to me and saying, "What are you doing with that bum?" And I would always say, "Because I like the guy." He never did anything without my advice. Why? Because I showed my personal attitude without kissing his behind. He told me that he knew he would have to learn to fight in prison, that he had worked as a goon for the telephone company back in St Louis, cracking heads, and that of all his managers, Blinky Palermo was the nicest to him. We'd be up at 6 every morning, running across the Las Vegas Sahara golf course. He was a loner. He didn't trust many people, and I didn't blame him. He never had a weight problem in my experience. I'd heard stories about the drink and the gambling, but I never saw him drink in five years. I couldn't fathom that it was true. When I told his lawyer this, he told me I was Sonny's conscience. But people used to come up to me and say, "You should have seen your boy, Liston, last night. Was he ever drunk!" I once asked him, "What is this? You leave me at night and go out and get drunk?" He just looked at me. I never suspected him of taking heroin: he wouldn't even take a shot for a cold. If he did he must have done it when his conscience wasn't looking.

'One time I was asked to ref for a few 9- and 10-year-old kids at an amateur show in a small town called Henderson. It was something I did every year. Sonny came with me on this occasion and, for a laugh, announced that he was going to show me how to ref. When he stopped one particular fight, the beaten kid was so embarrassed he tore off one of his gloves and threw it at Sonny. Sonny was so ashamed and shocked and upset that he never went back there again.'

Sonny, one must assume, was equally ashamed of his performances against Clay/Ali: not once did he ever talk to Pearl about either. His fiscal plight was more obvious. 'He was robbed of millions,' Pearl alleges. 'I used to write down every penny we spent. Before one fight, Geraldine asked me to pick up the money. She told me right in front of Sonny that I was not to give him any money.' Would Sonny have been better off without boxing? 'I don't think so. He lived like a king. They had a beautiful home, a beautiful wardrobe. They adopted that boy from Sweden, Danielle, a handsome kid. He was happy. What could he have been otherwise? A labourer?'

On one morning run through the congested Vegas streets, Pearl following in his car while Sonny trundled ahead, the exercise came to an abrupt halt. 'Sonny told me to stop the car. I said I couldn't because of the traffic, but he insisted and jumped in. Then I saw what he had seen: a woman sitting on some wheeled platform, selling pencils. Then he jumped up again and emptied his pockets for her.' On another occasion, Pearl was taking part in a radio sports show when a listener with a bad heart rang in. 'He didn't want charity, just to borrow $40 for some knife-sharpening equipment he could make a living out of. Sonny heard all this at home and, the next thing I knew, he had driven to the studio and was banging on the glass, trying to attract my attention. "What are ya doin', Sonny?" I mouthed at him. "We're on the air." Then he handed me two $20 bills. That was the kinda guy he was.'

On Thanksgiving Day, Sonny was involved in a traffic accident and detained in Nevada Memorial Hospital for a few days. How badly he was hurt was never divulged. During one visit, Johnny Tocco remembered being shown some needle marks in Sonny's right arm. These temporary scars were brandished in Pearl's presence as well. Look what those doctors had done to him! That dread of needles, camouflaged by Braverman's trick syringe in Boston, remained acute. Around this time, Lem Banker had been warned by a local sheriff to stay away from Sonny because the police were 'looking into a drug deal'. In turn, he told Sonny 'to keep away from the wrong people'. One morning, a couple of coppers were said to have marched into Tocco's gym and informed him that Sonny had been spotted at a house earmarked for a drug raid. For a week, Tocco contended, the law was camped opposite the gym, scrutinising Sonny's every coming and going.

A couple of days before Christmas 1970, Geraldine, Danielle (now 7) and Sonny went to the Pearl residence for dinner. 'Sonny was fine,' Davey recollects. 'He never had a drink – and I owned the biggest bar in Vegas.' Geraldine, who insists that Sonny was messing with the demon alcohol and suffering from high blood pressure at that juncture, took Danielle off to St Louis on Christmas Eve to stay with her mother for the holiday season. She tried to call Sonny on a number of occasions but failed to obtain an answer and assumed he was in LA painting the town red. On 28 December, she was awoken by a vivid dream. 'He [Sonny] was falling in the shower and calling my name, "Gerry, Gerry!",' she later told *Sports Illustrated*'s William Nack. 'I can still see it. So I got real nervous. I told my mother, "I think something's wrong." But my mother said, "Oh, don't think that. He's all right." '

He wasn't, of course. At some point between Geraldine's departure and her return at 9:30 p.m. on 5 January, Sonny died/ was murdered/committed suicide. Take your pick. Everyone else did at the time and, even now, none of us are any the wiser. Geraldine's pink Cadillac was parked under the carport alongside Sonny's black Fleetwood. Just as it should be. Next to the vehicles, however, lay an unusually large number of copies of the *Las Vegas Sun*, a good few days' worth. When foster-mother and foster-son entered the house, the lights were all on, the doors unlocked and the windows flung wide. The only noise emanated from the master bedroom at the top of the stairs as the television crackled away. Geraldine and Danielle headed for the patio at the back of the house, only to change direction when Geraldine detected a pungent, unpleasant odour. Thinking that Sonny might have left out some food that was beginning to rot, she walked up the three steps leading from the den to the kitchen. There was nothing amiss there. Finally, she and Danielle followed the sound of the cathode rays and went upstairs to the master bedroom. At the foot of the bed lay a smashed bench. Propped up against it they saw a rigid, inert figure wearing a shirt smeared with dried blood, head slumped to one side.

The autopsy ascertained not only that Sonny had been in that state for at least six days, but that his body contained traces of codeine and morphine of the type normally generated when heroin is broken down. Tests proved inconclusive. The state of decomposition was too advanced. On initial inspection by the local chief of detectives, Spencer W. Lemmon, Sonny appeared to have fallen heavily while preparing for bed and struck his head on the bench. Mark Herman, the Clark County coroner, ruled that death had been due to natural causes stemming from 'lung congestion brought on by poor oxygen and nutrient blood supply to the heart muscles'. Many believed, however, that Herman's verdict was diluted for some reason, probably in order to stave off adverse publicity for a city whose life-blood, ever since Bugsy Siegel conceived the Flamingo, had always been tourists and their wallets.

There was, nevertheless, circumstantial evidence of a drug-induced death. One of the investigating officers, Sgt Gary Beckwith, discovered a quarter of an ounce of heroin in a balloon in the bedroom, a syringe near the body, and a blob of marijuana in Sonny's trouser pocket, plus an unidentified black powder on the dresser. Needle tracks, moreover, littered Sonny's right arm, almost certainly too fresh to have been those he had displayed to Pearl and Tocco while laying in hospital six weeks earlier. But the amount of morphine and codeine found in his kidney tissue was held to be insufficient to cause fatality. One plausible scenario was furnished by Sonny's erstwhile press aide, Harold Conrad, who evidently had reason to believe that, besides associating rather too obviously with a white prostitute, Sonny was also involved with the Las Vegas loan sharks as a debt-collector (Jack McKinney said he had heard much the same). Sonny apparently wanted a bigger slice of the pie, Conrad calculated, so his bosses plied him with booze and the odd Mickey Finn, drove him home and administered the fatal dose which, under the circumstances, did not need to be that large.

Then again, there were many plausible scenarios. If people always believed the worst of Sonny, then they expected no better of those whose company he supposedly kept. Floyd Patterson and Bill Cayton both claim to have heard on the grape-vine that Sonny, in Cayton's words, had 'either alienated some very powerful people high in the wiseguys or been very fresh with one of the *capo de capos*', and that this was the aggrieved party's concept of a slap in the face. It was surely significant that, even before that loss to Martin hammered in the final nail, Sonny was existing on borrowed time as a professional boxer. In *The Godfather*, Michael Corleone instructs his henchmen to leave his brother, Fredo, in one piece so long as their mother is alive, then orders his death at her funeral. By the same token, maybe Sonny was permitted to remain upright for so long as he remained a legitimate – and therefore useful – contender, then terminated as soon as he began to slink into the background? Could Patterson and Cayton have been referring to Moe Dalitz, the ex-Cleveland Mob boss at whom Sonny once cocked his fist in Hollywood? Alternatively, Sonny could well have been requested to lie down against Wepner and was ultimately wiped out when his pride prevented him from taking an easy payday.

Another lobby had it that responsibility lay with the Black Muslims, who were allegedly anxious that Sonny might blurt out the truth (which truth was that, exactly?) about the Ali fights. A similar line of argument substituted mobsters for Muslims. Some Vegas law-enforcers were of the opinion – again, unsubstantiated – that Sonny had been bumped off at the behest of Ash Resnick, the gambler whose presence at Miami Beach had stoked the rumours that the first Ali fight was fixed. Sonny and Resnick, it was claimed, were in the midst of a financial imbroglio.

Resnick, like Father Murphy, Harold Conrad, Willie Reddish and so many other constituent parts to this sorry saga, is no longer available to clarify all this conjecture, or even mould theory into fact. For sheer volume of hypotheses, the Kennedy assassination had nothing on this. With his having danced with goodfellas throughout his career, the odds on someone as lippy as Sonny treading on a few influential toes were pretty good. If he had been forced to take an overdose – and that busted bench suggests there may well have been a struggle – the link is logical enough, since this was a *modus operandi* notoriously popular among Mob hitmen.

A brief segment of the HBO series *Unsolved Mysteries* a couple of years ago concentrated on this conundrum. 'I often wonder, but . . .' began a smartly-attired, remarkably cheery-looking Geraldine, who then resisted any temptation to elucidate. 'He never took any drugs as far as I knew, and I sure knew a dopehead when I saw one.' The dark, diminutive, tousle-haired Pearl imbued the Wepner fight with the greatest significance, suggesting that victory would have brought Sonny a big pay-day in his next fight (unlikely, since no such prizes materialised in the six months that followed). Johnny Tocco, furthermore, revealed that, two days before the Jersey City massacre, he had accompanied Sonny to a hotel bar for a rendezvous with a pair of dodgy-looking black dudes. Tocco never heard the ensuing conversation because Sonny had asked him to wait in the lobby, but that didn't prevent him from drawing conclusions. 'Sonny had to have been approached to drop the fight. The talk around was that they [the gamblers] wanted a Wepner victory, and the only way they could get that was if Sonny would have been involved.'

What does seem self-evident is that Sonny did not die of natural causes. The apparent freshness of the needle imprints surely undermines that proposition. No one I spoke to, moreover, could lend any credence whatsoever to the possibility that the jabs were made by Sonny's own hand. Given his hang-ups about injections, any other common or garden method of self-destruction would have been explicable, but not this one. At the time of his death, admittedly, he was sliding into a morass, albeit one only partly of his own making. He had money problems, sure, but no one had noted any suicidal tendencies. 'He was not depressed,' confirmed Mildred Stevenson, the Listons' housekeeper. Geraldine is alone in vouching that death was exclusively attributable to heart failure, but then perhaps she wanted an end to all the torment. By accepting the innocent option, she could rid herself of Frankie and Blinky and all the rest of the hoodlums, once and for all. Why would they bother her any more? She could keep her real beliefs to herself for ever.

The tributes ranged from the fulsome to the hollow. 'It was, perhaps, fitting that the man who in four title bouts amassed about £1.6 million should end up sprawled out on a gold bedspread,' wrote the misinformed Peter Wilson, 'like the dice which roll, day and night, on the green baize in Las Vegas where he died.' Sonny's death failed to get a mention in either *Keesing's* or the *Annual Register*. *Whitaker's Almanack* stated the date of death as 3 January, the *Chronicle of the 20th Century* as 6 January. The only Listons in the *Chambers Biographical Dictionary* (an expansive tome that includes both Jack Dempsey and Jack Johnson) are John (1776–1846), an 'English low comedian', and Robert (1794–1847), the Scottish surgeon who first used general anaesthetic in a public operation. The *Encyclopaedia Britannica* entry for Sonny begins: 'b. 8 May 1917? St Francis County, Arkansas. d. on or after 28 December 1970.' There was evidence, it continued, 'that he began his ring career as early as 1934, at the age of 17, under the name of Charles ("Sailor") Liston. If these statements are correct, he was a 45-year-old when he won the championship.' What if he was? For a 45-year-old to be the leading figure in a young man's trade is surely a cue for rejoicing. All Sonny ever got were cheap shots.

Joe Louis was one of the pallbearers as the funeral procession wended down the Strip. Doris Day and Ella Fitzgerald paid their respects. So did Father Murphy, who flew in from Denver to deliver the eulogy then wept for an hour upon his return home, partly out of remorse, partly out of disgust. Ironic, was it not, after all those years when the boot was on the other foot, that Sonny should attract a police escort and a supportive crowd on his way to the grave? 'People came out of the hotels to watch him pass,' Father Murphy once reminisced, less than fondly. 'They stopped everything. They used him all his life. They were still using him on the way to the cemetery. There he was, another Las Vegas show. God help us.' Father Stevens, whom Geraldine had rung a couple of days after she had stumbled across her husband's corpse, decided not to attend for precisely that reason. 'It was too far away, for one thing, and it was also a side-issue. I had a very large parish. But I didn't want to go because I knew they would make a circus out of it. I didn't want to be involved. I wanted to give him a chance, and my victory came in getting him that far. He was a victim of society early on, but later of the whole boxing business.'

Davey Pearl heard the news of his friend's demise soon after the police arrived. 'I got a call the morning after they found him, I can't remember who from. It was a total shock. I used to see him nearly every day. What happened? I don't suppose we'll ever know.' The body was laid to rest in Paradise Memorial Gardens, Las Vegas. Overhead, planes roar in and out of the adjacent McCarran International Airport, day and night. Beneath the flowers, as the brass plate on the grave indicates, lies 'A MAN'. Along with a rather large cache of secrets.

Thirteen

Born to Lose

The bad ones are the ones who seem to have all the power and be in these positions to block things that you and I need. You and I have to preserve the right to do what is necessary to bring an end to that situation, and it doesn't mean that I advocate violence, but at the same time I am not against using violence in self-defence. I don't even call it violence when it's self-defence. I call it intelligence.

(Malcolm X)

More, arguably, than any other boxer, Sonny employed violence as a means of self-defence, of self-preservation. Without it, he would surely have submitted far earlier to the racist proclivities of a world doing its damndest to keep the civil rights movement at bay, to keep the black man in his place. As it was, his triumph lay in delaying the inevitable.

As a pulpit for self-expression and self-assertion, the ring first loomed as the Negro Mecca when Jack Johnson pursued Tommy Burns half-way across the world and cut down his quarry in Rushcutter's Bay. Outside the ropes, blacks remained members of the downtrodden underclass; inside them, they became symbols, both of revolution and what the underdog, black or white, could achieve. By the 1960s, though, the goalposts had moved. Redemption through physical force merely strengthened the stereotype, a fact recognised in their differing ways by Floyd Patterson and Muhammad Ali. Sonny also acknowledged this, but he was too busy trying to evict the skeletons from his closet to pay his political responsibilities much heed. Having struggled vainly for attention throughout his childhood, he certainly made up for lost time with a vengeance. However, given that the pacifistic doctrine of Martin Luther King ultimately found greater favour than that of Malcolm X, it was scarcely surprising that his race should reject Sonny's one-dimensional demonstration of black power.

Sonny's, assuredly, was a career riddled with contradictions. The first challenger to win the world heavyweight title by flattening the champion in round one, Sonny also found himself on the rough end of the shortest world heavyweight title bout in history. The purse for his first duel with Patterson was the largest ever offered up to that point; the limp Lewiston crowd that attended his second defence against Ali remains the lowest for any world heavyweight championship fight.

Less equivocal are those who believe Sonny to have been one of the finest of all heavyweights. In the 1963 Christmas issue of *Esquire*, behind that cover shot of the baleful, doleful-eyed champ as the most unsuitable, unwelcome of Santa Clauses, lurked an article headlined 'THE GREATEST FIGHTS OF THE CENTURY'. Anticipating the computer contests of the 1970s, Robert Riger shrugged aside practicality to speculate the outcome were Sonny to have been matched, in turn, with Marciano, Louis and Dempsey. The scenarios, predictably, were lacking in credibility (no self-respecting boxing buff I know would fancy the 'Manassa Mauler's' chances of knocking Sonny out). But by having Sonny set up Joe in round two and send Rocky reeling 'at 2:16 of the most brutal first round ever seen', Riger made his feelings clear. For sheer power of punch, Sonny was The Man.

Granted, his capitulation to Ali emphasised once and for all that boxing is less about power than will-power, more mind than matter. Yet with better, more committed advice and a less stubborn belief in his own immortality, Sonny might have disproved this. The physique alone, alabaster-smooth, ebony curves outlining biceps and triceps of technicolour brute, was enough to frighten the bejesus out of any foe, Ali included. At 14in, his left fist was a grenade beyond compare; only that circus turn, Primo Carnera, ever launched a larger weapon in a ring. Above all there was The Look, that motionless, emotionless glare that defeated opponents at the weigh-in and inspired emulation in others. Rubin 'Hurricane' Carter, for one, proudly admitted to having spent endless hours in front of his bedroom mirror practising The Look.

These, though, were eyes weighed down by gloom, sagging with the dread of the inescapable. There was no spark to them, no speck of hope. When Sonny ended his life – or, rather, had it ended for him – not even the illustrious phalanx of mourners could disguise the true nature of a denouement that the producers of *Rocky* would have ripped up at the very first script meeting. Despite the esteem, despite the millions of dollars generated by his sweat and toil, Sonny ended his career as he had started it, an errand boy with undernourished pockets. Instead of enjoying his questionably-gotten gains and insuring his family's future, he still had to do a bit of moonlighting, and lending the loan sharks some extra teeth – as he was reputed to have done – constituted a handy source of extra cash. The tool remained a tool even as it rusted.

Bill Cayton sees many, too many, parallels between Sonny and his former charge, Mike Tyson. The comparison is unavoidable: weak, unhappy roots, next to no education, a penchant for petty (and not so petty) crime, inhuman strength, morally dodgy job and extremely dodgy advisers are common to both. 'They were both victims,' Cayton stresses, 'but they were both knowing victims. The difference, the tremendous difference, between them is that Jim Jacobs, Cus D'Amato and I really cared for Mike Tyson. The people around Sonny didn't care for him. If anyone was exploited, he was.' And who was Tyson's role model? Sonny, of course.

Sonny and Tyson both strove to assert their masculinity when off-duty. Tyson did so in his sexual dalliances; Sonny, it is said, was content with a white woman on his arm, an outrageous evocation of black power for its time. Neither found it sufficient merely to master opponents inside the ropes. Not that the sour science has had any shortage of exponents in need of extra-curricular hormone injections. In 1910, Stanley Kechtel was shot in the back by a jealous husband while breakfasting with the chap's wife at their

Illinois farmstead. Carlos Monzon, Diego Maradona's immediate predecessor as the Prince of the Plate, was sentenced to eleven years' imprisonment when found guilty of hurling his girlfriend to her death from the balcony of their Mar del Plata flat. Trevor Berbick, who lost his WBC heavyweight title to Tyson, was recently convicted of raping the family baby-sitter in Miami. 'Go ahead, report it – they'll never believe you,' he scoffed. Tony Ayala, a gifted light-middleweight from New Jersey, was the No. 1 contender when charged in 1983 with the rape of a schoolteacher: sentenced to thirty years, he won't be eligible for parole until 1998. Jake La Motta battered his wife as a matter of course and was jailed for hiring a minor as a hostess at his Florida night-club, but he was forgiven.

Tyson had the twin misfortune to have been born neither a Caucasian nor a Kennedy but, even if we defy all the evidence and accept that the judgement of his so-called peers was not the stitch-up it appeared, the keenness of the boxing fraternity to discuss the offender's post-incarceration prospects was sickening at best. Does a man stop being a rapist when his sentence ends? Only if he's worth a bob or two to someone else. As an armed robber, Sonny was not in the same judicial or even moral ballpark, yet he carried his lapse around as if his rump had been branded in neon.

Both men, however, were dispensed with in much the same fashion. Prior to being brought to book, Tyson had contrived to skirt a host of allegations pertaining to sexual impropriety, so why did the protection wear thin? Because he was no longer the champ. He had served his function. As a meal-ticket, he had been devalued. When Sonny was found dead he was no longer even a contender. He, too, had exceeded his sell-by date.

Geraldine stayed in Vegas until the end of the 1970s before returning to St Louis where, twenty long and trying years earlier, she had once left behind the drudgery of the munitions factory to dance the night away with Sonny. She now works as a medical assistant and has yet to remarry. 'He was a great guy, great with me, great with the kids, a gentle man,' she told *Sports Illustrated*. The last time we spoke, she was about to commit her version of the story to paper. Her only words to me were plaintive *in extremis*: 'What does it matter what happened?'

In many senses, she is right. But what does matter is how Sonny managed to get himself into a position to get shot at in the first place. One seemingly reputable diagnosis came from Dr Charles P. Larson, a former president of the NBA and WBA, later president of the College of American Pathologists and a leading crime expert to boot. He claimed to have known Sonny well. 'Sonny was a true illiterate. He was a poor, dumb man. When he was champion, we had a hell of a time giving him a decent image. He was always in trouble. He drank too much, he hung around with criminals, punks. We assigned detectives to tail him just to keep him in line . . . Through his childhood and early adult life, those associations (with hoodlums of the worst sort) made such an impression on him that he actually developed an adulation for the low-life criminal element. He especially idolised those who beat the law. To Sonny Liston, those who made a lot of tainted money and got away with it were heroes.'

Larson also asserted that Sonny's ability to discern between 'right' and 'wrong' had been distorted. 'But I do not blame him for this attitude, because most of his life he dealt with people in business who gave him the short end of the stick. I think it finally dawned on him that he seldom got a fair deal from anybody; the reason being, of course, that those who managed him and had a piece of him were crooks themselves. We never did find out who really owned his contract or who got his money.' Larson cast his mind back to one particularly shady confrontation in Chicago. 'This hoodlum walked up to me at one of our boxing conventions and offered me $50,000 under the table if I'd help Liston get a licence to fight in a certain state. I told him in no uncertain terms where he could go! Later, at our WBA meeting in this hotel conference room, one of our officials saw this same guy's pocket bulging. He walked up to him and purposely brushed past him to feel the pocket. Inside was a miniature tape recorder. The hood had been taping his bribe offer to frame me later. That's when I decided to clean up boxing.' Indeed, it was during Larson's tenure at the NBA that the rule obligating complete financial disclosure of a fighter's ownership was introduced. By then, though, Sonny had long since been disowned, discarded like a child adopted purely for the benefit of the new parents' self-gratification.

Unsurprisingly, what Dr Larson omitted to say was that boxing itself might have had a detrimental effect on Sonny. When Frank Bruno made his ill-advised come-back from an eye operation necessitated by one of Tyson's barbarous biffs, he declared that life is showbiz, 'and boxing's just show business with blood'. At that moment, two other British boxers lay in intensive care. One of them, middleweight Michael Watson, had described boxing as 'a dirty business' even before his tragic duel with Chris Eubank.

Sonny inhabited the smelliest edge of this dirty business. A caged lion released on the whim of callous zookeepers, he too was cast aside. The difference was that boxing killed his spirit, leaving his body intact, not unlike that neutron bomb Ronald Reagan used to be so fond of. From Doc Kearns to Don King, boxing has been poisoned by amoral men on the make, but then we are hardly talking honourable professions here. All right, so Sonny was the Mob's status symbol, but that surely says more about the nature of the business, and the baser instincts it represents, than it does about this particular employee. Above all, Sonny was the first black villain white America had had to taunt since Jack Johnson half a century earlier. And God knows they needed a punch-bag during the 1960s, if only to stop themselves from succumbing to the Martin Luther King line on race relations. Sonny was used to fuel every argument against civil rights. A knowing victim, yes, but a helpless one all the same.

Sonny was a shadowy figure all right, but what price a shadowy figure in this darkest of worlds? The sour science gave him the opportunity to transcend his reality, but all it really supplied was an illusion. Sadly, so long as professional boxing exists, the world will never run short of Sonny Listons to kick around.

Ring Record

Sonny Liston – Professional Career

Date, Opponent, Venue, Result, Round
World title fights in capitals

1953
2/9:   Don Smith (St Louis) KO 1
17/9:   Ponce De Leon (St Louis) W (pts) 4
21/11:   Benny Thomas (St Louis) W (pts) 6

1954
25/1:   Martin Lee (St Louis) KO 6
31/3:   Stan Howlett (St Louis) W (pts) 6
29/6:   Johnny Summerlin (Detroit) W (pts) 8
10/8:   Johnny Summerlin (Detroit) W (pts) 8
7/9:   Marty Marshall (Detroit) L (pts) 8

1955
1/3:   Neil Welch (St Louis) W (pts) 8
21/4:   Marty Marshall (St Louis) KO 6
5/5:   Emil Brtko (Pittsburgh) KO 5
23/5:   Calvin Butler (St Louis) KO 2
13/9:   Johnny Gray (Indianapolis) KO 6
13/12:   Larry Watson (East St Louis) KO 4

1956
6/3:   Marty Marshall (Pittsburgh) W (pts) 10

1958
29/1:   Bill Hunter (Chicago) KO 2
11/3:   Ben Wise (Chicago) KO 4

3/4:   Bert Whitehurst (St Louis) W (pts) 10
14/5:   Julio Mederos (Chicago) KO 3
6/8:   Wayne Bethea (Chicago) KO 1
7/10:   Frankie Daniels (Miami Beach) KO 1
24/10:   Bert Whitehurst (St Louis) W (pts) 10
18/11:   Ernie Cab (Miami Beach) KO 8

1959
18/2:   Mike De John (Miami Beach) KO 6
15/4:   Cleveland Williams (Miami Beach) KO 3
5/8:   Nino Valdes (Chicago) KO 3
9/12:   Willi Besmanoff (Cleveland) KO 7

1960
23/2:   Howard King (Miami Beach) KO 8
21/3:   Cleveland Williams (Houston) KO 2
25/4:   Roy Harris (Houston) KO 1
18/7:   Zora Folley (Denver) KO 3
7/9:   Eddie Machen (Seattle) W (pts) 12

1961
8/3:   Howard King (Miami Beach) KO 3
4/12:   Albert Westphal (Philadelphia) KO 1

1962
25/9:   FLOYD PATTERSON (CHICAGO) KO 1

1963
22/7:   FLOYD PATTERSON (LAS VEGAS) KO 1

1964
25/2:   CASSIUS CLAY (MIAMI BEACH) L (RTD) 7

1965
25/5:   MUHAMMAD ALI (LEWISTON, MAINE) L (KO) 1

1966
29/6:   Gerhard Zech (Stockholm) KO 7
19/8:   Amos Johnson (Gothenburg) KO 3

1967

30/3:   Dave Bailey (Gothenburg) KO 1

28/4:   Elmer Rush (Stockholm) KO 6

1968

16/3:   Bill McMurray (Reno) KO 4

25/5:   Billy Joiner (Los Angeles) KO 7

6/7:   Henry Clark (San Francisco) KO 7

14/10: Sonny Moore (Phoenix) KO 3

3/11:   Willis Earls (Juarez) KO 2

12/11: Roger Rischer (Pittsburgh) KO 3

12/12: Amos Lincoln (Baltimore) KO 2

1969

23/3:   Billy Joiner (St Louis) W (pts) 10

19/5:   George Johnson (Las Vegas) KO 7

23/9:   Sonny Moore (Houston) KO 3

6/12:   Leotis Martin (Las Vegas) L (KO) 9

1970

29/6:   Chuck Wepner (Jersey City) TKO 9

Overall Record: Fights 54 Won 50 Lost 4 KO 38

Bibliography

Anderson, Dave: *Ringmasters* (1991, Robson Books)

Andre, Sam, and Fleischer, Nat: *A Pictorial History of Boxing* (1975, Citadel Press)

Berube, Maurice: *Defeat of the Great Black Hope* (1971, *Commonweal* magazine)

Collins, Nigel: *Boxing Babylon* (1991, Citadel Press)

Congressional Record, 1950–70

Dubois, W. E. Burghardt: *The Souls of Black Folk* (First published 1903; reprinted by Crest in 1953)

Dundee, Angelo, with Winters, Mike: *I Only Talk Winning* (1985, Robson Books)

Hauser, Thomas: *Muhammad Ali* (1991, Robson Books)

Levine, Lawrence: *Black Culture and Black Consciousness: Afro-American Folk Thought from Slavery to Freedom* (1977, Oxford University Press)

Liebling, A. J.: *The Sweet Science* (1951, Simon and Schuster)

McCallum, John D.: *The World Heavyweight Boxing Championship* (1974, Chilton Book Company)

Mailer, Norman: *The Fight* (1975, Little, Brown and Co.; Penguin Books)

The Autobiography of Malcolm X (1965, Hutchinson)

Mead, Chris: *Champion: Joe Louis; Black Man in White America* (1985, Charles Scribner's Sons)

Muhammad Ali with Durham, Richard: *The Greatest* (1975, Book Club Associates)

Oates, Joyce Carol: *On Boxing* (1987, Bloomsbury)

Ed. Oates, Joyce Carol, and Halpern, Daniel: *Reading The Fights* (1988, Prentice Hall Press)

Patterson, Floyd, with Gross, Milton: *Victory Over Myself* (1962, Pelham Books)

Plimpton, George: *Shadow Box* (1977, Putnam; Simon and Schuster)

Roberts, Randy: *Jack Dempsey: The Manassa Mauler* (1979, Baton Rouge: Louisiana State University Press)

Sammons, Jeffrey T.: *Beyond the Ring: The Role of Boxing in American Society* (1988, University of Illinois Press)

Schulberg, Budd: *The Harder They Fall* (1947, Random House)

Summerskill, Baroness Edith: *The Ignoble Art* (1956, Heinemann)

Suster, Gerald: *Champions of the Ring* (1992, Robson Books)

Torres, Jose: *Fire and Fear: The Inside Story of Mike Tyson* (1989, Warner Books)

—: *Sting Like A Bee* (1971, Abelard-Schuman Ltd)

Wilson, Peter: *The Man They Couldn't Gag* (1977 Hutchinson, Stanley Paul)

Various newspapers and periodicals, including *Ebony, Esquire, New York Times, The Ring, Sports Illustrated* and *Time*

Index